YOUNG CENTER BOOKS IN ANABAPTIST & PIETIST STUDIES

Donald B. Kraybill, *Series Editor*

Growing Up Amish

The Teenage Years

Richard A. Stevick

THE JOHNS HOPKINS UNIVERSITY PRESS
Baltimore

© 2007 The Johns Hopkins University Press
All rights reserved. Published 2007
Printed in the United States of America on acid-free paper
2 4 6 8 9 7 5 3 1

The Johns Hopkins University Press
2715 North Charles Street
Baltimore, Maryland 21218-4363
www.press.jhu.edu

Library of Congress Cataloging-in-Publication Data

Stevick, Richard A., 1939–
Growing up Amish : the teenage years / Richard A. Stevick.
p. cm. — (Young Center books in Anabaptist and Pietist studies)
Includes bibliographical references and index.
ISBN-13: 978-0-8018-8567-9 (hardcover : alk. paper)
ISBN-10: 0-8018-8567-1 (hardcover : alk. paper)
1. Rumspringa. 2. Amish teenagers—United States—Social life and customs.
3. Amish teenagers—United States—Social conditions. 4. Amish teenagers—
United States—Religious life. 5. Amish—United States—Social life and customs.
6. Youth—United States—Social life and customs. I. Title.
E184.M45S75 2007
305.235089'31073—dc22   2006023119

A catalog record for this book is available from the British Library.

Frontispiece: Cornerball is a favorite game in some Amish communities.
Photo by Dennis Hughes.

To Pauline, of course,

My wife and friend of forty-five years

—◦◦—

Contents

Preface

With their quaint dress, horse transportation, and rejection of digital technology and mass entertainment, the Amish are arguably the most easily recognized minority group in America. In recent years, books and articles on the Amish have proliferated almost as fast as their booming population. Glossy coffee-table books feature bucolic scenes of horse-drawn carriages on the way to church, children hoeing corn, or swarms of Amish men raising a barn for a neighbor. Scores of writers analyze or eulogize these plain, hardworking people.

From New York to Los Angeles, newspapers feature Amish society with photos of families working together in the fields or of smiling teenage girls on in-line skates. In a typical year, nearly seven million tourists journey to Lancaster County, Pennsylvania, home of the nation's oldest Amish settlement. Many come to gaze at bearded farmers mowing hay or to buy homemade root beer or shoofly pies from barefooted children at roadside stands. Even abroad, interest in the Amish abounds. In Japan, for example, more than a dozen books on the Amish have been published.[1]

Some of the popular interest in the Amish probably stems from media portrayals such as a succession of films, articles, and books, including Paramount Pictures' *Witness* in 1985.[2] In 2004, the UPN television network produced *Amish in the City,* a controversial reality series featuring five youths who had grown up in Amish homes as they experienced the culture of Los Angeles.[3] Typically, media portrayals of the Amish show stable communities with little crime, violence, sexually transmitted disease, or family dysfunction.[4] Almost all Amish children learn to work hard at an early age and grow up to be self-supporting, responsible adults. Perhaps as modern society becomes more hurried, pressured, and complicated, the Amish lifestyle rouses some incipient yearning for their presumably simpler way of life. Mainstream parents, wearied with talk-show deviants or worried by school violence, teen suicides, and a seemingly endless stream of other bad news, may be especially attracted to these quiet people. For many, the Amish symbolize peaceful communities, stable families, and responsible youth. No wonder, then, that our fascination with the Amish continues.

My own interest in the Amish intensified when I moved to Lancaster County, Pennsylvania, in the 1960s. At the time, I knew almost nothing about the Amish except what I had read in a 1965 *National Geographic* article by Richard Gehman. As a newcomer, I was curious about the customs, values, and lifestyle of our quaint neighbors. I was interested not only in how they lived but also in how for three centuries they had maintained their unique culture despite outside influences and internal stresses. I found the literature published for tourists to be shallow and sketchy, but more disconcerting were the blatant inaccuracies—for example, that families with eligible daughters advertised to potential suitors by painting the front gate blue, or that Amish farmers placed hex signs on their barns as protection from bad luck.

The behavior of some Amish youth puzzled me more. I noticed Amish teenagers frequenting forbidden venues such as Dutch Wonderland amusement park, local movie theaters and drive-ins, and even bars and taverns. In the town of Intercourse, Pennsylvania, young men would often congregate outside the convenience store on a Saturday night, smoking cigarettes, buying bags of ice for the party later that night, and peeling out of the parking lot in high-performance cars. On most weekends, the clip-clopping along our back road in the early hours of the morning was evidence that even the plainest youth were staying out late. Newspapers occasionally carried articles describing weekend parties among Amish youth that resulted in public intoxication, driving while under the influence, disturbing the peace, vandalism, and subsequent arrests.

At that time, I was unaware that all of the young people were participat-

ing in *Rumspringa* (running around), a brief interlude of increased independence before they decide whether to take the lifetime vows of church membership. During this time, some of the more daring youth choose to sample
the outside world and indulge in non-Amish behavior. In addition, a division had split the conservative and "change-minded" adults over religious
and technology issues in the Lancaster Amish settlement. Soon dozens of
families left the Old Order church for more progressive ways.[5] I concluded
that the days of Amish society were numbered. Anyone could see that a
separatist culture like theirs that sought no converts and could not control
its own youth was obviously destined for extinction. To me, the signs were
unmistakable: the Amish not only would die out but would be extinct by the
end of the century, disappearing like the Shakers in America and the now-
vanished Amish in Europe.

The reality, however, is that instead of withering away like their European
forebears, the North American Amish population has quadrupled since my
1960s prediction.[6] In fact, their exponential increase makes them one of
the fastest growing religious groups in North America. Cars, cigarettes, and
rowdiness did not mean that Amish youth were abandoning the faith and
practice of their plain-living fathers and mothers. Their society's viability
had never been in doubt. I had totally misread the signs. Thus, I began my
long quest to understand how the Amish community transmitted a positive
Amish identity strong enough to overcome mainstream cultural values and
pull even the wanderers back into the fold.

In my search for answers, I sought out academic sources but was disappointed to find that most books devoted only a few pages to adolescent issues. Also, most authorities had studied a single settlement, which reduced
the relevance of their work to other Amish settlements. As a professor of
psychology, I was especially interested in the developmental tasks of youth
and wanted to learn all I could about how Amish youth related to their parents, their peers, and the community. I decided to cast the net wide and look
at Amish adolescence in a variety of communities and locations so I could
study the adolescent life of Amish youth in the broader context of family,
peers, schooling, work, and leisure.

When I started teaching a course on Amish life, I had no intention of
writing anything about Amish adolescence. My goal was simply to learn as

much about the Amish culture as I could and, in turn, help my students do the same. Of course, as I continued teaching and learning, my interests and opportunities to learn also grew. Thanks to the help of the late Abner Beiler, I placed my students with families in Lancaster County, Pennsylvania, and later with families in Holmes County, Ohio, the two largest Amish settlements. Eventually, I felt drawn to share my observations, insights, and questions not only with my students but also with many Amish individuals who had become friends.

With their encouragement, I eventually visited more than sixty Amish settlements in the United States and Canada and attended dozens of church services in Amish homes, Amish weddings, a baptismal service, Sunday night youth socials, one-room schools, German/vocational classes, softball games, school picnics, and benefit auctions. I witnessed these events in large and small settlements, Old Order and New Order affiliations, and plain and progressive groups in twenty states and provinces. I spent more than six hundred hours with Amish teenagers, parents, and ministers, in both formal interviews and informal conversation. Always I sought to understand how this unique culture so successfully transmitted a positive Amish identity to the next generation.

Most of the information on Amish adolescence and parenting in this book is either new information from my work or significantly expands upon previous work and should therefore interest readers in anthropology and psychology as well as Anabaptist or Amish studies. The book depicts what it means to grow up in a collectivist culture that values group goals over individualistic expression, and it tracks the developmental stages and tasks of Amish adolescence in a separatist society.

Chapter 1 recounts some of the important historic and cultural roots that anchor Amish life today and shows how the demographics of geography and settlement size affect the adolescent experience. The religious bedrock that provides the foundation and coherence for expectations and practices in Amish culture is described in chapter 2. The third chapter explores the ways in which the Amish identity is formed and cultivated.

I discuss Amish schooling in chapter 4 and show its importance in passing on the Amish culture and identity. Chapter 5 describes the high expectations Amish society places on Amish parents and children and shows some of the worries and stresses faced by parents of teenage children. Chapter 6, which is about work and play, demonstrates that hard work is a core Amish value that strengthens Amish identity, both as a society and as individuals. On the other hand, the kinds of recreation and play that youth participate in have the potential to either strengthen or weaken their Amish identity, depending on the choices they make.

Chapter 7 details a social event that is little known to outsiders but central in the social development of Amish adolescents—the weekly singing. "Going to the singing" is a rite—and right—of passage in virtually all Amish communities. Childhood is over, and life will never be the same. The practice of *Rumspringa*, which stirs so much interest in the media, is addressed in chapter 8. I focus primarily on a large community to show how adolescent social groups and peers influence the identity and behavior of Amish youth. Chapter 9, which is about dating and courtship, describes both the variety and similarity in the ways youth find each other and pair off in different Amish settings and affiliations. Marriage is the final rite of passage, and chapter 10 portrays the similarity of the wedding services but the diversity of the festivities that follow in a variety of settlements. The last chapter explores the importance of passing the cultural heritage on to the next generation and discusses the factors that strengthen and weaken the fabric of Amish life.

A Postscript to Amish Readers and Friends

In my search to understand Amish youth, I have met hundreds of your people, young and old, in large and small communities, who have been willing to talk with me about their experiences, hopes, joys, and concerns. Many of you freely related your stories and experiences to me, even though you realized that at times these things might be embarrassing to some Amish.[7] I have tried to avoid emphasizing flaws or pointing out only strengths. Instead, my goal has always been to be accurate and fair. Telling the truth is a virtue in Amish culture, and I have tried my best to be virtuous in this account.

Because of the wishes of dozens of you, my Amish friends, I have worked hard to conceal the names of individuals, sources, and, at times, even the locations of communities. I trust that I have succeeded. I might even hope that this book can be useful to Amish leaders, parents, and youth as you seek to live out your lives with faith and integrity. Where I have missed the truth, I claim full responsibility and apologize.

Acknowledgments

At times during the ten years I spent researching and writing this book, I would recall the observation of the writer of Ecclesiastes that "in the making of books there is no end." Thanks to the encouragement and help of many colleagues, friends, and students along the way, I have at least arrived at the end of this particular book.

First, I am grateful to many Amish friends and acquaintances, old and young, who not only assisted me in my quest to understand Amish adolescence but also made sure that the manuscript accurately reflected Amish experiences, beliefs, and practices. Multiple readers have read every chapter. I am respecting their wish to remain anonymous, but my gratitude to them is immense. *Unni dei hilf, veah des buch net meeglich. Dengi fer alles.* (Without your help, this book would not have been possible. Thanks for everything.)

In the early stages I used drafts of the manuscript as a supplemental reading in my adolescent development classes. The feedback from former students, especially from Faith Detweiler, Kristine Koslowsky Boyes, and Rachel Bennett, undoubtedly helped turn this into a better, more readable book. Four summer work-study students—Kimberly Arva Valvo, Carol Way Johnson, Ginger Little, and Jenna Hunsberger—also provided timely help in the intermediate stages of the manuscript, and my four Messiah College scholar interns—Lynn Keefer, Myron Sauder, Kristen Schwartz Dressler, and Anna Wendel—saved me countless hours in tracking down scholarly sources and in providing careful attention to endnotes and references. Anna deserves special mention for providing an extremely close and helpful late editing of the text, endnotes, and references and for compiling the index. Her level of competence and insight belie her years.

I also received significant help from a former colleague at Messiah College, Julia Kasdorf, now a professor at Penn State and one of the finest writers I know. She took time from her own writing to read carefully and comment extensively on an early draft. Her perceptive questions and challenges helped sharpen my focus and reduce some of my chaff and fluff. I was privileged to learn from her.

Several friends also deserve special recognition. I am indebted to the late Robert Smith, M.D., and his wife, Marilyn Byer Smith, whose financial support and commitment to excellence funded my four scholar interns and dozens more like them. I am also grateful to the late Reg Fisher, a friend to all at Messiah College and an especially ardent fan of my "Amish book." He never failed to check in on my progress and always asked to read each word I wrote, almost as soon as it appeared. I am appreciative to Laura Shaida, longtime friend and member of our book discussion group, who read the almost-final version and provided constructive and practical suggestions. I am indebted to Paul Hostetler, a fellow student of Pennsylvania German, who read through the manuscript on two different occasions. His careful eye, passion for clarity, and considerable editorial skills made this a much more readable book.

I am grateful for the help of Elizabeth Yoder, my copyeditor, whose suggestions contributed significantly to the final manuscript. I am also thankful to Claire McCabe Tamberino and Linda Forlifer of the Johns Hopkins University Press for their considerable skill and patience in attending to my many concerns and answering my numerous questions throughout all aspects of the publication process. These three women provided invaluable help and counsel.

Special thanks to Donald B. Kraybill, my colleague for five years at Messiah College. He graciously mentored and encouraged me in the early stages of this project. Recognized as the top Amish Studies scholar in the world, he set for me a rigorous example of careful scholarship and meticulous research. After he moved to Elizabethtown College and assumed the series editorship for the Young Center Books in Anabaptist and Pietist Studies, he became my editor. Even though his role changed, his interest and encouragement continued. This is a much better book because of him.

Without doubt, the most influential person in this entire process was my best friend, Pauline Stevick, who also happens to be my wife and the love of my life. She helped refine the manuscript with careful readings and with her perceptive insights and suggestions. Her faith that I would eventually . complete a publishable book was invaluable. (The fact that she wrote and finished a book of her own on Amish life during the time I was working on mine helped inspire and motivate me to persevere to the final endnote.)

I appreciate the generous permission to quote excerpts from *Rosanna of the Amish*, by Joseph W. Yoder (copyright © 1973, 1995 by Herald Press, Scottdale, PA 15683). Finally, I am indebted to Messiah College for providing several internal grants to work on this project, two sabbaticals (one to start the book and the other to finish it), and two faculty forums to share my manuscript-in-progress. Heartfelt thanks to all.

Growing Up Amish

Most Amish boys learn to handle horses at an early age.
Photo by Daniel Rodriguez.

Amish Life
Plain and Perplexing

All good things go to ruin if we don't work on them.
—Amish parent

Five Amish in the City

In the summer of 2004, UPN launched its first installment of *Amish in the City*. This so-called reality television series featured five young adults who had grown up in Amish homes in the Midwest and six "English" (non-Amish) counterparts who supposedly approximated a cross-section of middle-class American twenty-somethings. UPN prepared an upscale house for the group in Hollywood Hills and during the next several weeks dispatched their camera crews to document the encounters of the innocents and the sophisticates, both in their home with each other and in the glitzy life of Los Angeles with its diversity, attractions, and allures.

A new reality show often receives little attention from the mainstream media, but before its airing, writers and producers from a variety of news organizations, including the *Washington Post*, the *Washington Times*, the *Philadelphia Daily News*, the *Christian Science Monitor*, MSNBC News, NPR, and even the *Sunday Telegraph* of London not only noted the new series but often questioned UPN's motivation and taste in producing it. Even some politicians raised similar issues when word of the network's intentions leaked out. U.S. Representative Joe Pitts of Pennsylvania and fifty of his Republican colleagues petitioned UPN to cancel the show out of respect for Amish values. Pitts and his group charged that the media would make a mockery of down-home Amish values and would subject his plain constituents to public scorn and the ridicule of late-night comics. It turns out that their fears were unnecessary.

From the first episode, the five young people from Amish families quickly established themselves as the home team favorites. Despite their lack of sophistication ("Who is Reggae?" and "What is sushi?"), they demonstrated a refreshing curiosity regarding their surroundings and their companions, while displaying an affable cooperation and good-natured courtesy. Most of the time, the Amish youth were low-maintenance participants compared to their often whining, bored, and self-preoccupied counterparts. Representative Pitts must have been pleased with his television Amish.[1]

The parents of the six non-Amish participants were probably pleased that their children were on national television, and they probably taped every episode. Besides the notoriety and the twenty thousand dollars that each reportedly received, such national exposure might prove to be a foot in the door for a future career or even stardom. Such opportunities are not to be taken lightly. The English parents would undoubtedly watch each episode with great interest.

In contrast, none of the Amish parents would want to see even a single episode of *Amish in the City* because it would be too painful. Even though they would have known nothing about reality television, these parents would feel deep sadness and shame since first learning of their children's involvement with the medium. For these parents, this was more bad news that simply confirmed their worst fears—the worldly journey that had begun during their children's teenage years was leading into apostasy and eventual damnation. Undoubtedly, each of the Amish parents also struggled with self-condemnation, remorse, and guilt, and must have been plagued by the recurring question, "Where did we go wrong?" All of them knew that the Scriptures state, "Train up a child in the way he should go, and when he is old, he will not depart from it" (Proverbs 22:6).[2] Obviously, they had failed in their training.

The parents of one Amish youth, Miriam, may have been especially hurt, because her father was a bishop, the most honored and influential position in the church. However, the parents of the other Amish youth would have been equally worried, not just about the temptations their wayward children would face but also by their own awareness that if their sons or daughters married outside the Amish faith, they would surely be lost from the fold. Mose, an affable twenty-four-year-old, whom some viewers regarded as the star of the series, faced the most serious consequences because he had already joined the church at age seventeen and had then broken his lifetime vows to God and the church.[3] The other four would be accepted back more easily since they had not made or broken any solemn vows.

Deep Roots

Although all Amish have limited formal education and a limited knowledge of popular culture, most Amish, young and old, have some interest in history, both oral and written. Certainly these young Amish in the city would have at least known about their own early history in Europe and America. However, in a culture that reveres tradition, knowing one's past is more than a matter of idle curiosity. For the Amish, recalling their stories helps define who they are and gives them a standard for judging whether or not they are drifting into mainstream worldliness or following the biblical description of "keeping the faith once delivered to the saints" (Jude 3). According to sociologist Donald Kraybill, the Amish constantly negotiate with the press of modernity, and now post-modernity, by weighing present realities with their historical core values. Without this intentional reflection and assessment, they are in danger of losing their distinctiveness and ultimately their culture. Kraybill believes that this combination of scrutiny, vigilance, and compromise contributes to their survival (1994b, 21–50).

Several other things help explain why the Amish have been so successful in capturing the hearts and minds of their young. Historical, sociological, and demographic factors, such as their European roots, their population growth, their decentralized and autonomous church districts, and the relative density, size, and isolation of their settlements, are pieces in the surprising puzzle of Amish retention.

The Radicals

Historically, both secular and religious authorities regarded the forbears of today's peaceful Amish as dangerous radicals when they emerged in Switzerland during the early sixteenth century. Shortly after the reformer Martin Luther ruptured Christendom by challenging the established church in 1517, certain Swiss reformers decided that Luther's Reformation failed to go far enough or deep enough. Although they adhered to Luther's belief in the ultimate authority of Scripture (*sola scriptura*) and in the repudiation of the Roman Catholic Church, they criticized Luther, Calvin, and Zwingli for their refusal to sever ties with the political powers. These radical reformers agreed with the Protestant belief that the state was instituted by God to provide structure and to maintain order, even by force, if necessary. However, the dissenters believed that true Christians should separate themselves from earthly powers. As followers of Christ, they believed they should not be actively involved in any government that used force or violence to achieve its objectives. In essence, they believed in two separate kingdoms—the kingdom of this world and the kingdom of God. Those in God's kingdom were to be peaceable, nonviolent, and nonresistant.[4]

From their study of the New Testament, these radicals also concluded that only adults could make a meaningful confession of Christian faith. They believed that infants and children lacked the understanding to make an intelligent and informed commitment to Christ and the church. This idea contradicted the Lutheran, Reformed, and Roman Catholic practice of infant baptism. Not only did these dissidents rebaptize each other in 1525, but they also required all converts to be baptized again, hence earning the epithet *Anabaptists*, which means "re-baptizers."[5]

Hard Times

Because of their beliefs and practices, hundreds of Anabaptists were tortured, and many were drowned or burned at the stake, persecuted by both Catholics and Protestants. Also, because baptismal records established the future tax rolls, civil authorities were incensed by the potential loss of taxpayers. Since the Anabaptists initially rejected all forms of violence, including involvement in the military, the state joined in the persecutions. They feared that they would lose future soldiers who would be needed to fight the Ottoman Turks.

As a result of a violent uprising by Anabaptist zealots, civil and religious authorities executed many Anabaptist dissidents.[6] These persecutions are recounted in numerous songs in the *Ausbund,* the Amish hymnal, and in the graphic narratives in *Martyrs' Mirror,* a book owned and revered by most Amish families today.[7] Adversity scattered the survivors, and new groups took root in Holland, Germany, and France.[8]

Persecution of these Swiss Anabaptists, also known as the Swiss Brethren, waxed and waned for nearly a century, depending on current tensions or the whims of the powerful. Bloodless internal conflicts also wracked the Anabaptists. Nearly 170 years after the birth of the Anabaptist movement, some of their descendants, called Mennonites after an early leader, Menno Simons (1496–1561), faced a serious challenge by a zealous Swiss/Alsatian Anabaptist minister, Jakob Ammann. He charged that Mennonite leaders were drifting away from the teachings of the Bible and of Menno Simons and were becoming lax on important issues such as separation from the world, communion practices, and excommunication.

The heart of the conflict stemmed from the issue of the "shunning" of excommunicated members. Ammann and his followers believed that disobedient church members should not only be excommunicated and put out of the fellowship, but should also be socially isolated, as taught in the New Testament.[9] He brashly charged Swiss Anabaptist leaders to either discipline lax ministers and members or else face excommunication by Ammann and his followers. Eventually, the Swiss leaders and the Ammann group split over their disagreements, and the more conservative offshoot in both Switzerland and the Alsace became known as the Amish.

A Separate People

In light of the history of early and widespread persecution of the Anabaptists, the Amish belief in separation from the world and in the separation of church and state is understandable. Today, most Amish are decidedly wary of government, and relatively few vote in state and national elections.[10]

They follow the biblical injunctions in Matthew 22:21 and Romans 13:6–7 to pay taxes, but they have opted out of the federal social security system. Also, they rarely accept unemployment or health care assistance from the government. Since the mid-twentieth century, their distrust has often extended to public school boards and local officials, who had sometimes arrested, jailed, and fined Amish fathers for refusing to send their children to large consolidated schools or to high school. In general, the Amish avoid public education because of their persistent fear of the worldly influences and secularizing effects of higher education.

Their desire to be separate from the world (Romans 12:2) also helps explain their hallmark bonnets and broad-brimmed hats, suspenders and aprons, and straight pins or hooks and eyes instead of buttons. Their dress and characteristic grooming help maintain their identity and emphasize their distinctiveness. In the twentieth century, separation has also translated into the rejection of "worldly" technologies and practices such as car ownership, power-line electricity, telephones in the houses, and commercial insurance. Kraybill (1994b, 35–52) points out that the Amish do not automatically equate modern technology with sinful practices, but they do seek to limit anything that they believe will weaken or corrupt the community or endanger their society and youth.

Other aspects of their past also influence Amish society. Many men started as farmers or craftsmen in northern Europe, and when they migrated to America they maintained their love for rural life and their passion for agriculture. Even though many Amish have had to give up farming for lack of available farmland, they have traditionally viewed farming as the ideal occupation. They regard the farm to be an especially suitable environment for rearing a family. Parents can always find work for their children to do on the farm, and hard work is part of the Amish rural heritage. They regard the rural environment as wholesome in contrast to city life, which they see as both physically dangerous and morally corrupt.

Another remnant from their European heritage is their language. All Amish speak a German or Swiss dialect in the homes and use a mixture of the dialect and old German in their church services. Many Amish believe that their young children are protected from worldly influences by not knowing English during their early formative years. Thus their children, especially the oldest, typically do not learn English until they enter school.

The Center of Amish Life

Amish faith and practice stem from their literal understanding of the Bible, especially the New Testament teachings of Jesus. Because they take the Gospels seriously, particularly the Sermon on the Mount, they oppose war and retaliation, refuse to take oaths, and strive for a simple and peaceable life.[11] Within the church and home, the Amish unabashedly support a patriarchal system, again based on their understanding of the Scriptures.[12] Males are expected to be the head of the home and of the church; and females, married or single, are to wear head coverings, according to 1 Corinthians 11:2–16, to reflect an attitude of prayer and submission.[13] Socialization into community mores begins early because all able-bodied people, including infants, are expected to attend the local church service. Unless individuals marry or move, they attend church all their lives with the same friends, neighbors, and relatives. Services are held every other week in members' homes, barns, or shops.[14] The local congregation, called a church district, is an ecclesiastical unit based on geography and proximity. Typically, it consists of twenty-five to thirty families that live within a geographic boundary small enough to permit members to reach each others' houses by horse and carriage for church on Sundays.

Attending church from childhood, however, does not make a child a member of the church. Each young man and woman must decide in their late teens or early twenties whether or not they will take membership instruction, make the lifetime vows to follow Christ and the church, and be baptized into the faith. To freely choose to be baptized as an adult is one of the core practices of all Anabaptists.

Diverse Communities

If an outsider were to visit church services in several of the thirty states where Amish live, the visitor would likely observe few differences from one place to the next. The tone, the order of service, the cadences, and the songs and prayers would all be remarkably similar. To the uninitiated, most Amish look alike. All wear plain clothes, use horse-drawn transportation, resist many aspects of modern technology, and speak in "Dutch."[15] Outsiders typically conclude that if the Amish look alike, they must act alike. Even some scholars study only one Amish community and then make generalizations about all Amish based on such limited experience. Such generalizations and tendencies help explain why outsiders are surprised when they first encounter the diversity that exists in communities and in the behavior of their youth.

Today more than fourteen hundred Amish church districts or churches are scattered throughout nearly 350 settlements in thirty states and in Ontario, Canada (Luthy 2003). The local church district is the unit that organizes Amish life, and each has its own set of ministers and its own unwritten rules called the *Ordnung*. The *Ordnung* is the agreed-upon set of rules that prescribes the behavior in every district and is rarely written. With such a large number of churches, some diversity of customs and practice naturally emerges, because each local church district has some autonomy to establish its local *Ordnung*.

Other factors also lead to diverse traditions and behavior. For example, Amish groups in the same settlement sometimes belong to different affiliations (clusters of church districts that are governed by shared *Ordnung*). The Big Valley of central Pennsylvania has several Amish affiliations, including three main affiliations, each with its own set of standards.[16] For example, each affiliation has its own distinctive carriage. Members of the Renno group drive all-black carriages, the Byler people ride in yellow-topped carriages, and the so-called Nebraska Amish drive white-topped carriages.

These three affiliations can also be distinguished by the color and style of their clothing, by the length and cut of their hair, and by their use of technology. In contrast to the Renno and Byler Amish, the Nebraska men wear brown coats instead of black, and the women wear head scarves instead of organdy head coverings. The Renno and the Byler groups may use gas refrigerators, but most of the Nebraska groups forbid their use.

Adams County, Indiana, has five distinct affiliations, and in the Holmes-Wayne-Stark County settlement of Ohio at least six Amish affiliations coexist, often side by side. They range from the ultraconservative Swartzentruber Amish, who reject most modern technology, to the progressive New Order Amish, who have telephones, electricity in their houses, and tractors in their fields (Kraybill 1994a, 53–74). Differences also exist among the youth of the affiliations in recreation, dating, and wedding customs. These distinctives generally center on what each affiliation regards as moral or immoral behavior and how each group practices its Christian faith.

For example, the New Order Amish originated in Ohio in the late 1960s, splitting from the Old Orders over moral and theological issues, especially as they related to acceptable behavior among the youth (Kline and Beachy 1998). New Order founders objected to several traditional Old Order practices, such as using tobacco and certain courtship practices. The New Order Amish also adopted more intentional but nontraditional practices such as Sunday school and Wednesday night church gatherings for the youth. Additionally, they spoke out strongly against the Saturday night party behavior and certain courtship practices. These religious distinctions, more than external differences, became the defining issues that separated the two groups.[17]

A Snapshot of Two Communities

Adult-Centered Communities

Wherever the settlement or whatever visual images are associated with Amish communities, outsiders may be tempted to envision a picture-perfect Amish life, unchanged over the centuries. Especially in small traditional communities, Amish life may appear untouched by the present. On the Saturday night before the Sunday worship service, families will complete their farm or shop work in preparation for "the Lord's Day." Most of the activity will center around the kitchen, where the family may read, play games, or talk about plans for the next day. If tomorrow is an "off Sunday" instead of a "church Sunday," courting couples will see each other at the home of the young woman.

On church Sundays, virtually all teens attend the three-hour worship service and closely mirror their parents and grandparents in dress and grooming. Like their fathers, the young men wear their hair in the traditional "blunt cut," a squared-off Dutchboy style. The young women part their long hair in the middle and pull it back in a tight bun in the traditional fashion. They wear dark stockings, and dresses that reach at least midway down their calves. The congregation sings from the *Ausbund*, a venerable German hymnbook with no notes that has been used in Anabaptist worship for more than four hundred years. Those youth who do not sing at least turn to the right page and sit quietly during the sermons.

Following the service, all the young people stay for the light communal meal. Afterward they might chat with friends, go hiking, or play volleyball until supper or until the Sunday evening youth singing begins. These peaceful Sunday scenes are reminiscent of the simple rural life of a century ago with its horse-and-buggy pace and its cross-generational mix of family, relatives, and friends. Some communities do, in fact, approach this ideal, especially in the more isolated settlements such as those in Kentucky, Michigan, and Wisconsin.

Peer-Centered Communities

But life on the inside is rarely as simple or as perfect as it appears from the outside. Picture the same scene on any Saturday night in a large Amish settlement in Pennsylvania, Ohio, or Indiana, where thousands of Amish youth live in close proximity, not only to each other but also to surrounding urban centers. Here, clusters of Amish teenagers lounge outside the local 7-Eleven store on Saturday evening. Some have come to town by horse and buggy, but others drive cars, pickup trucks, or SUVs. If most girls wear Amish clothes, their organdy head coverings may be precariously perched far back on their heads, the hems of their dresses may be shortened to barely reach their knees, and they may wear ankle socks instead of traditional stockings. Some of the more daring girls may change into English clothes in the restroom of a local convenience store or fast food restaurant. In parts of the Midwest, girls sometimes appear in jeans or shorts.

Most of the boys sport "barber" haircuts, and some have hidden their plain clothing in plastic bags in the back of their buggies, in family mail boxes, or even between corn rows while they dress "English." Few, if any, wear the traditional broad-brimmed hats or suspenders. Some smoke cigarettes while discussing the latest standing of their local Amish softball team. Others talk about the band hop, hoedown, or party starting later that night that will attract hundreds of young people and may feature live music, dancing, and lots of alcohol.

Since parties often last till 3:00 or 4:00 a.m., fewer than half of the youth may show up for church in some districts. Those who do attend often slump or sleep through the singing, Scripture reading, and sermons. Afterward, many teens will skip the communal meal to join their friends from other church districts for afternoon recreation or more partying. Some of the youth, especially males, may still be feeling the effects from Saturday night or may be getting high or drunk again.

Just as the pastoral scene failed to depict all small-settlement youth, this large-settlement scene represents only the rowdier young people. Yet most Amish agree that these two vignettes accurately represent life today in both kinds of settlements. Whether compliant or rebellious, youth in both settlements are involved in the heady experience of *Rumspringa*. In their Pennsylvania German dialect, this term literally means "running around" and does not necessarily denote wild or deviant behavior. It simply means that youth have freedom at age sixteen to socialize and date without close supervision. To varying degrees, they begin socializing with their friends on weekends instead of staying at home.

Myths of *Rumspringa*

Most, if not all, Amish studies scholars do not believe that *Rumspringa* is a built-in "time out" period when young people are set free from parental and community restrictions. The phrase "time out" was coined by journalists writing about a major drug arrest among some Amish youth in Lancaster County in the 1990s. Many of these reporters incorrectly assumed that Amish adolescents are given total freedom, if not parental and community encouragement, to taste the forbidden pleasures of the world before rejecting them to join the church. Thus they equated "sowing wild oats" with *Rumspringa* and assumed that most Amish youth "go wild" during the running-around years. The journalists did not realize that they were reporting on the most deviant element in a large settlement. Writers who delved deeper discovered that the majority of the youth in large settlements and most of those in small settlements did not experiment with headline-making activities. Nor was *Rumspringa* deliberately created by Amish parents so that their youth could distance themselves in the outside world. Contrary to media myths, very few Amish youth move away from their families. Even though their focus shifts to their peers, the overwhelming majority of youth still live at home.

Why the Differences?

When asked to speculate on why such differences exist among communities in the behavior of the youth, most Amish parents and ministers do not mention specific rules or lack of them but quickly attribute the causes to adult or community failures. They mention dissension in the church, lax discipline by leaders, careless parents, or inconsistent adults. Many Amish also believe that those settlements where most of the fathers are farmers have fewer problems with their youth than those with fathers employed in factories, construction crews, or other work venues away from home.

Others cite factors such as the settlement's isolation, or more commonly, its size. "When it comes to the young folk," declared a bishop from Illinois, "the larger the settlement, the larger the problems." Similarly, a minister mused, "It's easier to corral ten calves than a hundred." Actually, the size of the settlement appears to be the major predictor of youth behavior. Settlements that consist of a single church district with a few families, such as in Oceola, Missouri, or only two or three church districts, such as Somerset County, Pennsylvania, tend to have few problems with their youth. On the other hand, the largest three settlements of Holmes-Wayne-Stark counties in Eastern Ohio, Lancaster County in Pennsylvania, and Elkhart-Lagrange counties in Indiana regularly encounter not only more problems with their youth but the conspicuous or illegal behaviors that catch the attention of the public and the media.[18]

Although most people would regard these three largest Amish enclaves as rural, someone has dubbed them the "Urban Amish" because of their large numbers. Together, these three settlements consist of several different Amish affiliations, contain hundreds of church districts, and are home to nearly two-thirds of all Amish. All other settlements are significantly smaller than the big three and are typically more isolated from urban areas.[19]

The relationship between settlement size and youth behavior likely stems from demographic changes that occurred in the 1930s and 40s. During the early decades of the twentieth century, while church districts were small and grew slowly, an Amish young person's peers consisted primarily of the family and childhood friends from the local church district and immediate vicinity. Before 1950, the Amish population in America barely exceeded the population of a single large settlement today, and, according to an Amish historian who lived during that period, was fairly static.[20] Improved health care and strong retention contributed to the exponential population growth among the Amish, especially apparent in the large settlements.[21]

Because of this growth, the demand for good farmland began to outstrip the supply. Farm sizes began to shrink as parents divided their property among their children.[22] As their communities grew, more families moved into nonfarming occupations. Of course, many more nonfarming family plots than farms could be squeezed into a given area. Thus, the growing numbers of people, coupled with the smaller farms and nonfarming households, resulted in a greater density of Amish families in the larger settlements. Now, instead of church districts being fifteen or twenty miles across, some became as small as four or five square miles. And instead of needing to travel long distances to visit friends, young people were able to easily associate with a variety of peers with a short buggy ride. These changes produced social influences with enormous implications for youth and their parents. As the Amish population expanded in the large settlements during the early 1950s, a few young people began to break away from the single large Sunday night singing to socialize with smaller groups of peers.[23] This had rarely, if ever, happened before among the Amish.

Another change that led to wider peer contacts began in the early 1950s when some of the teenage boys began driving cars during *Rumspringa*. Until then, a youth's birth community shaped the selection of friends more than one's social preferences. Now the new demographics and mobility provided greater opportunities to find like-minded companions who shared and reinforced their particular interests, values, and proclivities.[24]

It is unlikely that mid-twentieth-century Amish leaders and parents realized the impact that these demographic changes would have on their communities. As young people began socializing with other youth farther from home, accountability diminished. Youth discovered other peers whom they had not even known before but who, like themselves, left their home church district to enjoy the excitement and stimulation afforded by clusters of like-minded youth. A bishop's wife declared flatly, "It's the anonymity our youth have that leads to trouble."

In the larger settlements, the growing numbers of young people, coupled with a choice of peers, ushered in significant changes in social interactions that transformed Amish youth culture. Thus, the antecedents of present social networks and behavior in large settlements started to emerge with the peer choices made more than a half-century ago by the grandparents of today's Amish teenagers.

Whose Standards Anyway?

In Amish circles, especially in the large settlements, adults frequently express concerns about the attitudes and behaviors of the youth. Leaders may not connect past demographic changes with what is happening on weekends, but the behavior of the youth, or *Youngie* as they are affectionately called in the dialect, is a frequent topic. A perplexed father from a large settlement asked, "Why do our young people have to carry on like this? So many of the youth in this community do not care what us parents or church leaders think or believe. They only care about what their friends will think or say and about having a good time." Many adults add their concerns about adolescents in the large settlements and speculate as to why more problems and "fun-seekers" emerge there than in the smaller settlements.

Although neither Amish adults nor youth would use the terms *adult-centered* or *peer-centered,* most would recognize that these concepts describe the difference in orientation of the youth in large and small settlements. During *Rumspringa,* adult-youth interaction tends to be much higher in the small settlements than in the larger ones. In a future chapter, we will see that many large-settlement youth spend almost all weekend every week with their peers, whereas their small-settlement counterparts typically spend only a few hours a month at the singing socials with their peers.

Small-settlement youth have more opportunity to absorb adult standards and thus behave and think more conservatively. On the other hand, youth with extensive peer contact may behave in ways that are less acceptable to adults.

A major indicator of adult-centered settlements is the continuity of behavior from the teen years to adulthood. Continuity refers to a fairly smooth or seamless transition from childhood to adulthood in areas of dress, mode of transportation, recreation, and dating and courting practices.[25] Conservative youth behave in ways that are consistent with adult behavior and expectations. When these sixteen-year-olds begin "going with the youth," their actions primarily reflect the traditional standards of their parents and great grandparents.

Likewise, conservative young people sound more like the adults of the community, especially when they condemn certain changes, which they refer to as "drift," meaning the growing tendency of the youth to violate church rules or act disobediently to the parents. For example, a seventeen-year-old boy from a small settlement who had recently visited one of the larger settlements exclaimed, "I think it's awful the way the young folk behave over there. They drink and smoke and carry on at the singings. It's a disgrace." He also added, "When some young people from their settlement visited us, they got bored right away; they didn't know what to do out here." His grandfather would have undoubtedly agreed with the young man's assessment.

Peer-centered settlements demonstrate much more discontinuity between adult expectations and youth behavior. When these sixteen-year-olds begin their *Rumspringa,* many show a dramatic change in behavior, especially the boys. They often ignore or modify traditional dress standards and engage in activities that would result in excommunication for church members. Their *Rumspringa* behavior is more disconnected from traditional Amish behavior, before and after their running-around time.

Determining whether a community is adult-centered or peer-centered is not simply a matter of settlement size, however, because adult-peer orientation also reflects a community's local history, tradition, and moral beliefs. Peers can either oppose or reinforce the adult values and mores in communities of any size. Because of strong negative peer pressures, some small settlements also struggle with the rowdy behavior more common in large settlements. For example, although one of the young women who participated in *Amish in the City* grew up in a large settlement, two of the small settlement young men experienced many of the same behaviors that more typically characterize the fringes of the larger settlements.

Despite the exceptions, most Amish would agree that settlement size is a useful factor in predicting youthful attitudes and behaviors. But many other factors, past and present, help build an Amish mindset that retains the faithful and brings the wayward back to the fold. We turn first to the religious underpinnings upon which Amish society is constructed.

*Every other Sunday, young and old meet for a three-hour
church service in a member's home.*
Photo by Keith Baum.

CHAPTER TWO

Socialization

Passing on the Faith

When I was baptized, I felt clean as a whistle.
—Amish father

A Faith Community

Although most textbooks on adolescence devote little attention to religious practices and faith development, any study of Amish youth that neglects the subject would be seriously deficient. Much has been written to describe Amish worship rituals and beliefs, but little attention has been directed to moral or spiritual development, the transmission of faith to the young, and the religious practices of the youth.[1] Most young people, no matter how neglectful or wayward, would agree with the words of an elderly bishop: "Our faith is at the heart of Amish life, the foundation on which we seek to build our relationships, vocations, family, and communal life. If anyone fails to understand that, they will never really understand who we are and what we are about."

A non-Amish observer, accustomed to the compartmentalizing of secular and religious life, might assume that in the highly structured Amish society, every facet of community life rigorously instructs and enforces the tenets of Amish faith. Outsiders might expect Amish practices to resemble the extremism of David Koresh's Davidian compound or Sun Myung Moon's Unification Church. Actually, for a religious culture that strives to leave nothing to chance or to the outside world, Amish communities provide relatively little *formal* religious instruction in the home or even in Amish schools.

Of course, parents admonish their children and youth to obey God and their parents, revere the Scriptures, recognize God as the creator and sustainer of life, and submit themselves to Christ and the teachings of the Bible. In most communities, however, formal religious instruction occurs only after the youth, usually in their late teens, have expressed their intention to join the church. Prior to that, according to Kraybill and Bowman, "religion is not formally taught in the school or in other Amish settings" (2001, 114). Formal instruction in the faith occurs only during the preparatory class for church membership.

Youth and Worship

Although church leaders do not adapt traditional forms and practices to the interest level or preferences of the young, an estimated 90 percent choose to join the church and to remain Amish for life (Kraybill 2001, 186). Neither does the church employ age-appropriate curricula, junior church, or interactive instruction. Infants, children, and youth sit through adult-centered services along with their grandparents, parents, siblings, and neighbors. They sing the same songs and hear the same sermons as the adults. Moreover, everyone expects the young to sit quietly through a long, thoroughly predictable, adult-oriented worship service. A bishop observed, "The reason there are so many good deer hunters with bow and arrow among the Amish is because they are used to sitting still for three hours in church."

As a further challenge, all hymns, prayers, and scriptures are written in old sixteenth-century "high" German, the language Martin Luther used to translate the Bible. Since the Amish never use this idiom in daily discourse, the youth face a challenge similar to that of mainstream youth listening to Chaucer's *Canterbury Tales*. "When I was younger," a man recalled, "I had to concentrate so hard to understand High German that I would eventually give up and start to think about the Phillies' game in the afternoon." A twenty-five-year-old man admitted, "Our family sometimes reads the Bible at home in English, but in church I understand very little of the scripture readings and hymns."

When asked how members learn the old German, he replied that most learn throughout their adult years.[2] Ministers preach in the Pennsylvania German vernacular, their first language, but sermons may last nearly an hour and a half, which is beyond the attention span of many adults, let alone children and youth. In the plainest settlements, some ministers still preach in an old-fashioned sing-song or chant-like style, rarely establishing eye contact with the faithful. A few even preach with their eyes closed. Finally, everyone must endure the discomfort of cramped seating, hard benches —and depending on the season, a hot stuffy house, dusty barn, or drafty shop. Despite these conditions, the Amish transmit their faith effectively, if their high retention rate is any indication.

In most settlements, children and most youth regularly attend church. Although they always sit with their peers, they rarely "carry on" or disturb worship by talking. However, parents admit that it is hard to know how many youth are actually engaged in the prayers and sermons. During the reading of the scriptures in some settlements, half or more of the young men leave for an ostensible bathroom break. And if posture or eye contact is an indicator, youth generally appear to be less involved in worship than the adults, but that also varies from place to place. One parent indicated, "I think they are listening. When they get home, young people can be quite critical of boring sermons. They will also get upset when ministers harp on things such as dress or the behavior of the *Youngie*. 'They should be preaching from the Bible,' our youngest son says."

The Religious "Curriculum"

Most Old Order communities do not supplement the Sunday services with any of the traditional Protestant programs such as Sunday schools, summer vacation Bible schools, or Bible study groups. Traditionally, Amish have associated Sunday schools with more liberal Anabaptists and mainline churches.[3] Expressing a negative attitude toward typical Sunday schools, an

Amish minister voiced his disapproval of non-ordained men or women instructing in matters of faith. Another elder stated, "We are concerned about what might be taught to our children and the lack of safeguards against error." Finally, a leader argued that if the Sunday school was such a good idea, it would have been part of the New Testament church.[4]

This belief that the family and the ordained leaders carry primary responsibility for religious interpretation and instruction may explain why Amish schools provide little specific religious teaching. This differs significantly from many non-Amish conservative religious groups who regard the parochial school as a mainstay for the teaching and propagation of their faith. The curriculum in many private religious schools presents doctrinal beliefs in a systematic fashion. By contrast, most Amish schools do not use an explicitly religious curriculum. Additionally, the teachers are usually women, and based on 1 Corinthians 14:34–35, the Amish consider it wrong for females to instruct their students in matters of faith.

This does not mean that classes are devoid of religious content. In most Amish schools, teachers start the day by reading a biblical passage, leading the children in singing hymns and gospel songs, and reciting the Lord's Prayer. Teachers typically assign "memory verses" from the King James Version of the Bible, especially from the Sermon on the Mount, a favorite Anabaptist passage. In some communities, pupils in the upper grades memorize both scripture and songs in old German for the equivalent of one or two class periods per week.

However, teachers are instructed to simply make the assignments and not explain the scripture passages. A section addressed to teachers from the booklet *Standards of the Old Order Amish and Old Order Mennonite Parochial and Vocational Schools of Pennsylvania* (1981) admonishes, "Instructors are advised not to include Sunday school lessons, not induce the child to be Scripture-smart for religious show. Scripture teaches simplicity by examples. Do not beguile [sic] that which belongs to the Church and its leaders." In one large Amish affiliation, some leaders consider writings about God too sacred to be printed in textbooks. Consequently, their curriculum and textbooks are generally morality-based rather than specifically religious. They emphasize the values of hard work, thrift, honesty, and humility, with some references to the Bible.

Teaching by Word and Deed

Ideally, the community expects all adults to teach the faith through examples of consistent living. They believe that the young come to spiritual maturity more from what they see than from what they hear. The Amish believe that one's life is the most important text. As we will soon see, the first requisite for an Amish schoolteacher is that she provide a positive example to her students. Everyone regards her knowledge, mental abilities, teaching, and management skills as secondary. Although the teacher is certainly an arm and a voice for the community, Amish parents strongly believe that they have the ultimate responsibility to "prepare the soil," plant the seeds of faith, and nurture the spiritual development of their families: "Our major task as parents," explained an Amish father, "is to pass our faith on to our children."[5]

In many Old Order settlements, parents have traditionally used the off-Sunday mornings for religious readings and reflection. "We were taught that off-Sunday should be used for the family *Sunndaagschul* (Sunday school). We would read the Bible, memorize Bible verses in English or German, and pray together, but we were not supposed to explain the Word of God—just read it," explained a grandfather from a large settlement.

Most Old Order Amish believe that religious discussions are more appropriate among adults and that the final interpretation comes from the ordained ministers in communal worship. Parents are expected to teach their children in the "nurture and admonition of the Lord" (Ephesians 6:4), providing a loving Christian family and being faithful examples to the children. Parents are also the guardians to protect their offspring from unhealthy worldly influences and reinforce the teachings of the church.

In daily discourse, parents admonish their children to live obedient, faithful, and moral lives. One Amishman recalled his parents' admonitions and reminders of forty years ago:

> God sees what we do . . . He can see into our hearts . . . When we do wrong, it is sin . . . Don't lie . . . Don't harm others . . . Play nice with other children . . . Keep yourself clean . . . Look constantly to God . . . Remember that Christ has the forgiveness for sins.

Depending on the family and community, many households routinely start or end the day by reading a passage from the Bible and a prayer from *Die Ernsthafte Christenpflicht,* a prayer book.[6] In typical homes, fathers read the scripture and prayer in old German. Amish adults rarely pray extemporaneously, nor are family times designed for scriptural or religious interpretation or religious dialogue with their children or youth.

This lack of individual religious discourse cannot be equated with an absence of devotion; rather, it may simply indicate that a majority of Amish accept the religious teachings and practices of the church with few serious questions or reservations. Adults do not encourage their youth to analyze their beliefs and practices or subject them to critical scrutiny. Most embrace their religious faith without questions or simply absorb it from the "landscape" of daily life.[7]

This does not mean, however, that conscientious parents are disengaged from their children's moral and spiritual development. For example, in most families parents are involved in the careful selection and monitoring of reading materials available to their children. Many families own a copy of *Martyrs' Mirror,* an eleven-hundred-page book that describes the persecution and suffering of the early Anabaptist martyrs through graphic accounts and vivid engravings. Amish periodicals such as *Young Companion* and *Family Life* are popular in many homes. The stories and articles in both magazines emphasize adherence to Christian ideals and strict moral standards.[8]

Unlike mainline and evangelical church publications, Amish magazines rarely feature devotional guides, scriptural analyses, or even Bible stories. Rather, they are filled with stories and short essays by Amish and Old Order Mennonites, often written anonymously to avoid pride or pretentiousness. The articles emphasize religious values and themes such as the responsibility of parents, obedience to those in authority, submission to God's will, nonresistance, and separation from worldly temptations and activities. Youth and adults commonly read both magazines, despite the different target groups.

The Ultimate Decision

About the time Amish children finish their formal schooling in early adolescence, they are considered to be approaching the "age of accountability,"
the stage at which they are assumed to fully know right from wrong and
understand the implications of their choices. After they begin attending the
youth singings, the adults consider them to be accountable for their choices
and behaviors.

As the youth approach this age, the bishop and ministers, especially in
the smaller settlements, increasingly admonish them to set aside any sinful
behaviors and to start "counting the cost" of becoming a baptized member of
the church. Even though most Old Order ministers preach about the necessity of the new birth, their emphasis is much more on being baptized into the
community of faith than on a personal salvation experience with God.

The age at which young people decide to join the church varies. In most
Old Order groups, parents hope that their children will take instruction and
then receive baptism between the ages of sixteen and nineteen. In some
large settlements, however, youth typically join between the ages of eighteen
and twenty-one. Females almost always join the church at a younger age
than males. Youth in small, isolated settlements or in New Order churches
typically join earlier than do youth from the larger settlements. Leaders in
the larger communities observe that in the last thirty years, youth have been
waiting longer to join than their parents and grandparents did, especially
the males. Some of them have even been delaying membership instruction
beyond their mid-twenties. The adults almost always attribute this delay to
the young men's desire to "keep their vehicles and have a good time for a
while longer." Some Amish observers believe that the trend has begun to
move toward earlier membership since the 1990s.

Amish Catechism

No young person joins the church without first receiving teaching in religious beliefs and practices from the local bishop and ministers. During the
first hymn on a Sunday morning, usually in the spring, the self-declared
candidates for church membership join their clergy in the "council room,"

usually an upstairs bedroom of the home. This is an important day in the life of the church, a day of both anticipation and apprehension. The ministers, and even the parents, do not always know who will decide to take instruction and who will delay for yet another year or more.[9]

One minister reported, "My wife and I were holding our breath Sunday morning, watching to see if our son would enter the room with the youth or remain outside with the candidates, waiting to meet the ministers. He was only sixteen, and we weren't sure he was ready. When we went out to lead the waiting candidates up to the council room, I was greatly relieved to find him there along with the others who were starting in the instruction class." In all settlements, parents hope and pray that their children's closest friends and relatives take instruction at the "right age," since youth tend to join at the same time as their closest friends.

Some parents, especially in the large settlements, experience the disappointment of facing another year of waiting, hoping, and praying if their children fail to take the membership step. One father hoped that his son might give up playing in the local softball league in order to enter the current class but admitted it was very unlikely: "He is really good, and softball has taken over in his life. It looks like he is out [of church] for another year." Meanwhile, a bishop asked, "If a young man is not willing to give up softball, what kind of church member is he going to make anyway?"

Those who decide to "take instruction" meet every other Sunday with the bishop, ministers, and deacon during the first thirty or forty minutes of the worship service for eight or nine sessions. At the beginning of every meeting, each candidate affirms, "I am a seeker desiring to be part of this church of God." In most districts, the classes are devoted to explaining the articles of the Dordrecht Confession, two articles per class, for a total of nine sessions.

This 1632 document summarizes the historic beliefs and practice of the early Dutch Anabaptists.[10] Although candidates may not know scriptural references or be able to recall specific points, they are already familiar with the themes. They have repeatedly heard all of the beliefs and practices from the Confession in past sermons at church and in conversations at home. Thus, the content of the classes may be less important than the symbolic submission of oneself to the instruction by those who have been ordained by God to lead the church.

The eighteen articles begin with the foundational belief in God the Creator and proceed through the second coming of Christ as the final judge. They also explain the basis for the Amish adherence to the typical Anabaptist practices of adult baptism, separation from the world, non-swearing of oaths, nonparticipation in the civil government, nonresistance, foot washing, excommunication, and shunning, or social avoidance.[11] In Lancaster County, the third session covers each point of the local *Ordnung*.

All young people who are preparing for membership are expected to move into compliance with the local church *Ordnung*, especially if they have been lax or straying in their behavior. Ministers and church members seek evidence of sincerity, especially from youth who have practiced behavior "outside of the *Ordnung*," such as car ownership, worldly dress, and partying. By the end of the classes, if the young men have failed to let their hair grow to the proper length or the young women's hemlines are too short, they will be "held back" from baptism.

At the church service following fall communion, the ministers and members determine whether the candidates have come into full compliance. "If there is an improvement in whatever the problem is, they are baptized the same day. I would say 99 percent of the time it would be this way," a young Amishman wrote. Those who have still not fully complied will be "worked with," and if they change, they will be baptized within a few weeks. Otherwise, they will have another opportunity to prepare for membership when the next class forms. Such delays are relatively rare.

However, in a conservative settlement in Pennsylvania, the ministers "held back" a young man for membership three times because they felt he was too questioning and rebellious. He subsequently left the Amish. One test of the seriousness of the youth in Lancaster County is that they are not to go out at night with their peers on the first, third, ninth, and tenth weekends of instruction. After the bishop reviews the local *Ordnung* in the third session, the candidates must unequivocally discontinue all unacceptable behavior and move into total compliance with the rules. Some young people react like two sixteen-year-olds in a large settlement did. They simply dropped out of instruction after the deacon confronted them about their worldly behavior at Saturday night parties. They returned two years later for instruction, were baptized, and subsequently joined the church.

On the Saturday prior to baptism, the youth and their parents meet with the ministers a final time to review the Dordrecht Confession and the vows they will take. The ministers ask the candidates one final time if they still wish to be baptized and join the church. This is also the time when the bishops typically ask each young man if he is willing to serve in the ministry if the lot or choice should ever fall on him, as described in Acts 1:23–26. Undoubtedly, asking the candidates on several occasions if they still wish to continue their instruction emphasizes the informed choice that Anabaptists value so highly.

Normally, baptism and reception into membership occur during a Sunday morning following the fall communion. The service is considerably longer than a regular church service. After four or five hours of singing, prayer, scripture reading, and two sermons, the candidates for baptism, who have been sitting together on a bench, rise and answer the following questions that the presiding bishop asks:

Q. Can you confess as the Ethiopian eunuch confessed?
A. *Yes, I believe that Jesus Christ is the Son of God.*
Q. Do you acknowledge it to be a Christian order, church, and fellowship of God, under which you now submit yourselves?
A. *Yes.*
Q. Do you renounce the world, the devil with all his doings, as well as your own flesh and blood, and do you desire to live for Jesus Christ alone, who died on the cross for you and rose again?
A. *Yes.*
Q. Do you also promise in the presence of the Lord and the church to support these teachings and regulations, help to counsel and work in the congregation, and not to forsake the faith, whether it leads to life or death?
A. *Yes.*

The candidates then kneel before the bishop, who says, "Upon your faith, which you have confessed, you are baptized in the name of the Father, the Son, and the Holy Spirit. Amen."[12]

As the bishop mentions each member of the Trinity, the deacon pours water from a pitcher through the bishop's cupped hands, which have been resting on the candidate's head. After everyone is baptized, the bishop grasps the hand of each kneeling young man and raises him to his feet saying, "In the name of the Lord and the church, I extend to you the hand of fellowship. Rise up." He then gives the new member a handshake and places a holy kiss on his lips. The bishop's wife extends the same greeting to each new female member.[13]

Of course, baptism affects each candidate differently. One father, recounting his baptism thirty-five years earlier, recalled, "When I was baptized, I felt clean as a whistle—I could have died right then and I knew that I would have gone straight to heaven." "You don't always stay at that level," he added. "For some people, they are converted right then. For others, I believe it's the start of something gradual."

Some Amish describe coming to faith before they ever attended instruction class or became baptized. A mother describes how her life changed because of a dream. "I was sixteen or seventeen, and I would come home from a weekend with my friends feeling terrible about the things I was doing. But I would be back at the same things the next weekend. One night I had a dream that I was waiting in line at the final judgment, but when Jesus got to me, he looked doubtful and said that He would have to think about it. He said my record was not too good. I woke up and decided to change. Within a month I was going in a different direction, and I was eventually baptized." However one responds, the intensity, instruction, scrutiny, and ceremony surrounding baptism underscore the importance the Amish place on an informed and volitional covenant in becoming part of the church.

Passing on the Faith

Because the candidates receive less than eight hours of formal religious instruction, other factors must account for why Amish communities and families are so successful in transmitting their faith. Ideally, the Amish believe that all of life has religious significance and should be lived carefully and intentionally for the Lord. They implicitly acknowledge God's sovereignty in both the mundane and extraordinary events of life. They recognize God's hand in providing the daily blessings of good weather and good health and also acknowledge his sustaining grace in times of drought or disaster. They see evidence of God in the cycles of life, the circles of the seasons, their daily work, and their designated "lot in life." The entire community authenticates these shared beliefs and reaffirms them individually and corporately. The Amish are imbued with the sense that they have been privileged and are responsible for being God's children "in the midst of a crooked and perverse nation" (Philippians 2:15).

The Amish ideal is submission to God's will, to divinely appointed leaders, and to the community of faith. This means that after they join the church, they promise to remain Amish until death. These lessons are not lost on the children and youth. God's will, whether revealed through the Bible and the church or through selection to ministry by the casting of lots, transcends personal preference or convenience.

As parents submit themselves to the teaching and discipline of the church, they are in turn teaching their children about ultimate priorities, faith, and commitment. No wonder their children follow the way of faith. Through "precept and example," the soil has been prepared to nurture the seeds of faith and commitment.

As Kraybill has pointed out, spirituality for the Old Order churches is more communal and traditional than individual, and the children learn through modeling and assimilation more than from direct instruction.[14] The responsibility of transmitting the faith to the next generation belongs not only to individual couples but also to the extended family and the entire community. Everyone understands the parameters and expectations. As one aged grandmother remarked, "We have some who don't do [practice], but we have none who don't know."[15] To assure that no one forgets, before each spring and fall communion, ministers review the *Ordnung* with the entire church and then ask each individual member, young and old, if he or she is in agreement and compliance with it. Thus the vows of faithfulness are renewed twice each year.

The New Order Challenge

Although the more progressive New Order churches share many of the same practices and assumptions of their Old Order counterparts, the religious environment for youth growing up in New Order churches differs in some significant ways. One is the age at which young people typically join the church. In most settlements, New Order youth join around the age of sixteen, two or three years earlier than their typical Old Order counterparts. Some have even joined as young as fourteen years of age.

Also, if the content and sheer number of their publications are any indicators, New Order leaders are much more intentional in discussing and disseminating their religious convictions, both to members and to outsiders. For example, several New Order ministers and lay leaders have written and published booklets on plain dress, godly homes, theological errors, and the evils of bed courtship. [16]

New Order definitions of living separate and faithful lives include a strong emphasis on a spiritual new birth and the belief that one can know that he or she is in right standing with God. These theological issues also characterize the progressive Beachy Amish, a small plain-dressing offshoot that permits car ownership.[17] Also, similar to the Beachy Amish, some New Order members support missionary activities and witnessing to their faith—explaining to outsiders their need for salvation through repentance of their sins, obedience to Christ, and the acceptance of God's salvation.

Occasionally, New Order members may even offer outsiders religious tracts or pamphlets or speak about the necessity of being born again to go to heaven. In contrast, Old Order members generally speak about their "hope of salvation" or the quiet witness of a faithful life, but only when they are directly asked about their beliefs and lifestyle. When asked about his Christian life, an Old Order man reportedly answered, "Ask my friends, family, and people I work with. They know how I live and should be able to answer that question."[18]

Although the general format of worship remains virtually the same in both groups, visitors often note a different tone, tempo, and emphasis between them. New Order services are characterized by faster singing, a more conversational tone in the sermons, and the use of more English words and eye contact.[19] A New Order minister who visited a Swartzentruber Amish service reported, "During the sermon, I happened to catch the bishop's eye while he was speaking. He totally lost his train of thought when we established eye contact. Their ministers are not used to that."

Even the level of involvement of the young people in the services appears to be different. In general, New Order youth participate in singing more consistently than their Old Order cousins. Also, relatively few New Order youth leave during the scripture reading for the traditional bathroom break. "If our young people begin leaving too often or staying too long," said one New Order man, "the ministers will bring it up in the members' meeting following the church service."[20]

New Order churches in most places still maintain the cultural distinctiveness of plain dress, house church, German singing and preaching, and horse and carriage transportation. However, their theological distinctives have, in fact, led to practices more typical of their conservative Mennonite cousins or even religious practices typical of some conservative evangelical or fundamentalist groups. For example, New Order parents are expected to conduct family worship or devotions each day. Unless outside employment interferes, everyone living at home attends. In at least one district, parental failure in this area brought censure by the ministers. This kind of scrutiny of family worship practices is not typical among the Old Order Amish.

Unlike their traditional Old Order neighbors, many New Order parents prefer to read the Bible and pray in English. Additionally, they are more likely to discuss with their children the meaning and implications of the scriptural passages that have been read. Also, they may ask family members to say a spontaneous prayer.

Another basic difference is that both New Order adults and youth will more frequently voice their disapproval of the use of tobacco or alcohol, involvement in worldly activities such as card playing, reading romance or Western novels, or dancing of any kind. Their strict courtship requirements discourage physical involvement, such as holding hands or kissing.[21]

Youth Concerns

New Order Amish adults have typically been more intentional in assessing the needs and concerns of their youth. For example, adult leaders often invite the young people at their annual youth gatherings to submit questions to a panel of ministers. Their questions provide a window into the moral issues and religious concerns which engage their youth: "What are some subtle sins that we should be careful not to let creep into our youth group? In what areas could we as youth improve in the church? How can we best keep from drifting along with the tide? What is the best way to keep our flesh [human temptations] crucified? Can you give some advice as how to keep our thought life pure and holy?"

Conspicuously absent in this sample were questions challenging the status quo or requesting explanations from the ministers as to why certain practices are forbidden. Rather than revealing dissatisfaction with the group expectations or prohibitions, these questions focused more on internal moral and religious concerns. The questions, at least from this group, reflected a sense of accountability to God for high moral and spiritual standards as opposed to simply abiding by traditional expectations. These young people were not trying to wrest concessions from their leaders or seeking to "crowd the fence." Rather, they expressed a desire to align their inner lives and outward behavior with their understanding of the Bible and the teachings of the church.[22]

Of course, such spiritual concerns are not limited to one group or affiliation of Amish. But given the differences that exist between New and Old Order groups, New Order youth appear to be more intensely invested in religious matters than their Old Order counterparts. Although some of their communities have compromised with the telephone, tractor, and power-line electricity, New Order young people must still conform to most other traditional Amish practices—plain dress, the German dialect, horse transportation, nonresistance, and excommunication—which set them apart from the world, mainstream Christianity, and most other Anabaptist groups.

In addition, New Order Amish must adhere to rigorous moral standards in dating and recreational activities. Most important, they need to profess to having a personal experience of God's salvation. They must practice "private daily devotions" consisting of Bible study and prayer. Also they are expected to demonstrate a willingness to share their faith with those who have not been saved.

These internal and external demands likely make their faith and practice more salient on both cognitive and emotional levels. For the New Order youth, their faith and practice must always be in the foreground. Their experiencing of faith with its inherent joys and responsibilities may be similar to that of conscientious young people in evangelical churches. On the other hand, Old Order youth may feel fewer demands to verbalize their faith or engage in evangelizing. The deep meanings of their faith are found, not in individual experience, cognitive claims, or verbal statements. Such differences between the two groups might suggest at first blush that New Orders would retain a higher percent of their youth, but this is not the case, as we shall see later.

New Order / Old Order Tensions

In some instances, especially in the 1970s and 1980s, differences between the New and the Old Orders were great enough to strain relationships. From the start, New Order members and youth were critical of groups that used tobacco and alcohol or tolerated dancing, partying, and certain courtship practices. When the New Order split first occurred in Ohio in the 1960s, members reported that some rowdy or overzealous Old Order youth occasionally disrupted their singings. They called the singers "goodie-good-ies" and criticized them for having a "holier-than-thou" attitude.[23] Recalling those days, a middle-aged New Order minister said, "I believe those things actually made us stronger. Nowadays, our young people have it so easy that they can just drift along without being challenged."

New Order members sometimes questioned the sincerity of some Old Order youths' decision to join the church. They would likely agree with the writer in *Family Life* who wrote the following: "When I was taking instructions for baptism, there were several in my [Old Order] group who were not permitted to date until they were baptized. On the evening of the day of their baptism, all of them dated. How sad that they should cast a dark shadow of suspicion upon their motives for being baptized."[24]

An Old Order minister who eventually left the Amish also questioned some of the practices of his day in a column in *Family Life*: "Young people sow their wild oats, living undisciplined and lustful lives until they want to get married. Then all of a sudden, they decide to join the church. Many people suspect deep down inside that they are joining the church to get married, and not because they have repented of their sins. Yet parents and ministers go along with this mockery, remarking to one another how thankful they are that the young people still have a desire to join the church. Sure enough, they are barely baptized until they get published and married."[25] The writer might have cringed to hear the father of a twenty-one-year-old say, "Daniel is sorry now that he didn't 'follow church' last time around because I think he has marriage on his mind."

Most Amish have heard of instances where youth reportedly had one last party fling before submitting to baptism and church membership the next day. Since these parties frequently involve alcohol, they occasionally end in accidents or death on the Saturday night before the Sunday that the young person is to be "taken up" into membership. These incidents have caused New Order members to wonder aloud how much Old Order "faithfulness" is primarily external and cultural. "Too many of them think they will get to heaven by simply living the Amish lifestyle." An elderly convert to the New Order charged that "for too many of them, it's simply following the culture instead of the Holy Spirit."[26] A critic stated, "The reason they have trouble with their young folk is that they have not been born again."

While admitting that some of these stories are true, Old Order members often regard the New Orders as simply "Mennonites in Amish clothing" or "Beachy Amish without the cars." They see them as sliding down the slippery slope of liberalism and loss of Amish identity. They charge the New Orders with "abandoning the ancient landmarks" and simply using talk of spirituality as a cover for their underlying desire for technology and the material trappings permitted in the more liberal groups.

However, not all Old Order members regard their New Order neighbors and relatives negatively. In candid moments, some ministers confess that they wish that their teens were "under control" as well as the youth in the New Order. They admit that far fewer New Order teenagers have cars or drivers' licenses than do their own teenagers, and they recognize that this, along with other differences, is attractive to many Amish parents.[27] One Old Order mother in a large settlement confessed, "I would rather see my child become New Order than join one of the youth groups that carries on like some of them do in this area."

On the other hand, Old Order members report private conversations with New Order neighbors who express regret for ever having left because their children tend to leave the Amish in much greater numbers from the

New Order. In fact, some New Order districts or settlements reportedly lose at least half of their youth, compared to the less than 20 percent loss estimated for the most progressive Old Order groups with the highest defection rates.[28] Needless to say, these defections both perplex and disturb New Order parents and leaders. They also provide powerful evidence to Old Order parents that if they want their youth to be Amish, their best hope is to remain faithful to their Old Order heritage.

Nonetheless, virtually all Amish, Old Order or New Order, affirm that affiliation, family, community life, and the security of tradition are all inadequate foundations or reasons for their group to survive. They point to their religious faith as the center for who they are and what they do. They find it unthinkable that any Amish community could continue without the centrality of that faith.

"When seekers from the outside come to us wanting to be Amish," explained a bishop, "they are often attracted for the wrong reasons. They could have fallen in love with one of our *Youngie*. Or they may have fallen in love with what they think is a simpler way of life. What they fail to recognize is that our faith in Christ is at the center. Horses, buggies, and kerosene lanterns will quickly grow stale without the faith foundation."

Most Amish would agree with his assessment, not only for seekers from the outside but for their own sons and daughters as well. They believe that ultimately their Christian faith provides the core that nurtures the faithful and the magnet that draws the wandering youth back to the fold. But as realists, they also know that a host of tangible cultural influences and practices nurture a strong Amish identity. It is to these we now turn our attention.

In some communities young women in a "buddy bunch" wear
identical colors to Sunday evening singings.
Photo by Blair Seitz.

Adolescence

Testing an Amish Identity

*It's a mistake for parents to think they can teach their children
right and wrong when they turn sixteen. You have to start when
they are in diapers.*
—Amish father

Identity and Autonomy

Although few Amish would articulate the importance of nurturing an
Amish identity in their children and youth, virtually all sense that the
formation of a such an identity is crucial for the retention of their young
and the continuation of their culture. In contrast, developmental psychologists contend that attaining both a clear identity and autonomy are critical
tasks in establishing a sharply defined, independent self. The Amish emphasize identifying with their culture, whereas psychologists focus more
on those attributes and choices that make an individual unique and provide
the sense of self that distinguishes someone from other people.[1] Autonomy
involves owning and taking personal control of one's own decisions, values,
and emotional life (Steinberg 2005, 299–300). Since developmental psychology regards identity and independence as equally important, it is not

surprising that college textbook writers usually devote separate chapters to identity and autonomy.

For the Amish, however, identity and autonomy are in tension, because autonomy tends to promote independence rather than the interdependence and compliance that the collectivist Amish demand. A second inherent tension emerges from the conflict between Amish collectivism and their Anabaptist belief in adult choice. Amish youth frequently face the conflicting demands of being expected to freely choose to be Amish while at the same time feeling the weight of the entire culture pushing them to follow the Amish way. Forming an Amish identity may not be as simple as it seems.

Erik Erikson (1968, 1980), the most influential psychologist in identity theory, contends that the resolution of identity is a universal psychosocial crisis for adolescents. If they resolve the crisis successfully, they will attain an achieved identity and a focused life. If they do not resolve it, they will remain in a state of identity confusion or diffusion. Fear, withdrawal, and hedonism impede the formation of a positive identity. James Marcia (1980) argues that the key to successful identity resolution hinges first upon exploring one's options and subsequently choosing—or failing to choose— from among the options. In both theories, the importance of struggling with options and choosing for oneself is central in achieving an authentic identity.

Identity theorists almost universally discuss identity in the context of an individualistic, pluralistic society. They focus on self issues such as self-esteem, self-concept, and self-efficacy—important subjects in mainstream American culture. By contrast, the Amish always think in terms of a web of relationships rather than a complex stage of development or hyphenated words beginning with *self*.

When the Amish think about a person's identity, it is much more likely to be plural than singular. They identify someone by their place within an extended family that reaches back for generations. It is not uncommon to hear an Amishman inquire, "How is Bill Joe Josie's Junior getting along?" Newlyweds Samuel Stoltzfus and Rebecca Lapp are "Caleb's Elam's Samuel" (grandfather-father-son), and "Daniel's Reuben's Rebecca" (her paternal lineage). In a society that knows both families' members and stories, weddings join for life two families and their histories every bit as much as they join two individuals. An example of what Pauline Stevick (2006) calls "the web of relationships" comes from a scribe's letter in *Die Botschaft* (9 August 2000): "We extend our sympathy to the Jake Smucker family. Jake died suddenly July 28. Jake served as preacher for 42 years. Jake's wife was in Doddy Sams relation. Her mother, Sadie King, married to Chris L. King was grandmother's Salome's niece. A daughter of Joel Fishers Lovina, the second wife of Chris K. Stoltzfus. This is the Lovina that was the second wife of Daniel S. Esh." The Amish care about such connections.

In the same manner, an important part of Samuel's and Rebecca's identity is also their church affiliation and even church district. In the Big Valley of Pennsylvania, being a "Nebraskan white-topper" and not a "Byler yellow-topper" provides instant recognition and information about a person's cultural identity to all Amish in the Valley, both within and outside of their particular group. Everyone knows that "low" Nebraska Amish dress and live more plainly than their "high," more progressive Byler neighbors. Each affiliation's *Ordnung* clearly delineates the expectations and distinctives of that particular group, key components of each member's identity.

Identity in a Collectivist Society

Whether conservative or progressive, however, the strictures against choosing for one's self-gratification or searching for self actualization reflect the collectivist nature of Amish society. As cross-cultural psychologist Harry Triandis (1990, 1995) points out, in collectivist societies such as in Japan, India, or West Africa, the group's well-being and priorities take precedence over the individuals' desires and preferences. Choice is appropriate only within group-approved options and only if it maintains and strengthens the group. Understanding this difference is central in comprehending the heart of Amish identity.

The task of Amish young people is not to distinguish themselves from others by their uniqueness and achievement but rather by their willingness to conform to the group. They are expected to strengthen the cohesion of the community through "giving up the self," as they term it. Despite their personal preferences or tendencies, they are expected to accept their district's collective *Ordnung* with its explicit rules for dress and behavior. An

Amish person's identity is achieved only by sacrificing much of his or her personal autonomy.

Because humans are weak and sacrifices difficult, the Amish believe that forming an Amish identity is too important to be left solely to the individual and her family. All members, individually and collectively, share the responsibility of helping each child form a firm identity as a member of the Amish community.

In mainstream society, young people may flounder for years as they seek to know who they are and where their niche is in a complex, individualistic world. Many modern youth find the struggle long, lonely, and sometimes unsuccessful. They tend to start both their movement toward independence from parents and their growing involvement with peers at puberty, but they may not develop financial independence and intimate relationships until their mid-twenties or later. On the other hand, Amish young people do not begin to seriously socialize with their peers until they are sixteen. By this age most are working full-time. By the time they are twenty-one or twenty-two, most are married and starting families. Instead of a ten- or twelve-year exploratory period on their way to full-fledged adulthood, Amish youth typically spend five or six years from the time they enter their *Rumspringa* until they reach full Amish adult status.[2] Everyone, young and old, knows what is expected in the community.

Members of successful Amish communities work together to impart to every child the explicit knowledge of what it means to be Amish and to provide the skills and support to make it possible. Unlike mainstream youth, who are confronted with a multitude of vocational, value, and lifestyle choices, the Amish youth's ultimate task is deciding whether or not to embrace the Amish identity. This culminates either in being baptized and joining the church or in leaving the community, the most crucial decision an Amish young person will ever make. Becoming a church member means freely embracing the community's all-encompassing expectations. These have been systematically modeled, taught, and reinforced from infancy.

Although youth are not officially Amish until they join the church as adults, their Amish identity begins to form in infancy. Identity emerges from intentional training and instruction combined with the cultural influences that surround a person. Some aspects of Amish identity are achieved, such as their approach to work, and some emerge from relationships and associations.

A teenager's family of origin is an important source in defining self-identity. Children and youth from highly esteemed families are likely to form positive self-identities since they benefit directly from the accomplishments and status of their grandparents and parents. Family success is usually measured by hard work, thrift, good management, and the outcome of their children. Young people whose parents fail to meet the community ideals may struggle more with identity issues, both personally and socially, because of these family liabilities.

In Amish society, a major component of one's identity is influenced by how industrious and intelligent a worker he or she is. We have already seen that most Amish children learn to work early and thus develop a sense of their own efficacy and competence. By their mid-teens, most are able to assume adult work responsibilities.

A fifteen-year-old girl in Franklin County, Pennsylvania, taught twenty-five children in grades one through eight. Some of her students were scarcely a year younger than she. During her second year of teaching, her twelve-year-old sister transferred into her one-room school so that she could help by teaching the eight first-graders how to read. Parents of the school children reported that the sisters did well. If Amish youth are not supposed to take pride in their work, they are at least permitted to feel satisfaction in working hard and accomplishing tasks like these. Since hard workers are highly esteemed by adults and peers alike, they have a good foundation on which to develop a positive and robust sense of self-worth.

Another major identity component of Amish youth, whether positive or negative, is shaped by their peers, especially in the large settlements. In Lancaster County, peer groups, known as "gangs," provide an important arena for identity formation, especially through one's age mates and best friend, known as a "sidekick." Most settlements have their contingents of both compliant and resistant youth. In a Lancaster County daughter settlement, a father observed, "Youth from farm families tend to hang out with each other, and those whose dads work away find their friends in that group." As in mainstream society, young people tend to gravitate toward those who are like themselves.

"I hang out with the rowdy boys," explained a boy from a small, conservative settlement. "Almost all the other *Youngie* do what they are supposed to do, but my friends and me like to have fun together. Sometimes it gets us in trouble." Despite the increased impact of peers, especially during the first two or three years of *Rumspringa,* the power of the community and the family exerts a constant counterbalance to the excesses of the young, tacitly reminding them of adult values and expected behavior.

Identity and Dressing Amish

The symbolic aspects of attire promote and reinforce the desired Amish identity. The majority of Americans, from children to grandparents, distinguish themselves through their dress. A person's attire often reveals his or her personal or family income, social class, sense of taste, extravagance, love of adventure, travel history, political or sexual preferences, or nonconformity. Amish clothing, on the other hand, is designed to minimize individual tastes and differences. It demonstrates one's willingness to squelch personal preferences and uniqueness by accepting the group's costume. By minimizing individual or economic differences, clothing symbolizes that an Amish person is a part of the group rather than apart from or above it. Whether teenager or grandparent, conformity in dress reinforces a person's identity as an obedient and yielding member of the community. Deviance from those expectations frequently occurs in the *Rumspringa* years as youth explore identity and autonomy issues.

Another aspect of Amish identity strengthened through dress is their intentional separation from the dominant culture. Amish garb functions as a distinctive marker, both to others and to themselves, of the gulf between the two societies. For the Amish, seeing themselves and their peers in capes and bonnets or old-fashioned broadfall pants and broad-brimmed hats serves as a constant visual reminder of their uniqueness. It shows both their separate status and their shared values and distinctiveness as a countercultural group.

Wherever the Amish travel, they instantly recognize each other as a source of support, rapport, and camaraderie. A father related his experience of seeing an Amish couple at the far end of a bus terminal in Chicago: "We never seen these people before, but we knew them." One bishop urged his members to think of their garb as a uniform symbolizing their separation from the world and their accord with their community.

Amish clothing supports the core values of simplicity, practicality, and frugality. Their apparel is so plain and their styles change so slowly that most wives, mothers, and daughters are confident that they can make whatever clothes they and their entire family need. They know precisely what materials and colors are acceptable. No one needs to waste money on expensive store-bought clothes. The Amish do not have to keep up with the latest fashions or worry about disposing of outmoded clothing. Instead, they pass usable clothes along to younger siblings or relatives, and the women transform outworn clothing into rugs or quilts. Their clothing affirms their identity as frugal, practical people.[3]

Clothing styles also demonstrate the community's high regard for tradition and the past. One outsider, invited to attend an Amish church service, remarked that when she first saw the group, she felt that she had entered a painting of one of the old Dutch masters, with their subdued colors and the peasant style. Such plainness reflects their simple rural beginnings and provides another visual link with the past. It is an affirmation to all that the old days and old ways are best.

Although parents and elders deliberately teach some of these distinctives, such as the importance of modesty and plainness of dress, the young more often absorb these standards in daily living. Parents need not tell their growing children, for example, that their apparel will immediately mark them as different. As they mature, they implicitly recognize the contrasts between themselves and the tourists or English neighbors with their jewelry, shorts, slacks, and "loud" colors and patterns. Fancy clothing with buttons and bows or neckties and belts has always belonged to the worldly minded, not to the plain people of God.[4] And of course most Amish believe that any apparel that is form-fitting or revealing, whether shorts, short skirts, or sleeveless or low-cut blouses, indicate a worldly and wayward heart. Because children and youth are immersed from infancy in these communal clothing expectations and examples, their Amish identity formation is constantly strengthened and reinforced.

A Sense of Self

Non-Amish, accustomed to the autonomy and choice that are inherent in an individualistic culture, might wonder if collectivist restrictions result in "stunted" or "cookie-cutter" personalities and impaired self-esteem. If such is the case, most outsiders who have face-to-face or extended contact with Amish children and youth fail to detect such damage. In fact, observers often comment that Amish young people appear to have high levels of maturity and self-confidence (L. Stoltzfus 1998). They also note the poise with which the youngsters and teens relate to peers and adults, both friends and strangers. Little formal research has focused on the social skills and psychological well-being of Amish youth, but relatively few of them appear to be depressed, sad, lonely, or hostile.[5] If anything, their sense of who they are seems to be both clear and positive.[6]

Amish parents, teachers, or ministers rarely talk about building children's self-esteem. That idea, with its self-focus, is contrary to their way of thinking. They believe that children will learn to feel good about themselves by finding and fulfilling their God-given roles within the Amish community. If the majority of Amish youth are in fact psychologically robust, it should not come as a surprise. Compared to the complex and often vague demands placed upon youth in competitive mainstream society, the demands faced by Amish youth are clear and within reach of most. As Kraybill observes, "Achieving the Amish dream is much more attainable for the typical Amish individual than achieving the American dream is for the average mainstream individual."[7]

For example, Amish society values learning to work hard and well in whatever one does much more than achieving a lucrative but elusive position in a high-status profession. The entire community values, models, and reinforces hard work. Children and youth absorb this value at an early age and in the process learn to feel good about themselves when they overcome difficulties and persevere through tough tasks. Work competence is attainable by virtually all Amish youth and likely plays an important role in both their self-esteem and identity formation.

Another more attainable expectation is in the area of appearance. In mainstream society, a person's attitude toward his or her physical appearance is the single best indicator of self-esteem according to Harter's research (1999). Advertisers foster insecurity among youthful consumers by creating needs that can only be met by purchasing the right look or clothing. Unless Amish teenagers have very strict parents who demand conformity to more conservative adult standards, youth can easily dress in the style of their peers, despite their economic status or fashion limitations.

Because Amish children and youth are not bombarded by the unattainable standards of material affluence portrayed in the media, they are less likely to feel deprived because they cannot afford expensive jewelry, makeup, designer jeans, footwear, or NFL team jackets. Likewise, their lack of exposure to fashionably thin models and media stars may help explain the relative scarcity of anorexia and bulimia reported in these communities.[8] This seems to be especially true in the more traditional Amish groups, where physical attractiveness appears to be less important to self-worth and identity than are character traits or personality.[9]

Another factor that helps develop confidence and a secure identity in any young person is the sense of being highly valued and loved by one's family and community. The society's love for children manifests itself in a number of ways. For example, the Amish traditionally fail to understand why English couples would routinely want to postpone having a family. A parent stated, "Newlyweds expect and want to begin having children as soon as they get married."

Even Amish couples who learn that their baby will be born with severe birth defects do not consider abortion. Rather, children with physical and mental disabilities appear to be treated with special care by the community. Instead of stigmatizing individuals with disabilities, people often express the belief that families with these challenging children and youth are chosen by God to care for these "special ones."

Many Amish settlements have special schools for their impaired children and youth. If a family has a deaf child, community members often learn sign language along with the family. Whenever children are wanted, loved, and nurtured by a caring mother, father, extended family, and community, they are likely to develop both a confidence in their self-worth and a positive sense of themselves as Amish.

Gender-Role Matters

As in all societies, a major component of Amish identity is found in one's gender role. For the Amish, gender roles are clearly delineated and based on their traditional understanding of the Bible. They interpret the Scriptures as teaching the headship of the husband in the family and the submission of wives to their husbands. Women are to be "helpmeets" and supporters of their husbands, and husbands, in turn, are to love their wives as Christ loved the church and gave himself for it (Ephesians 5:25).

Likewise, Amish women are to respect and support men's leadership and authority in the church.[10] Women may nominate men for the ministry but can never serve in that position themselves. Amish society clearly defines and models expected sex-role attitudes and behavior for young and old. People who deviate from these roles and act like "bossy wives" or "henpecked husbands" are likely to be stigmatized.

Sex-role distinctions exist in virtually all areas of their culture. Dress and grooming standards for males and females are highly differentiated and maintained. The Amish cite Deuteronomy 22:5 from the Old Testament as their basis for prohibiting females from wearing jeans or slacks: "The woman shall not wear that which pertaineth unto a man, neither shall a man put on a woman's garment: for all that do so are an abomination unto the Lord thy God." Following the instructions of Saint Paul, women and girls, married or unmarried, must wear a head covering, or *Kapp*, as a sign of piety, submission, and prayer. Although some teenage girls will discreetly trim their hair so that their head covering fits better, they are not supposed to cut their hair, because "if a woman have long hair, it is a glory to her: for her hair is given her for a covering" (1 Corinthians 11:15).

By the same token, males are not to have long hair: "Doth not even nature itself teach you, that, if a man have long hair, it is a shame unto him?" (1 Corinthians 11:14). Men and boys traditionally wear bangs in the front, and square-cut their hair on the sides and back. After joining the church or marrying, young men further differentiate themselves from women by growing beards.[11]

In most settings, males and females traditionally interact and relate in same-sex groups. This sex separation is apparent even in church, where the married males enter and sit separately from the married females, the unmarried males and unmarried females enter and sit separately, and the boys and girls, except for the youngest, do the same. After church, everyone eats at same-sex tables and later socializes primarily with their own sex.

In some settlements, sex segregation continues during Sunday afternoon youth activities and through the evening singing. Courting couples rarely pair off until they are ready to go home. Even at most social gatherings, such as auctions and family reunions, males and females usually cluster in same-sex groups. Boys and girls may mix at work bees and Sunday afternoon volleyball, but actual pairing off is almost always reserved for courting couples or assigned pairs at a wedding meal.

Sex-role differentiation also reaches into the world of work. From early childhood on, children learn that males and females have different work domains. On the farm, men and boys work in the barn and fields, and women and girls care for the house, yard, and garden. Crossovers occur if a farmer has no or few sons. Then his wife and daughters will help with the milking and care of the animals. In especially busy times, the women will even assist with field work such as planting, haying, or harvesting.

Likewise, men will sometimes help in the kitchen with food preparation or washing dishes, especially when the children are young. Also, in families where all of the children are males, boys are expected to help their mothers in certain "female" tasks. "All of us were boys, and we had to take turns cooking, helping with the washing, and doing other things for our mother," said a middle-aged father. Another father explained, "Some boys help to wash dishes and do laundry if there are few girls in a family. But the boys want no one to see them doing these chores." As in mainstream society, females more frequently cross over to help in male roles than the reverse.

In work outside of the home, gender role differences are again apparent. Married men more typically work away from home than do married women. Men generally work in shops, construction, or even factories. Women, on the other hand, usually work as teachers, housekeepers, clerks, or waitresses. In certain communities, some men will teach school and some women will work in factories, but these are the exceptions.

Mothers with young children rarely work away from home, although in recent years women in some communities have begun developing home-based business enterprises of their own.[12] Both sexes in certain settlements may travel to distant farmers' markets to run their stands, but they rarely work away from home for more than three days per week and seldom stay away overnight. However, in all domains, males have more freedom and latitude in work choices than do females.

Another gender difference in Amish children and youth emerges in their interaction with same-sex friends. At school, boys and girls play softball together, and after they turn sixteen, teenagers of both sexes play volleyball together in the more progressive settlements. Otherwise, adolescent Amish males generally relate to each other through physical activities such as hunting, ice hockey, and softball or other sports. Where Amish youth participate in organized sports, boys invariably play and girls watch. Although girls play softball at school, no female softball teams or leagues exist. At the boys' games, the girls will intermittently cheer the players on, but observers note that the girls are as often focused on their conversations with each other as they are the game.

This difference in female intimacy and male activity manifests itself in the decor of the teenagers' bedrooms, especially in the large settlements. The walls or bulletin boards of a typical girl's room are often covered with birthday cards and notes, wedding announcements and mementos, and handwritten letters from her "secret pal," her "sidekick" (best friend), relatives, and pen pals from other communities.[13] She typically chooses a theme color, and the quilt or bedspread, wall coverings, throw rugs, artificial flowers, vases, and china accent this shade. In large settlements, she may sometimes display photos of her gang or sidekick on a shelf or on her desk.

As in mainstream society, Amish boys, especially in the faster crowds of large settlements, will typically clutter their rooms with mementos such as hunting trophies, guns, archery equipment, or athletic gear and souvenirs, depending on their interests. For example, the bedroom of a nineteen-year-old in a large settlement reflected his preoccupation with sports. It was flooded by sports paraphernalia and clothing. An expensive Weider weight training station dominated the room. Photos of professional athletes from the Pittsburgh Pirates and Steelers, an "I play to win" poster, and a football clock decorated the walls. A phalanx of trophies from his softball league, eight in all, lined his desk and bookshelves—one was nearly two feet tall. With the exception of a work jacket and a couple pairs of Wrangler jeans, almost all of his clothes were sports-related—four Pittsburgh Steelers hats and a Steelers warm-up jacket, a Nike cap and Nike sneakers, his local team's warm-up jacket and hat, and a sports equipment bag. A large Magnavox boom box sat on the bed, connected with a heavy yellow extension cord from some distant outside outlet. No straw hat or suspenders were in sight. With the exception of a bottled-gas lamp, a battery-operated horse collar clock on the wall, and a picture of his ten-year-old sister in plain garb stuck in the corner of his dresser mirror, almost nothing in his room resembled the plainness of a boy's room in a conservative group. By adding a TV and DVD player or computer, it could have easily passed for the bedroom of an active mainstream nineteen-year-old male.

Although such worldly trappings would not be tolerated among preadolescent children, some parents may simply stay out of the teenager's bedrooms or at least refrain from looking under the bed, a convenient spot to stash a forbidden boom box or camera. Such a room would be extremely rare in a small or conservative settlement or affiliation, however.[14]

Autonomy in a Collectivist Society

Perhaps because of their Anabaptist emphasis on the adult decision to join the church and follow Christ, most Amish allow their youth more latitude for exploration and experimentation than one might expect, especially in the larger communities. Many parents make an abrupt shift in their treatment of their children when they reach sixteen and begin their *Rumspringa* period. Throughout the formative years, the most common Amish parenting approach would be labeled authoritarian or traditional, according to family specialist, Diana Baumrind (1971, 1978). The parents are the undisputed authorities, and obedience is expected and required. Until their children are ten or eleven, almost all parents will not hesitate to spank them for disobedience or defiance. However, after their children begin "going with the young folks," most parents become much more permissive as they recognize the new status of their sixteen- or seventeen-year-olds.

The most tangible way that they acknowledge their children's new-found status is to provide them the freedom to socialize with their friends without being dependent on their parents for transportation. This freedom is recognized routinely by parents providing a horse and carriage to each son when he begins going to the singings. Unless their parents cannot afford it, virtually all males over sixteen have their own horse and carriage. This means that these boys have increased privacy and freedom.

Although girls rarely have their own carriages, they too are granted the freedom to fully enter the social life and attend singings along with their male cohorts.[15] With their new freedom, males are much more likely than females to deviate from adult and community expectations in areas of dress, car ownership, drinking alcohol, friendship with outsiders, and church membership. The tendency for single males to leave the Amish disproportionately more than do females likely reflects the males' higher need for independence or autonomy.[16]

Decisional Autonomy

Besides having new opportunities to travel with their peers, youth have other areas in which to express their autonomy. Because attire and appearance are such central components of Amish life and expectations, some youth find this a convenient target for asserting their autonomy, especially in the larger communities. In Lancaster County, many boys trade their plain clothes for what they believe to be the English look—in some cases, knit shirts, black jeans, and sneakers; in other cases, stylish polo shirts, khaki cargo pants, and sandals or expensive athletic footwear, depending on their peer group. To the embarrassment of their parents, a few young men even sprout forbidden moustaches.

Girls, who almost always dress more conventionally, may still hitch up their skirts, shave their legs, sport gold pins on their sweaters or jackets, and wear flip-flops or sandals. Also, they are more likely to dress English only when they are around their peers. For example, one girl related that she told her date to wait for her at the end of the lane. Before she met him, she had quickly changed into English clothes and stored her Amish clothes in a bag in the carriage.[17]

Even in the church setting, however, many youth in peer-centered settlements exert some independence. In most churches, the young men file into the Sunday service last so that church does not begin until they are seated. Occasionally the host father must go out and prod them to enter in a timely fashion. Once they are settled, many or most of the youth may simply sit passively instead of singing the hymns. During the scripture reading, some will leave for a presumed bathroom break, returning twenty minutes later smelling of tobacco smoke.

Once the sermons begin, youth often slump on the benches, head in their hands, elbows on their knees. As soon as the last song is sung and the service ends, they will exit immediately. If the cooks fail to serve the meal promptly or if the "first seating" of elders lingers too long at the tables, many youth will simply leave to join their friends. All of this serves as an unspoken but clear reminder to the parents and elders that these youth are in charge of their own destinies. The tacit message may be, "Don't push too hard because we are no longer under your control, nor yet under the control of the church."

Of course, parents and church leaders are very cognizant that the youth are "betwixt and between" in this sometimes unpredictable borderland where the scrutiny of the parents is ending and the control of the church has not yet taken over. However, the young person who wishes to become Amish will ultimately yield to that control. During their formative childhood years, most youth have learned to unquestionably obey their parents.

Childhood training prepares the youth to submit to the demands of the community, because once they join the church they are expected to follow the established rules. Sometimes rules might be "bent," for example, while traveling or while visiting other Amish affiliations with different standards, but their community *Ordnung* can be changed only by the consensus of the group. Until that happens, the rules are binding on all members, old and young alike.

Consequently, young people aspiring to church membership rarely struggle about whether they should go to high school or college, become physicians or lawyers, marry outsiders, move away from the Amish community, or postpone having children until after they have been married for a time. One reason is that in most cases their primary reference group consists of other Amish, youth and adults. Therefore, most do not feel deprived because they must work so hard, end their formal education at age fifteen, and severely restrict their vocational choices.

Having a group of like-minded peers helps them to minimize mainstream values and influences. For most youth, joining the church is a natural choice and indicates a willingness to strictly curtail one's autonomy in order to follow the community's requirements. All other choices naturally flow out of the ultimate choice—whether or not to become a baptized Amish member. Once an individual has joined the church, there is no turning back from that covenant. As one elder stated, "Joining church is a spiritual marriage, and just as in an earthly marriage, we cannot divorce the church and still be Amish."

Giving Up or Breaking Out?

Given the limited range of choices in this collectivist society, is identity development as important for Amish youth as for mainstream teenagers? Everyone needs to know how he or she is different from everybody else, so in that sense, identity formation is a universal task. But are identity issues equally important for all cultures? Certainly, in an Amish culture that stresses uniformity and conformity, the task of identity acquisition differs from the mainstream society that stresses individualism and independence. For the majority of Amish youth who choose to remain Amish, it might appear that acquiring a clear identity would be a relatively simple task because of limited choices and well-defined expectations.

Once again, things are rarely as simple as they seem. Sociologist Denise Reiling studied Amish life and culture for nearly ten years in a large settlement in a Midwestern state. During that time, she spent more than three hundred hours interviewing a randomly selected group of sixty Amish-reared youth and adults about their *Rumspringa*. She reported that in her sample, "identity during this decision-making period [whether or not to be baptized or leave the community] was reported to be highly ambiguous. Almost every participant's description depicted this decision-making period as one of limbo, wherein the child does not identify as Amish, even though continuing to live in an Amish home and to engage in Amish cultural practices. . . . Virtually every participant reported that they experienced social isolation during this time, which generated a high level of depression and anxiety" (2002, 155). Reiling concluded that these participants experienced strong levels of "negative affective response" and "angst." She attributed these effects, at least in part, to the length and seriousness of the deviant activities of the youth of that particular group and to the conflict between cultural and parental expectations.

Even in settlements where most youth do not participate in deviant activities or feel confused about adult expectations, Amish young people with a high need for personal independence or who are dissatisfied with their way of life have a much more complex task, also fraught with the potential for psychological and emotional stress or damage. A poignant illustration of this complexity occurs in a novel about the Nebraska Amish, *No Strange Fire* by Ted Wojtasik. When Jacob, the youthful protagonist, abandons his predictable and prescribed Amish world, he struggles with a deep sense of loss upon entering a new world of ambiguity, confusion, and alienation. Certainly, some youth seem to break free without severe emotional repercussions. Around any large Amish community, one can find many ex-Amish who say that they are glad to be out or glad that they never joined.[18]

However, evidence of how deep the Amish identity influences the youth may be found in the way that even those who are flaunting the community rules treat outsiders seeking to know the inner workings of Amish life. When a graduate student sought information from teenagers on Amish music preferences and practices at hoedowns and parties, he reported that he was "stonewalled." He finally completed his dissertation, but only by collecting most of his data from adults who had left the Amish over the years.[19] Another researcher attempted to interview a former Amish band member who reportedly had a vision of hell during a bad drug trip. Although he was asked to talk only about the kinds of music his band played, he declined to give any details "because that is our business." Within the next year, he received church instruction, was baptized, and joined the church.

Even if some youth were impressed by the media attention after a 1998 drug bust in which two Amish-raised young men were arrested for selling cocaine, most Amish youth presented a cool reception to the swarm of reporters that crisscrossed the county. Amish young men, dressed in

"English" clothes and driving cars, still refused to disclose to reporters what happened at their hoedowns and parties.[20]

This noncooperation reflects a deep loyalty to their separatist community. Despite their deviance, in a relatively short time most youth plan to abandon their worldly ways and return to their Amish roots.[21] This fundamental sense of who they are, now and in the future, is both pervasive and powerful enough to maintain their primary identity as Amish. This identity provides the core that allows them to give up their autonomy, their right to do as they please, and to accept the restrictions and proscriptions of the community. This "giving up" is necessary if they are going to be contented, committed members of this collectivist community. One of the places where children are taught to "give up" their prideful, self-centered ways and to fit in with their society's expectations for children is in the eight years of schooling that the community provides. We turn now to Amish education.

Most Amish children study in one-room schools operated by Amish parents. Young women with an eighth-grade education typically serve as teachers. Photo by Lucian Niemeyer.

CHAPTER FOUR

Schooling

Read'n, Writ'n, and Learning the Basics

*Our schools is our way of guarding against
bad company for our children.*
—*Family Life* Editorial

Carefully Tended Education

In mainstream society, many young people are only halfway through their formal education when they enter puberty. Not so in Amish society, where all youth complete their formal education by age fifteen at the latest. The Amish believe that eight grades are more than adequate to prepare youth to earn a livelihood, fill adult roles, and function as responsible, God-fearing church members both in their community and in the larger society. In fact, they believe that *high* school and *higher* education produce *Hochmut*, or high-mindedness and pride. Mainstream education results in "prideful thinking," the antithesis of simplicity and humility. Hostetler wrote, "The word *education* as used in American society is regarded with suspicion by most Amish people. To them it signifies ego advancement, independence, and cutting the ties that bind one to the community of faith and work" (1992, 561). In the crucial task of transmitting their culture and faith to the next generation, Amish education is both traditional and intentional. It is traditional in that it has changed little over many generations. It is highly intentional in that virtually nothing is left to chance in their eight years of schooling.[1]

A nineteenth-century child would probably feel at home in an Amish classroom today. One teacher typically instructs eight grades of a no-frills curriculum in a one- or two-room schoolhouse. However, a cursory look at contemporary Amish life reveals many changes outside of the classroom. For instance, the decline of farming, the rise of Amish industries and an entrepreneurial class, increased mobility and travel between settlements, and more discretionary wealth describes but a few of the changes in most communities (Kraybill and Nolt 2004). Similarly, incremental but continuing acceptance of technology and scientific farming methods such as automatic milkers, bulk milk tanks, hay balers, diesels, weed whackers, artificial insemination of dairy cattle, cell phones, battery-operated word processors, and even clandestine computers infiltrate some settlements.[2]

The Amish school curriculum, nevertheless, remains relatively impervious to the realities of these changes. In fact, in some communities leaders have attempted, with varying success, to revive the *Alice and Jerry* series of a half-century ago with their small-town and rural life settings. The conservative Swartzentruber Amish still use reprints of the 1853 revision of the *McGuffey's Readers,* and the Amish-produced textbooks used by the majority of schools today still reflect little on the changes affecting daily Amish life.

Compared to mainstream classes, Amish classes are characterized by much recitation and rote memorization. An Amish teacher would never offer a unit on scientific discovery or critical thinking. She avoids anything that might promote a questioning attitude or a rejection of Amish values and behaviors. She would be distressed if one of her brightest and best eighth graders began challenging Amish traditions or sought more education in high school or college. The teacher's task is to reinforce the status quo.

Until the school consolidation movement began in the 1940s, Amish children attended public schools along with the children of their English neighbors. These one-room neighborhood schools were funded and staffed by small local school districts. When public school boards decided to consolidate and bus children to distant buildings with hundreds of other children, Amish parents and ministers objected because these large consolidations went counter to the Amish values of smallness, proximity, and local control.

In addition, the state began enacting mandatory attendance laws that would require Amish youth to enroll in high school. These things put the Amish and the local and state educational establishments on a collision course. School officials warned the Amish to cooperate. When they refused, authorities arrested, fined, and sometimes jailed the recalcitrant fathers. Officials and parents eventually reached a compromise permitting the Amish to establish their own schools taught by uncertified Amish teachers.[3] Finally, in 1972, the U.S. Supreme Court in *Wisconsin v. Yoder* decided that in the interests of freedom of religion, the Amish had a right to restrict their formal education to eight grades.[4]

The restricted vision of Amish education at times produces tensions.[5] Limiting education to eight grades strikes many moderns as archaic, if not abusive. Mainstream observers, with their deep commitment to secondary and higher education, typically find this restriction one of the hardest to understand or accept. "What an unfair stifling of talent and tragic loss for that individual and society! What if a bright Amish student wants to go to high school or college or would like to be a doctor, nurse, or engineer?" outsiders ask. Some critics even charge that the Amish have deliberately structured their education to limit their children's capacity for critical thinking. Others regard it as a sinister form of social control designed to keep young people in the Amish fold by inadequately preparing them to compete in a complex, high-tech world (Garrett 1998).

Because the Amish believe that their children need to be protected from the contamination and sinfulness of worldly ideas taught in secondary schools, few appear defensive or disturbed over these charges. As Hostetler says, "The Amish educate for social cohesion and not for technical competence" (1977, 359). Most are convinced that eight years of practical education are more than adequate to lead fulfilled, productive, and faithful lives. In fact, most Amish express satisfaction with the quality of their education.

If demographic and quantitative data are accurate indicators of school success, the Amish appear to be correct about their education being sufficient for their lives. Unemployment is virtually unknown, and although their cash flow may be limited, probably no Amish are destitute, even in areas where farming and small business opportunities are marginally productive.

In terms of achievement test scores, Amish "scholars," as students are called in the community, score at or above the national norms in most areas, even though English is their second language. Hostetler and Huntington (1992) published the results of the first formal study done on Amish students' school achievement. They found that of the six subtests measured in the Iowa Test of Basic Skills, Amish children outscored their public counterparts in every area except English vocabulary. The Amish scored higher in spelling, word usage, and arithmetic. No differences were found in reading comprehension or the use of reference materials. Results from other standardized tests were similar. The authors concluded: "These standardized test results indicate that the Amish parochial schools, now taught by teachers educated in Amish schools, are continuing to give their students an adequate academic education, even when judged by measures designed to test students in our modern, technological society. Amish parochial schools are preparing their students for successful, responsible adulthood within their own culture and within the larger society" (1992, 94).[6]

Certainly the majority of Amish children and adults become capable readers—many are "book worms," to use their term—most write acceptably in English, and their mathematical skills are adequate for carpentry, business, and household finances. In many communities, adults who need bookkeeping and accounting skills or more advanced math usually teach themselves, learn from a relative or co-workers, or take correspondence or extension courses at home. In rare cases when members need a high school diploma for their employment, a few communities permit them to meet this requirement by passing the GED (high school equivalency exam) or by taking correspondence courses.[7]

Today, the Amish are decidedly wary of public education's emphasis on individual expression and creativity. They see it as the antithesis of a community-based society that values humility and cooperation. They also worry about the influence of non-Amish teachers and peers and a totally secular curriculum. In addition, they regard secondary schooling's focus on critical thinking and its intensified peer pressures as especially dangerous to the young and to their traditional way of life. In general, the Amish believe that most public education leads to pride and self-sufficiency instead of to humility and God-centeredness. First Corinthians 8:1 asserts that "knowledge puffeth up."

The Classroom and Curriculum

In virtually all states, the law requires that classes in Amish schools be taught in English.[8] Firstborn Amish children often understand only the Pennsylvania German dialect when they enter school, although some bright first-graders with older siblings may have already begun reading English at home. Besides the three Rs, children study penmanship, geography, German, and more. School boards will accept "nature study," but they reject almost all other science as suspect and worldly.

After a U.S. astronaut first walked on the moon, a Beachy Amish woman asked her Amish neighbor, a schoolteacher, if she had told her students about the moon landing. The teacher answered with an emphatic "No!" and refused to say anything more about it, even though her neighbor urged her to inform her students. Thirty-five years later, an Amishman reported hearing about the deathbed confession of an American astronaut who admitted that nobody had ever walked on the moon. "The whole thing was made up," he declared.

When a parent was asked what science was taught in their school systems, he wrote tersely, "No Science classes taught!" In fact, Amish schools do not use science textbooks, and most distrust science as it is taught in the public schools. They regard it as being not only impractical but, more importantly, promoting the theory of evolution. Nevertheless, many Amish, old and young, appear to be interested in aspects of science. A retired teacher wrote, "We do not use Science textbooks, but I believe we have teachers and students who would love to discuss 'moon landings' and other topics of this nature. There are those who are well-read and quite broad-minded."[9]

Despite Amish suspicions of science, evolution, and higher education, many first-time visitors to an Amish school express surprise at the level of vitality and student engagement they observe in many classrooms. While touring through Lancaster County, a professor from a major university who specialized in educational research visited a one-room school. In reporting his experiences to the author, he was visibly moved in recounting the interaction of the students with each other and of the pupils with their teacher. Although the teacher was obviously in charge, all her pupils called her by first name or simply "Teacher." In addition, she knew the families of each student. The visitor watched as the eighth-graders listened to the second graders read or helped them with their times tables and spelling words.

If the professor had interviewed the other teachers, he would have learned that parents were welcomed at school and were often involved in their children's education. A mother from Indiana said, "I'm expected to stop by on occasion to touch base with the teacher and keep up with what's going on. You don't just send your kids off to school and expect the teacher to raise them. It's a parent's responsibility."[10] "One-hundred percent of my parents are behind me and involved with the school," the teacher reported. They visited school from time to time to encourage and to help where needed.

Teachers often invite their "scholars" home for dinner or a birthday celebration. At least once a year, many invite every student, in groups of five or six, to stay overnight, and some teachers invite their scholars home during the summer. Another visiting educator remarked, "That school is modeling what we profess to value. The classes are manageable, and the teacher cares about each pupil, both as an individual and a learner. She clearly knows what she is about. It is obvious that students feel valued, competent, and safe with her and with each other. We have a lot to learn from them!"

In certain parts of the country a small number of Amish children still attend public schools. They tend to be in locales where the Amish are highly concentrated among neighbors who have historically accepted and understood their distinctives, such as in rural Ohio, Indiana, or Kansas. However, almost all Amish now prefer locally controlled private schools under the oversight of an Amish-elected school board. Three to six fathers serve as board members, whose task is to monitor the selection of teachers, curriculum, and texts.

In many settlements, curricular materials are chosen by a "Book Society" composed of several selected men who have oversight and control. They generally choose books and materials from two or three main sources. In Lancaster County and its daughter settlements, many schools have traditionally used discarded public school textbooks and workbooks from the 1950s. Now they are likely to use texts and workbooks from Amish-owned Gordonville Print Shop in Lancaster County, Pennsylvania, or curricular materials from Schoolaid Publishing Company, another Lancaster County enterprise, which was started by Old Order Mennonites. Among other things, Schoolaid produces English, health, mathematics, and German phonics and reading books. Another source of materials for plain schools is Study Time, in northern Indiana, which publishes an arithmetic series, a geography text, and even preschool activity materials.

There is no dearth of curricular offerings. Pathway Publishers in Aylmer, Ontario, is another Amish-owned curricular source. Founded in 1964 by three influential Amishmen, they publish *Pathway Readers* and a host of other materials designed to provide Anabaptist themes and values-based curricula to their Old Order Amish and Old Order Mennonite constituencies. While not exclusively religious, their curricula emphasize basic education within a morality-based context. For example, the eighth-grade reader specifically recounts aspects of Anabaptist history, both in Europe and in North America.[11]

Just Call Me Teacher

Most teachers are single Amish women in their late teens or early twenties "with a knack for learning and a flair for teaching."[12] Men sometimes teach, especially in the Midwest, but they often have difficulty supporting a family on a teacher's salary.[13] They are usually paid more than women, especially if they have a family, but in general the pay is relatively low since a teacher's work is seen as a service to the community. Because Amish teachers are themselves products of an Amish education, they rarely express frustration with local restrictions on their teaching. Most appear to be content with the curriculum and structure of their system. After all, the students will not be "spoiled" by high school with its godless curricula and teachers, permissive discipline, sex education, coed gym classes and immodest uniforms, computers, televised lessons, and the latest educational fads. Both teachers and the community they represent believe the primary key to success in Amish education is a carefully chosen curriculum taught by a teacher who models for the children what it means to be a committed Amish woman or man. The teacher's preparation, style, and classroom management are of secondary importance.

This does not mean that the Amish do not care about the quality of instruction. In most places they support both informal and formal teacher training. An Amish teacher's professional training generally consists of a brief pre-teaching "internship" with an experienced teacher. It also includes extensive reading in *Blackboard Bulletin,* a Pathway monthly dedicated to improved curriculum and instruction in Old Order schools. Teachers will also have periodic "in-service days" or meetings prior to and during their teaching careers "for discussion and learning from each other." There they consider practical issues and problem situations with other teachers and board members. Also, groups of teachers and board members customarily visit other schools and observe classes once or twice yearly.

School boards periodically arrange for a group of their teachers to spend a day with an experienced teacher to study and review the teaching of some specific skill, such as phonics instruction. In Lancaster County, Pennsylvania, a highly regarded Old Order Mennonite teacher regularly offers in-service instructional classes in phonics for current and prospective teachers from settlements throughout the state. Other in-service discussions frequently center on preparation, classroom management, discipline, and practical "how-to" techniques focusing on anything from improving handwriting to planning for the Christmas program.

Despite these efforts to provide growth opportunities for the teachers, not all Amish are pleased with the quality of teaching and the commitment of the teachers. A respected retired teacher wrote, "With no testing required for one to become a teacher in an Amish school, it is a REAL challenge to keep our education level up to a good, solid 8th-grade level. Anymore, most of our teachers were educated in our own schools, and we are losing a little here, a little there. The majority are young women (girls) who will soon be married, therefore the whole heart is not in teaching. I fear that too many board members are somewhat blind to what is happening; also, they are not familiar with the curriculum used."[14]

Vocational School

All states require Amish students to complete the eighth grade, but in Pennsylvania, state law mandates that they stay in school until age fifteen. Since most students complete the eighth grade before they reach that age, the Department of Education and the parents reached a compromise on this dilemma.[15] The Amish promised that they would require their eighth-grade graduates to attend an Amish-controlled "vocational educational" program until their fifteenth birthday. This schooling consists of a weekly three-hour class, often held at the teacher's house on an evening or a Saturday morning during the school year. In some districts the fourteen-year-olds return to their own school building for their instruction during the school day.

In Lancaster County, a vocational class may have twenty or more fourteen-year-olds when the program opens in August. Both parents and teachers carefully monitor the children's attendance because they do not want the community to jeopardize their good relations with the state. In Lancaster County, students are required to bring a German songbook, German-English New Testament, and a diary of their week's work activities to class.

Because of the language component, in some areas the Amish call this last year of education German *Schul* or school. Most vocational classes begin with an opening exercise, often in German, and with a distinctly Christian focus. Each student may take a turn reading a verse in the New Testament, first in German and then in English, until that day's chapter or chapters are completed. This reading is done without commentary by the teacher. At some point students recite the Lord's Prayer in German. Additionally, the class will sing several songs in German, some from songbooks, some from copies provided by the teacher. Frequently the songs are sung to tunes of gospel songs such as "Just a Closer Walk with Thee" or "I'll Fly Away." These devotional activities may sometimes take an hour.

In most vocational schools, teachers have the "scholars" take turns copying their diary entries from the previous week into their official classroom diary. "The reason pupils copy their work into the school diary," explained a former teacher, "is to encourage neat handwriting and correct spelling and punctuation." These entries record what each student did and how long he or she spent during the week doing farm, shop, or homemaking-related activities. A typical entry consists of one to six sentences, like this one, written by a fourteen-year-old boy in Franklin County, Pennsylvania:

> Feb. 24, Tues.
>
> I did chores and worked up in the log house. Finished the hay racks for the calf and made a thing to hold the bottle while the calf sucks milk.
>
> Matthew and me cleaned out the shop.
>
> This afternoon we started getting the old chicken house ready for farrowing hogs. We hauled the chicken nests out and the slats.
>
> We put a heifer down in the meadow and a dry cow up in the heifer pen.

While students copy their diary entries or translate German passages from the New Testament or hymnbooks, the teacher may have each one come up to his or her desk to recite the German "memory work" for the week.

More than a few students regard these weekly classes and requirements as busywork. Thinking back on his vocational school experience, an Amishman in his thirties declared, "Our vocational schools were useless. They were a total waste!" He and other critics see German *Schul* as either an intrusion that interferes with the "real" world of work in which they are now engaged or an absence of any substantive preparation. Almost all students report that they look forward to the end of their formal schooling. When asked if students who turn fifteen during the school year ever stay on to the end, informants universally answered, "Never!" This does not mean, however, that students abandon all school-related endeavors. From early childhood on, most Amish children and youth indicate that they enjoy reading, and they may read as much if not more than do their non-Amish counterparts.[16] This should not be surprising in a culture that rejects radio, television, and computers.

Reading the Right Stuff

If an ongoing interest in reading after graduation can be attributed to schooling, Amish schools appear to be highly successful. Histories, both secular and religious, are perennial favorites everywhere with readers of all ages. Small Amish-owned bookstores do a brisk trade in books dealing with Anabaptist history and issues. Many Amish readers, young and old, also like books about Native Americans and pioneer life. Family bookshelves often contain books on Revolutionary and Civil War history. Also, many readers are deeply curious about other lands and peoples. Except in the most conservative settlements, readers especially enjoy *National Geographic* magazines and books.

Librarians report that certain novels, such as *Heidi, Pollyanna,* and *Black Beauty,* and books with Amish themes, such as Yoder's *Rosanna of the Amish* and *Rosanna's Boys,* are popular among children and young teens. *The Little House on the Prairie* series by Laura Ingalls Wilder has been a perennial favorite. Mrs. Gideon Byler, a well-known *Die Botschaft* scribe from Franklin County, Pennsylvania, has written a six-book Lizzie series, which some readers have dubbed "the Amish Little House on the Prairie."[17] In some settlements, teens and preteens also borrow mystery and adventure stories, such as books by Zane Grey and the Hardy Boys. Westerns by Louis L'Amour are very popular in some settlements. Teenage girls often read books that their grandmothers and mothers read when they were young, romance novels by Grace Livingston Hill or the Nancy Drew mysteries, for example. Many girls—and often their mothers—read religious romance novels by Janette Oke. Frequently, both boys and girls enjoy suspenseful classics like *Tom Sawyer, Treasure Island,* or *Kidnapped.*[18]

Acceptable reading materials vary from settlement to settlement. Many families subscribe to at least one of the three Amish periodicals devoted to family, community, and church news throughout the settlements. The best-known is *The Budget* from Sugarcreek, Ohio, which has been published weekly for over a century. It is especially popular in Ohio and the Midwest. *Die Botschaft* (The Message), published in Lancaster County, Pennsylvania, originated as a conservative alternative to some "questionable" advertising in *The Budget*. In addition, *The Diary,* also from Lancaster County, prints monthly settlement news but features regular special interest columns on greenhouse management, bird watching, astronomy, and many other topics. With the exception of an occasional old German or Pennsylvania German word or phrase, these three periodicals are written exclusively in English. Farming magazines are popular, and families frequently subscribe to the local newspaper.

Many teenage boys, and more than a few of their fathers, faithfully read the sports section. In the more progressive settlements, families may get *Newsweek, Time,* or *U.S. News and World Report,* although some places prohibit any kind of news magazine. *Reader's Digest,* followed by *National Geographic,* seem to be the most popular secular magazines for Amish readers of all ages.

Parents and church leaders freely monitor their children's or young people's reading matter, and they will censor material that they believe promotes anti-Christian thinking or living. A father succinctly expressed the sentiments of most Amish parents: "It is the responsibility of parents to provide decent reading material." They routinely reject any books or articles that mention evolution, dinosaurs, or an ice age, since virtually all Amish accept the young earth theory espoused by many conservative Christians. "How could dinosaurs live millions of years ago when the Bible teaches that God created the earth only six thousand years ago?" they ask.

Most Amish also consider books that feature fairy tales, talking animals, fantasy, and science fiction as foolish. "There are enough true things to write about without wasting your time reading stuff that is made up," they say. For this reason, some parents include fiction in the time-wasting category, since it too was made up. Referring to a novel centering around a rash of Amish barn fires started by an arsonist in the Big Valley of Pennsylvania in 1992, one parent objected, "I wouldn't want my children reading this because the author spends too much time describing the sinful behavior of the world rather than what really happened. Besides, nobody actually died in the fire like he says in the book."[19]

Parents also try to prohibit books or magazines that use profanity or allude in any way to sexual or vulgar behavior. A minister criticized a novel portraying the struggles of an Amish young man coming of age in Ohio "because the author made it look like it's common for all of the young men to leave the Sunday morning church service and take a break during the reading of the scripture. Besides, he actually wrote that they went out and peed. This should not be written about in any book." A parent related that he routinely monitored his children's bookshelves and even the mail to check for "trashy ads and catalogs coming to our mailboxes, with very

descriptive illustrations." Parents may base their decisions on the accept-
ability of a book from unofficial reviews in *Die Botschaft* or *The Budget* written by David Wagler, a well-known "scribe" (community letter writer) from
Iowa, a man who is himself a widely read Amish author and co-founder of
the Amish-owned Pathway publishing enterprise in Alymer, Ontario.

Pathway Books

In many Amish homes, shelves contain books from Pathway Publishers,
and magazine racks bulge with current issues of their monthly periodicals. Besides the well-known *Pathway Readers*, Pathway has published many
other perennial favorites. An Amish teenager reported that he had read his
favorite Pathway book, *One Way Street*, three times.[20] It is a fictional account
of an Amish youth who is led astray when he is attracted to a more liberal
Anabaptist church that emphasizes expressiveness in worship and an out-
spoken assurance of salvation.

Another Pathway favorite is *Henry and the Great Society*, a story in which
the protagonist loses his contented life through the grip of materialism and
change. Both books have been popular with youth and their parents over
the years. *Henry and the Great Society* was serialized in the 1980s in both
The Diary and *Young Companion*.

The Amish editors of *Young Companion* aim to reach young people, but
most parents read it also. It features carefully selected fiction, moral admonitions, and a "Can You Help Me?" column, a monthly question and answer
section that focuses on adolescent problems and concerns, such as, "Is it
all right for a couple to hold hands or touch lightly?" *Family Life*, aimed
at a broader readership, also features a monthly column, "The Problem
Corner," that deals at times with adolescent concerns or concerns of their
parents. Among other things, the Pathway's editorial stance consistently
opposes partying, alcohol, and the use and cultivation of tobacco. This latter issue has resulted in some of the more traditional communities rejecting Pathway's position as being too similar to the Mennonites' and therefore suspect.[21] Despite some opposition, the majority of Amish families
subscribe to these two periodicals, and a number of Amish leaders believe

that the influence of these magazines has been substantial on both youth and adults in raising moral issues related to tobacco, alcohol, partying, and courtship practices.

Although it is aimed at a broader audience, *Family Life* seems to interest teenage readers as much as *Young Companion,* perhaps because it occasionally features issues rarely discussed by parents or ministers. A few years ago, an editorial on Saturday night partying in a large settlement provoked widespread comment and a flurry of letters to the editor. Articles or letters occasionally mention problems of alcohol abuse or drug use in certain unnamed settlements.

Each month a panel of ministers responds anonymously to a potentially difficult problem, question, or situation. Some issues focus on troubling or embarrassing youth issues such as questionable entertainment, dress standards among teenagers, dating behavior, rowdiness at singings, and vandalism. One forum that captured widespread attention a few years ago dealt with "self-abuse," or masturbation, an issue acknowledged but rarely mentioned openly in Amish circles.[22] That children and parents often vie over who will be the first to read the latest issues attests to their popularity. Many families have their copies of both periodicals bound annually.

Perils in Reading

Occasionally young people's love for reading or simple curiosity about ideas or the outside world entices them to delve into reading materials that the community finds objectionable. Non-Amish co-workers or local librarians sometimes recommend and even provide books that promote critical thinking or encourage additional formal education.[23] For some readers, these ideas provoke a discontent with their limited education and stimulate a desire for more learning. Some of these Amish young people eventually leave.

The best-known example is the late John A. Hostetler, formerly a professor of sociology at Temple University and author of a number of best-selling books on Amish life. In *American Scholar,* he reported that he had never joined the Amish church because he knew from childhood that he wanted more education than the community permitted.[24]

Another avid childhood reader left the Amish at the age of eighteen. He explained, "Reading is probably what got me into trouble in the first place." He believes that this activity planted those thoughts and ideas which led to dissatisfaction with the Amish way of life. After spending several years in the military, he returned from Japan, was discharged, and enrolled in engineering at a nearby university under the G.I. bill. As a result of a brief trip home to tell his parents of his college plans, he changed his mind and decided to return to his roots: "I realized that was where I belonged." He is now a Swartzentruber Amish bishop—and still an avid reader.

For every reader who leaves the Amish, many more Old Order youth remain to become self-educated. They now function as successful draftsmen, veterinary technicians, midwives, unofficial chiropractors, mechanics, hydraulic and pneumatic technicians, inventors, tax accountants, writers, historians, and even occasionally computer programmers for outside businesses—all without the benefit of high school or college.[25] Most of them demonstrate the ability to analyze both mainstream and Amish society. In articles, reviews, and letters to the editor appearing in Amish publications, readers can find carefully reasoned critiques of public education, consumerism, and environmental practices. The Amish are not adverse to self-scrutiny and criticism as they lament some of their own inconsistencies and questionable assumptions. Their depth of analysis belies their limited formal education.[26]

To mainstream parents and educators accustomed to the rhetoric of flexible curricula, interactive learning, and student engagement, Amish education may appear to be rather sterile or stifling. But it has proven to be widely effective, given their cultural context and goals. Hostetler wrote, "Today the Amish are quietly developing a school system that is integrated with their way of life. The Amish schools protect their youth from alienation inherent in the loss of community life and generally produce stable, dedicated adults who are productive members in both their faith community and in American Society" (1992, 562).

Hostetler grew up in an Amish family in Iowa and attended school in a simple rural schoolhouse. Despite the absence of curricular innovations or expensive learning resources, he, along with some other Amish children both then and now, embarked on their careers as lifetime learners. Unlike Hostetler, however, the majority of Amish accept the communal limitations on education as part of their heritage. Most do not appear to long for freedom to seek more schooling or to challenge or question their values, assumptions, and the status quo.

Rather than seeing their societal restrictions on education as arbitrary or harsh, most Amish regard them as necessary in order to avoid the pitfalls and excesses of mainstream society with its emphasis on individualism, materialism, and worldly concerns. They view too much education as dangerous to the character development of their youth—a danger that they fear would corrupt their life of simplicity, obedience, and integrity. Thus they give careful and ongoing attention to the form, content, and scope of their children's education. They believe that what happens during these formative years will help establish an Amish core that will see them through the new challenges and temptations they face both in the outside world and in the company of their peers.

Father and daughters enjoy a day at a public auction.
Photo by Daniel Rodriguez.

Parenting
Holding On and Letting Go

We love our children. They are the only things on this earth
we hope to take along to heaven.
—Amish father

Parenting Paradise or Pressure Cooker?

Outsiders who gain entrance into the Amish community often note the richness of their family life. These visitors frequently report much interaction, conversation, and laughter between parents and their children. A college professor who visited Amish families for many years noted a comparative absence of open conflict among the generations. She observed that in farming families the children, youth, parents, and grandparents frequently "chored" together. Even teenagers seemed to relate well to their younger brothers and sisters. Often older children, both male and female, cuddled, carried, or played with the infants, toddlers, and other younger siblings.[1] She also noticed that when the youth lost interest in adult-centered activities, they usually went elsewhere to play or socialize rather than disturbing their parents. Only once during hundreds of hours of visiting did the professor witness an angry outburst between Amish parents and children or observe rebellion, disobedience, or physical punishment. "Perhaps," she admitted, "this was true in part because they knew they were being watched."

Nevertheless, if the professor's experience and impressions reflect typical parent-child relations, family life and parenting receive high priority in Amish society. The Amish regard parenting as a profound calling from God, to whom they are accountable. Virtually all of them believe that parents carry a heavy responsibility for the outcome of their children. After all, Amish leaders teach that faithful parents produce faithful children. Proverbs 22:6 says, "Train up a child in the way he should go, and when he is old, he will not depart from it." That Amish retain 90 percent of their youth suggests that parents, for the most part, successfully transmit the faith to their children.[2]

If parenting success can be determined by social indicators, the Amish appear to be successful. Despite the fact that some youth use recreational drugs or drink and drive on weekends, the majority are law-abiding and responsible, both inside and outside the Amish community.[3] Relatively few are involved in serious deviance or criminal activity, and virtually all are reliable, hard workers. Almost all youth profess deep respect for their parents and families, even those who never join the church or those who join but later leave. Such love, responsibility, and caring are hardly accidental.

A quick perusal of the Amish periodicals *Family Life* and *Young Companion* reveals article after article focusing on both the challenges and the privileges of conscientious parenting and the obligations of children to respect and obey their parents. As Christians, these parents feel the responsibility of influencing the eternal destiny of their offspring by encouraging them to embrace the faith of their forebears, extended family, and community.

Finally, because they are a separatist group, the Amish realize instinctively that the transmission of their culture to their children is a crucial task for the survival of their community. This is especially true because they do not seek converts. They know that they are only a generation or two away from the loss of their distinctives. Therefore, the future of their society is wrapped up in their ability to transmit their Amish heritage—a very sobering responsibility for conscientious Amish fathers and mothers.

The structure of certain aspects of Amish society helps parents in their task of socializing the young. The roles of parents and children are clearly defined. Not surprisingly, Wittmer (1973) found that Amish youth compared with their non-Amish counterparts perceived their parents to be much more unified and congruent in their parenting roles and values. Young and old alike believe that God has appointed parents, with their years of life experience and accumulated wisdom, to lovingly care for, nurture, and correct their offspring. Parents teach children that they have the God-given responsibility to love, honor, and obey their parents "in the Lord."[4] Because the Amish consider the Bible the authority for parent-child relationships, everyone regards these roles as divine mandates.

Although children are cherished, Amish society is not child-centered. With confidence, fathers and mothers allot work assignments around the house and determine the frequency and duration of family activities. Children and teenagers rarely argue with their parents. Many Amish regard with surprise or quiet amusement their non-Amish neighbors who read the latest books on child-rearing or attend parenting workshops.[5]

For the Amish, all the wisdom of child-rearing can be found in the pool of social capital stored up in their extended family and community. One Amish woman, noting the middle-class tendency toward child-centered homes, declared, "You English [non-Amish] spend far too much time explaining things to your young children. Just let them know what you expect and then have them do it."[6] A writer in the Amish periodical *Blackboard Bulletin* advised, "Never let your child say 'No' when you ask him to do something. Expect nothing short of prompt and complete obedience. Remember, delayed obedience is disobedience. Get the child's attention; assign the task, and expect it to be completed with *no* reminders. Repeating instructions develops irresponsible habits."[7] The Amish are not trying to rear assertive, critical thinking individualists. Instead, they value children who are obedient to parents as future adults who will be obedient to the *Ordnung*.

Another feature of Amish life that helps parents is that the general pace of life is slower than that in the typical middle-class home, thus allowing for more quality parent-child interaction. Compared to many of their middle-class American counterparts, few Amish parents have to balance hectic work schedules with family demands. Amish couples rarely face the problems of finding sitters or day care for their preschoolers or of juggling their job responsibilities with the busy extracurricular lives of their school-aged children. Amish mothers almost always work at home, and older siblings learn to care for their younger brothers and sisters. Nor do Amish parents need to taxi family members to Girl Scout cookie sales or Cub Scout camp-outs, 4-H exhibits or science fairs, music or ballet lessons, gymnastics or swimming practice—in short, to the multitude of activities characteristic of typical suburban households. In farming families, both parents are present to direct, instruct, and monitor their children.

Moreover, Amish parents rarely encounter the dilemmas facing conscientious mainstream parents in a media-saturated society. They never have to decide how much TV their children should watch or if they should block the MTV or HBO options on cable. Whether they should give their twelve-year-old son the video game "Street Fighter" for his birthday or allow their fourteen-year-old to rent *Indecent Proposal* for her sleep-over are simply irrelevant issues.

Few Amish parents need to worry about the negative impact of the ads, images, and articles in teen magazines or the explicit lyrics on the latest gangster-rap CD. Nor do they fear that their teens will discover Internet pornography when their children visit friends whose mother, father, or guardian they barely know. Few Amish parents worry that the latest sitcom or movie star will influence their children to come home with a nose ring, a tattoo, or a shaved head. Little wonder, then, that on the surface, Amish parenting seems to be simpler and less stressful than mainstream parenting.

The Quiet Years

One stage of development that appears to be relatively uneventful for most Amish parents, especially when compared to the same period in mainstream society, is the early teen years. Developmental psychologists suggest that in mainstream society, the onset of puberty, the growing influence of peers, and society's push towards independence contribute towards an increase in the youngsters' need for more autonomy and in subsequent parent-teen conflict. Both cross-sectional and longitudinal research findings indicate that this conflict most often peaks when the child is around thirteen or fourteen (Steinberg 1990, 2001). Most Amish report, however, that the years from thirteen through fifteen are tranquil for both youngsters and their parents.[8]

This relative tranquility likely stems from a combination of factors. First, Amish children complete their full-time schooling at the end of the eighth grade. Most students report that they look forward to being done with school so that they can start their life "in the real world." Initially, this "real world" consists of either working full-time at home or gradually transitioning into full-time employment away from the home when they reach the allowable legal age. They have been taught from childhood to value work; and for most Amish, work has traditionally meant manual, tangible, sweat-of-the-brow work rather than studying books or dealing with abstractions. Now they can finally work, unencumbered by the requirements of formal schooling.

Another likely contributor to these quiet years is that the family, rather than peers, is still the center of activity. A fourteen-year-old celebrates her birthday mostly with immediate family and relatives. Also, almost no organized activities or group recreation exists for Amish youth in the early teenage years. If a fifteen-year-old wants to play softball, he does so with his siblings and neighbors. Contrast that with the multiple activities and frenetic pace that fill the hours of many middle-class children and early adolescents. For the most part, young Amish teens interact with their peers only on church Sundays every other week or at the occasional school sale, benefit sale, or farm auction.

Parenting Perplexities

Whether dealing with their young teens or with their *rumspringa* children, Amish parents still face unique parenting pressures, both internally and externally. They believe that their effectiveness as parents will be a crucial factor in determining the Christian commitment and, ultimately, the eternal destiny of their children. Regarding such faithfulness, one parent wrote, "Remember that virtues can often be lost in a two-step, two-generation manner. The first generation fails to see the danger, and neglects to provide basic and sound teaching against sin. Naturally, the next generation will not have true convictions against it."[9] A minister declared, "We parents . . . have to be constantly vigilant if we are going to maintain high standards among the young ones in our community."

Not only do they fear a loss of standards, but they recognize that they could lose their children to "the world." Even if only one child left the faith and became a successful and respected member of the outside world, most parents would feel a deep sense of failure and loss. A middle-aged Amish father lamented, "We have buried five children, but that has not given us as much grief as the one who has strayed."

A mother wrote poignantly of her feelings of losing her children to the world: "How do parents feel when children leave home? It is so heartbreaking. At first I cried and cried, and when I got over that, it just made me sick. Still, I had to do my daily work. Sometimes I feel I didn't treat them right when they were growing up. I didn't show enough love, didn't talk nice and kind, didn't teach them enough about God and pray, and so on. Whenever I think about it, such as now when writing about it, it brings tears to my eyes. We can't change what already happened. I will keep praying for them as long as I live. Signed, A Lonely Mother"[10]

The parents' respect from the community relates directly to their success in rearing children who become committed, conscientious Amish adults. "You can judge the parents by looking at their children," a Nebraska Amishman asserted. In those communities where family directories list the membership status of each child in every home, the "failures" of parents with non-Amish children are published for all to read.[11] In one settlement, a minister will not be considered for the office of bishop if all his children are not safely in the church or at least preparing for membership.[12] Some Amish even evaluate parents on the outcome of their grandchildren, as did an older Amishman who maintained that "the real test of parents is to see how their grandchildren turn out." In the same vein, a young Amishman announced, "All of the grandchildren on my mother's side are still Amish, and only one grandchild on Dad's side left the Amish."

In many places, communities hold parents in high esteem if their children are among the first to join the church. Conversely, parents lose status when a child delays membership beyond the expected age of joining. Such postponement puts stress on the parents, and the longer the delay, the more tensions rise among them, their wavering son or daughter, and the church.

Although many parents can tolerate the deviance and disobedience of the middle teen years, when a child reaches the expected time for joining the church, parents are less likely to remain tolerant and patient with their children's reluctance.

In some places, community tolerance also ends when the uncommitted son or daughter reaches a certain age, usually twenty-one. This holds true especially for children who are dressing or acting in objectionable ways. At that point, the community expects the child to come into full compliance and join the church or else permanently leave the home and community. "Ephraim will be twenty-one this summer," reported a father. "If he doesn't give up baseball and join the instruction class this time around, we will come into trouble with the church if we let him live at home."

Parents regarded as lax or inconsistent in either their personal lives or parental responsibilities may be counseled, pressured, and occasionally disciplined if they fail to enforce church standards. This is most common in the smaller, plainer communities or in some New Order settlements. Both parents and their delaying children may be stigmatized. One minister's wife commented, "It's a disgrace that Amanda has still not become a member at twenty-one. But what can you expect, since her mother was also pretty wild when she was Amanda's age." Even if young people join the church but fail to comply with community values, observers often attribute this to parental failure.

In many places, behavioral expectations are high not only for parents but also for teenagers. In *Young Companion*, parents listed the desired characteristics of a "normal" teenager. A father of sixteen children declared, "A normal Christian youth should respect his parents, be friendly, and if reminded of any wrong on his part, should be ready to make amends." Another writer responded this way: "Christian youth should be Christlike, compassionate, humble, meek, full of love, and an example to the believers. They should respect their parents and obey them in the Lord. They should enjoy and cherish Christian fellowship, singing, helping others, and above all they should enjoy their time spent at home with their families." A third writer described the role of parents in nurturing these Christian traits in their children: "The concerned parent will watch to avoid bad habits, worldliness, laziness, wastefulness, intemperance, disrespect, pride, and other such traits that might show up in young folks. Also, the parents should encourage humbleness, love, respect, temperance, as well as learning to work and being a help in the home."[13]

Amish parents must struggle constantly with the challenge of influencing their children, while at the same time allowing them the freedom to choose or reject their teachings and influence. Reiling (2002) believes that in certain settlements, parents are expected to allow, if not encourage, youthful deviance during the *Rumspringa* so that their teenagers will have a genuine choice to make in deciding whether to be baptized or to leave the Amish. In a cultural setting that promotes "parental complicity," to use Reiling's term, parents as well as their children feel stressed because of the conflicting expectations, she believes. Whatever the setting, Amish parents constantly face pressure to succeed in this high-stakes parenting task. Although they have considerable influence, it is nonetheless limited, especially during the *rumspringa* years when their children face equally daunting and sometimes conflicting expectations from both parents and peers.

Conflicting Demands

Parents of teens may also feel caught between the conflicting pressures from their growing children and their own adult peers in the church. Some teenagers may pressure their parents to go away for the weekend so that the house will be available for unsupervised weekend partying. If the teenage children host singings or parties, they may push the parents not to report group misbehavior to the church leaders or not call the police if some of the participants become overly boisterous or destructive.

Some parents claim that other parents also pressure them not to report illegal activities to the authorities. "They say they don't want to give the church and the Amish a bad name in the community. What's a person to do?" a father asked. A *Die Botschaft* writer suggested that in dealing with rowdiness "to call out the law for help is again not letting our light shine. [If] the police have our sons' names on record, then what will it come to, if they are called to service as trying to go for C.O. [conscientious objector status] of which we don't know how soon it could come to such."[14] Sometimes parents fear possible retribution from some of the rebellious youth if they crack down or call the authorities. A father said he disapproved of the carrying on, "but the boys would get down on me if I didn't allow it."[15]

Some parents occasionally succumb to pressures in order to please their children and their peers. One man recalled an after-singing party when the host father came out to the barn to check in on the young people. Although he found that a number of boys were drinking openly, he conversed and joked with them. During the conversation, one boy came up behind him and poured a bottle of beer over the father's head. As everyone laughed, he said, "Since I'm here, I might as well have a beer too. Give me one of those things," and drank it along with the boys.

Although this kind of behavior is uncommon, bishops have at times threatened to discipline parents who allow their children to engage in forbidden activities such as hosting a party or parking a car on the premises. According to one Amish informant, a Lancaster County bishop warned parents that if their children attended hoedowns "with antisocial behavior . . . their parents will have to answer to the church leaders."[16] Also, some Lancaster County bishops reportedly warned that parents who knowingly permitted gangs to party on their property would be brought before the church council. In one case, a father was "held back" from communion twice for permitting his wayward son to park his car behind their barn. "What can I do?" he lamented. "If I make him quit parking at home, he'll just leave, but if I am held back the third time, I will be put in the *Bann*."

At times Amish youth deliberately separate themselves from both parental and community influences and make choices that distance themselves from home and church. For example, parents typically experience high stress if their sons or daughters begin to socialize with non-Amish youth, whether from another Anabaptist group or with the "English." Parents know both intuitively and experientially that these friendships threaten the fabric and integrity of their separatist society and the future of their children as Amish.

In some communities, young people have become involved with youth whose parents left the church or never joined. Elsewhere, parents reported that some of their youth had begun socializing with marginalized, alienated, or deviant outsiders in partying and vandalism. When a small settlement failed in Gettysburg, Pennsylvania, in 1997, some Amish attributed it, at least in part, to their youths' worldly friendships that eventually led to problems and defections.

The major concern of Amish parents is that if their children dally with English teenagers, they may become romantically or sexually involved with an outsider whom they will eventually marry. Parents especially worry if their daughters date non-Amish youth. A father explained, "Boys may fool around with English girls for a while and then 'tell them off' [break up], but girls naturally become more attached in a relationship."

When Amish children marry outsiders, they almost never return. Unless the spouse converts to the Amish—an unlikely event—this "unequal yoking" in marriage spells the end of the parents' hopes for the child's return to the fold.[17] Furthermore, if the son or daughter should divorce and remarry, he or she would be disqualified from returning to the Amish as long as the spouse lives.

One reason that Amish do not actively seek converts may be their caution of outsiders. They fear that however sincere the "seeker" might be, he or she could unwittingly bring in deeply ingrained worldly influences, attitudes, and habits to contaminate their church and the youth.[18] A parent explained, "Young people who sow their wild oats still have the basic Amish core that draws them back. However, converts do not have that same base."

A Breach in the Wall

Separation between Amish youth and the world was seriously breached during World War II when nearly eight hundred young men received draft notices from the government. Draft boards required that Amish young men, along with other conscientious objectors, participate in Civilian Public Service (CPS) or its Canadian counterpart during World War II. Fifty of the young men decided to serve in the military, either as soldiers or in noncombatant roles. Virtually all of the others joined CPS as conscientious objectors (Nolt 2003, 288). Officials often sent these conscripts hundreds of miles from home to work with non-Amish personnel. Parents and church leaders believed that such isolation from the community would lead to increased defections.[19]

During the 1950s and 1960s, parents worried even more about their sons who were sent to urban centers to fulfill their alternative service obligations in hospitals and other nonprofit organizations. "This kind of voluntary service was a more dangerous environment for our boys than when they were working in remote areas as fire fighters or in conservation projects," an Amishman explained. More than one young Amishman became attracted to a nurse or nurses' aide. Many Amishmen wrote that they faced temptations at their workplace. A grandfather recalled that in his alternative service about twenty new student nurses rotated into his hospital every thirteen weeks. Predictably, some Amish young men were attracted to these young women.

Another Amishman recalled his experiences as an orderly in a hospital in the 1950s: "I am not proud of some things in those two years. Things were not always what they should have been. There were many temptations. Working in a hospital, we were working with women mostly as fellow workers. These hardworking, dependable boys were eye-catching to some of these girls. Some boys ended up getting hooked" (Beechy and Beechy n.d., 140). Similarly, a grandfather opined that "many of these girls wanted a boy, and it didn't matter whether he was Amish or not."

Overall, relatively few conscripts were swept away by the pleasures of the world, the flesh, and the devil. More often they were influenced through contact with members of more progressive Anabaptist groups. CPS inductees from more liberal denominations challenged their Old Order counterparts with arguments favoring evangelical beliefs and practices. At the same time, most of the more progressive Anabaptist volunteers reportedly modeled a conscientious, responsible, and devout lifestyle, without the trappings of Amish austerity. "I was working in Wooster and driving a car at the time, even though I was a member of the church," one man recalled. "One of my Mennonite buddies asked me if I was going to go back to the church when I got out. I couldn't really tell him because I didn't know what I was going to do." Another young man had decided that he wanted to become an airline pilot after his alternate service duties were over. Both eventually returned home. The first man confessed his wanderings and was "taken up" again in the church. The second returned to join the church and eventually became a bishop. Another who returned said that he was not sure what he would have done if he had not had a girlfriend waiting for him back home. Despite these stories of happy returns, a number of Amish youth left the Amish during or after their voluntary service experience.[20]

During World War II, Amish parents and leaders, sensing the potential danger to their youth, launched an alternative plan of their own. They selected ministers to regularly visit CPS centers and work sites to provide worship, counsel, contact from home, and accountability for their youth. Meanwhile, Amish leaders lobbied the government to allow more of their sons to stay at home. They sought farm deferments rather than placements that would put their boys in questionable surroundings and activities (Nolt 2003, 299–300).

However, parents and leaders were less successful in the 1950s and 60s at keeping in touch with their young men in urban settings, despite their worries for their sons' welfare and future. Although the number of Amish young men who participated in alternate service was relatively small, the concern of Amish adults clearly shows their fears of having their youth mix with the world away from home.

Sowing Oats Back Home

Besides concerns over their children's liaisons with non-Amish youth, parents also worry about their children's participation with each other in activities back home that would surely result in their being disciplined if they were church members. For example, some youth, especially in large communities, attend movies. (*Witness* was popular when it came out in the 1980s.) Others rent videos. They often watch them at a non-Amish relative's house, in a home where one of the girls housecleans, or at an Amish home on a battery-rigged TV and VCR when the parents are away.

Occasionally, friends will rent a room in a nearby motel as the venue for hanging out and watching rented movies. An eighteen-year-old disclosed, "Our gang used to be conservative, but some sixteen-year-olds have started renting videos on Saturdays. They are the ones who are most likely to do that." A convenience store clerk in the same settlement reported that Saturday was video night for many Amish youth. Both males and females rented videos, but usually in same-sex groups.[21]

Of course, others want more excitement than watching videos on a Saturday night. Numbers of Amish youth from Ohio have traditionally traveled to Wheeling, West Virginia, for the Saturday night WWVA country music Jamboree in the Hills, or to Sea World Ohio or Geauga Lake, amusement parks in northern Ohio. Their counterparts from Lancaster County, Pennsylvania, drive to Atlantic City, New Jersey, or Rehoboth Beach, Delaware, where they periodically spend summer weekends lounging on the beach, swimming in the ocean, or hanging out on the boardwalk. Others flock to Six Flags in Jackson, New Jersey. For a while, many Amish youth enjoyed getting their pictures taken at a vintage photo establishment, where some of the girls reportedly posed as barmaids.

In the winter, some youth go skiing in Pennsylvania's Pocono Mountains or in New England, and not a few have traveled as far away as the Rockies for winter activities. Parents often worry about the increased peer pressure and diminished accountability on these trips, which sometimes result in injury or even death. Closer to home, a Pennsylvania mother wept as she related that police arrested their oldest son at the Delaware shore for driving under the influence. While traveling to a cabin in the mountains, another young man in the same community died of a diabetic condition aggravated by heavy alcohol consumption. Amish parents of children who drink and drive worry just as much as their mainstream counterparts do about their offsprings' safety and future.

Perhaps Amish parents have greater concern about unsanctioned activities that take place right in their own communities. In the large settlements, the most notorious problem and the most troublesome to church leaders and parents are parties, hoedowns, or band hops, the name depending on the location and emphasis. Most occur on Saturday nights, but a young man from southern Indiana reported that many youth there party every night from Thursday through Sunday. The more rebellious youth and those who belong to "faster" groups tend to be most deeply involved. However, some normally conservative young people may also show up in their carriages, drawn by the action and the chance to meet other Amish youth. Most parents object to these activities but have felt powerless to change a tradition that existed long before they were teenagers themselves.

Sliding into Liberalism

Although parents understandably worry about the attractions of "the world, the flesh, and the devil," many Amish believe that the appeal of more liberal Anabaptist groups poses a greater danger to their plain communities' continuation than the lure of the world. "When young people go out drinking and partying," an Amishman explained, "they know that they are acting wrong and need to stop it before they come back. When they start going with the Mennonites, they begin to question the whole Amish way of life. And that's dangerous."

Another man who eventually left the Amish concurred: "My parents worried more about me visiting a Mennonite church than about my brother who was out partying and carrying on. I would be the one to come home with questions." In *One Way Street* (Stoll 1972), a novel written by an Amishman, the winsomeness, warmth, and apparent freedom of the local Mennonites attract the Old Order teenage protagonist. Although he finds these qualities initially appealing, the young man later decides that this "one way street" too often ends in liberalism and eventual ruin.

A more subtle but perhaps equally dangerous way to get onto the one way street, the Amish believe, is through moral and spiritual "drift." They see this as the gradual tendency to abandon practices, beliefs, and behaviors that once characterized the Old Order Amish. The number of former Amish now on the membership roles of the "higher" Amish-Mennonite, Beachy Amish, and Mennonite churches provides them with ample evidence that drift leads to defection. They believe that drift within the church is dangerous, but they especially worry about its impact and influence on the younger generation.

Losing the Language

An ominous sign to many parents and grandparents in some settlements is an apparent decline in the use of German, the language of worship and of their Bible. They believe that facility in High German has been deteriorating, both in the church and among the young. "Many of the youth do not even know the German hymns anymore," lamented a minister. A young man admitted that he understood very little of the German he heard in the worship services, and a young woman from northern Indiana claims she did not understand what she was committing to in her vows because she knew very little German. Moreover, adults complain that many youth rarely speak Pennsylvania German, the language of the home, at social gatherings or work. In Lancaster County, for example, Amish softball players and fans speak virtually no Pennsylvania German at their softball league games.

An unmarried young man from a peer-centered settlement described his experience and that of his peers with regard to the Pennsylvania German dialect. He claimed that their youth "begin to speak exclusively in English at about the age of 10. Thenceforth, they will never use Dutch amongst their peers. It makes them uncomfortable. Conversely, it is just as unpleasant to speak to one's parents in English. Isn't that curious. . . . Parents decry the erosion of their maternal tongue for their children [but] when unsure of the proper Dutch word, will immediately reach for the English."[22] An Amish waitress in Pinecraft, Florida, said, "I don't like to speak in *Deitsch* [Pennsylvania German]. It's too hard. Hardly anybody speaks *Deitsch* where we live in southern Indiana, adults or teenagers. We feel much more comfortable in English."

Many Amish parents intuitively recognize that their German language and dialect are not only symbols of their distinctiveness but a de facto barrier between them and the world. A father stated that it was a very good thing that their children typically do not speak English before entering first grade. "This acts as a shield against the influence of the outside world," he explained.

Similarly, A Michigan father thought that if teenagers became too fluent in English, they would be able to make the transition to "out there" too easily. In an anonymous article, the author admonished the readers of *Family Life* to use the dialect: "Anybody who speaks English around home when just family members are around, or while working or visiting with others who know Pennsylvania Dutch, is putting in a vote to drop a rich heritage that will never again be brought back if we lose it. The value of that heritage is so great that we can't afford to lose it."[23]

One writer in *Blackboard Bulletin* regarded limited education as a strategy in retention of the young: "My mind goes back almost thirty years to when I taught school. On two occasions our senior bishop reminded me not to over-emphasize speaking English in school. The pupils should learn to speak well enough to do business in town but being somewhat hindered in speech could serve as a barrier to their fitting in with worldly associations."[24] A number of youth interviewed for *Devil's Playground* (2002) reported a fear of not being able to cope in the outside world if they left the Amish (Shachtman 2006).

Most Old Order people can quickly cite groups, such as a New Order church in North Carolina, that started an outreach in English to several families who were "seekers" expressing an interest in becoming Amish. The New Order bishop stated, "We wanted it to be open to whoever wants to come, and we wanted English services for people who were not raised in the Amish church." However, it was only a short time until the English-speaking group decided to become Mennonite, and most of the members purchased cars (Tomlin 2003). Although speaking English in daily interaction is the exception in most places, a minister wondered, "Can we still keep our Amish ways if we lose our language?" He, along with many of his New Order counterparts, believes that as groups become more progressive, their use of both old German and Pennsylvania German diminishes, along with the group's Amish identity. Thus, some adults wonder if their youth's careless language use reflects potential drift and loss of a cultural distinctive or is merely a passing stage in their journey to Amish adulthood.

The Lunch Pail Threat

The most frequently expressed concern voiced by parents and ministers is the potential impact of thousands of Amish children and youth growing up off the farm today. Like their predecessors and most nineteenth-century Americans, the Amish have associated farming and a rural environment with wholesomeness and hard work.

Conversely, they have linked an urban environment with worldliness, corruption, temptation, and sin. For most parents, "going into town," whether for work or play, symbolizes Lot's sojourn into the biblical city of Sodom, the prototypic urban image of wickedness and degradation described in Genesis 13:10–13. If the producers of the UPN "reality series" on *Rumspringa* had tried to find a title to upset Amish parents, they could have found nothing better than *Amish in the City*.

With the exponential growth of the Amish in the last several decades and the reduced availability of affordable farmland, the old dream of fathers helping each son obtain a farm is just that—a dream (Kraybill and Nolt 2004, 19–35). Moreover, Amish leaders express dismay that growing numbers of their young people show little interest in farming, traditionally their occupation of choice. They fear that the prospect of enormous mortgage payments, increased governmental regulations, and working countless hours for little profit has diminished farming's appeal for many youth and even adults.

Finding meaningful work for each child in a large nonfarm family poses a difficult challenge for parents with a rigorous work ethic; garden and yard work are seasonal, and care of the driving horses takes a limited amount of time. Family-run businesses may provide work for the older children, but they believe that nothing teaches self-sacrifice, perseverance, delayed gratification, and obedience as much as submitting to the never-ending chores of milking, feeding cattle, haying, and forking manure.[25]

This exodus from farming has raised many concerns. Not only are parents uneasy when their offspring find employment in town, but they are equally uneasy when their teenagers and young adults work alongside non-Amish employees in factories or on construction crews. An Amish elder wrote, "Here in northern Indiana, with all the factories, and our boys and girls working there, they have more money than is good for them, to do and buy whatever they want. Many drift out in the world and get hooked with outside partners, never to come back" (Beechy and Beechy n.d., 141). A mother wrote, "Are we as parents fair to our children if we expect them to take an interest in our church hymns or in our singings if they have been exposed all week to radio music while going to and from their work? Or if they work in factories where the radio is blaring? Or baby sitting, or cleaning homes where TV is waiting at the flip of a button?"[26] Because of outside work, many Amish teenagers may be spending more time with non-Amish people than with their own.

Another fear related to the move off the farm and the increased outside contact is the parents' concern that the young people will lose their dedication to hard work. Many Amish are offended by what they perceive to be a defective work ethic among non-Amish employees. They fear the debilitating effects of too much contact with people who work primarily for their paychecks and do as little as they can on the job.

Tourist Traps

Similarly, many parents in large settlements worry about the possible negative impact of tourism on the youth in the large communities. Although many parents perceive inquisitive, camera-toting tourists as more of an irritation than a threat, parents worry more about the influx of money, the dangers of materialism, and the growing dependency on tourist dollars. Both a minister and an Amish mother from a Missouri community that has become a destination for Amish-based tourism declared that, for whatever reason, they could see a change: "Our young people seem to have developed a harder attitude since the tourists came," they said. A parent from a small settlement said, "Even though it appears to you that we are isolated from the world, the trends that affect your children also affect ours because we have so much more contact with you than we used to."

Perilous Times

Whether their children encounter tourists or not, most Amish parents are convinced that being an adolescent and being a parent are more difficult today than when they themselves or their parents were young. They see the outside world as making constant inroads into their lifestyle, either subtly or directly. "When I was with the young people in the fifties," said one grandfather, "a few of the most rebellious boys had cars. Today all of the boys in some groups have them." Another grandfather reported, "Back then if drinking went on, it was almost always the boys. Now some of the girls join in, and they are just about as bad as the boys." A minister reported that in one settlement, girls would drive the boys home because they were too drunk to drive.

A mother maintained that drugs were unheard of in Amish communities until the 1970s. "Today if somebody wants to find drugs, he can," she said. In some settlements, parents worry about the availability and use of pornography. "It's available everywhere," lamented one father. "Our youngest son got involved with pornography through the influence of the van driver who hauled his carpentry crew to and from work." A bishop agreed that pornography was a growing problem.

Parents worry that instead of their children learning the value of money and hard work, they will become slothful and self-indulgent. "In my generation," recalled one great-grandfather, "nobody had enough money to buy a car, or even go to town and buy drinks. What little we did earn went to our parents until we came of age at twenty-one. Now young people are making big money and many of them are keeping all of it for themselves." A father made a similar point: "When I was a boy, our parents kept what we earned until we were twenty-one and responsible enough to spend it wisely. They would save as much as they could on our behalf until we came of age. It was also a good way to be sure we didn't spend it on cars and such foolishness. My own son has worked in construction for the past three years, and he has nothing to show for it. I'm sure that he has wasted $45,000 on vehicles and other foolishness." An Indiana father lamented the fact that "our boys working in factories can earn $1000 or $1200 a week. It's not good for them."

For the Amish, more money, coupled with more leisure time, seems like a devil's mixture fraught with both financial and moral danger. An Amish market owner complained, "Nowadays, you can't get young people who want to work for us on Saturdays. We can't compete with carpentry or factory wages. There they make good money. Besides, they want their weekends free to go camping, tear off to the shore, or go on other out-of-town trips with their friends." Many adults share his concern about what kind of church members high-spending, pleasure-seeking youth will become.

Tiptoeing a Fine Line

Considering these concerns and changes, how do Amish parents respond to their adolescent children? People who equate plainness with sternness might expect Amish parents to be harsh and authoritarian, demanding respect and instant obedience. Some parents do attempt to become more controlling with their teenage children. For example, as a punishment for unacceptable behavior they may keep their sixteen-year-old home from the next singing or two, or forbid him or her from getting together on a holiday with friends. However, this is rare.

In the large settlements, at least, many youth get an enormous amount of freedom. Some spend entire weekends with their peers, totally absent from home and supervision. Their parents may not know where they are, who they are with, or what they are doing. When learning of this, many outsiders react like the bus drivers who drove three busloads of Amish youth to an Ascension Day get-together. According to the *Die Botschaft* scribe, when the drivers observed how little Amish parents monitored their children, "[they] were surprised the church doesn't require chaperones with the young people at such times, they said they would have [an] older person to [every] 10 younger in a bus trip. It made us feel guilty as our youth have traveled the same way."[27]

In many churches, Amish youth have enjoyed freedom from adult restrictions for generations. One reason is that a major tenet of Anabaptist belief and practice is voluntary adult baptism. Because the church has no direct control over the youth before they become members, parents know that their sons and daughters have the final decision about whether to join the church. This gives young people considerable leverage during their *rumspringa* years. "Our parents don't push too hard," explained one young man, "for fear that they will make the children bitter." A father concurred: "If I or the ministers push my son too hard now to get rid of his car, he will just up and leave for good."

A young man who left his family to spend the winter in Florida agreed: "My parents are not happy that I am down here, but they are afraid that pushing too hard will cause me to rebel." Perhaps these factors help explain the shift from the traditional authoritarian parenting style to a more indulgent approach when their sixteen-year-olds formally begin attending singings with their peers.

Church leaders are also likely to ignore infractions rather than confront their teenagers who are not yet members. "Sometimes the church will just overlook some things," explained an independent-minded single male who had his picture taken for a passport. "Don't ask, don't tell" seems to be an acceptable way in many communities to reduce confrontations and conflict. Although a father will sometimes smash his teen's radio or guitar if he finds it in the house, he will more often simply ignore the offensive item if he can. Similarly, if parents hear rumors that their daughter has been watching television while cleaning house for an English neighbor or find evidence that their son is playing in a softball league, they may turn the proverbial blind eye or deaf ear.

Parents are more likely to confront their children only when they engage in flagrantly disrespectful or deviant behavior that will bring shame on the parents or the church. For example, the local paper reported that an Amish youth doused a state policeman with beer as authorities attempted to break up a large party.[28] In another state, a news article reported that in an attempt to break up a Saturday night party, "officers were greeted by several rocks, beer bottles, and beer cans, each thrown by persons in the group."[29] When the youth can be identified, parents and church leaders will, in their words, "try to work with the offenders." However, the adults may proceed slowly if they recall incidents when local youth retaliated against those adults whom they regarded as too punitive.

Pushing Past the Limits

Actually, destructive acts by youth towards other members of their community are nothing new. Nearly a century ago, an article in *The Budget* reported that Menno Graber and Bud Yoder were arraigned before Squire Lenacher and fined four dollars for amputating the tail of Daniel Knepp's horse.[30] In the late 1990s, national media carried stories of a rampage directed against an Amishman in a small Iowa community. At least four youth were arrested for breaking forty-four windows, upsetting family carriages, and damaging household property.[31] A community in Missouri also has a reputation for similar outbreaks over the years.

Most youthful acts of vandalism share several characteristics. The perpetrators are invariably unmarried males who have not joined the church. They have usually been drinking, rarely act alone, and target a man or men in the community with whom they have real or imagined grievances. These targets have often been parents, bishops, or ministers who are regarded as harsh, unfair, or who have reported misbehavior to the police or the miscreants' parents. In the Iowa rampage, the vandals believed that their victim had reported their underage drinking to local authorities. In another settle-ment, young men, upset with the strictness of their bishop, put fly spray in the cattle feed, cut down and broke limbs off fruit trees, and damaged carriages.[32]

In Ohio, a Swartzentruber Amish minister was disturbed one night by a group of young men who were outside playing music on a forbidden radio. When the boys refused to stop or to cooperate, the minister tried to detain them by unhitching the horse of one of the offenders. One of them struck him on the arm with a jockey stick before they all fled. A passing milk truck driver observed the boys and later identified them. The minister agreed that they were the offenders. Later, four of the boys returned, overpowered the minister, and in retaliation cut his hair short. This incident subsequently led to church problems and a serious breach in the local church.

Occasionally, scribes in Amish newspapers allude to malicious acts and worry about possible retaliation. A writer to *Die Botschaft* expressed such a concern: "Write-ups are in the daily papers about the wild drinking parties and hoe-downs among our young folks etc. But it is NOT to be mentioned in our papers like *Die Botschaft* etc. And if any of the young folks get into trouble; whoever reports it will have some of their property damaged later on etc. So the people just more or less keep quiet about such things and 'look the other way as if they hadn't noticed.' Yes, we're too weak to stand up to persecution—from our OWN people."[33]

Such aggressive actions are rare in most communities, but a deacon from Pennsylvania who visited two of those settlements with a history of vandalism concluded, "These problems will happen when the local adults check the young peoples' buggies for things, such as radios. When they find something forbidden, they'll break it up. Then the young folks will destroy the adults' property to get revenge. In the one settlement, quite a few of the ministers have moved away because of this." Some observers believe that the extensive migrations out of the Missouri community occurred because of fear of retaliation from disgruntled or angry youth. As an afterthought, the deacon concluded, "You can't force the young. You have to sweet-talk [*sic*] them into joining the church."

Coping with Deviance

In rare situations, individual youth exhibit repeated destructive or rebellious tendencies beyond the control of their parents.[34] Upon encountering such open defiance or serious deviance, parents may resort to more drastic attempts to bring their resistant child—usually a son—into compliance. If the child is not yet sixteen, the family may send him or her to a relative in the same community or, less frequently, to relatives in a distant, often more conservative, settlement. For example, parents of a rebellious fourteen-year-old in upstate New York sent their daughter to live with her grandparents in Ohio. Similarly, a man who had grown up in an Amish home claimed that his parents sent him away to work when he was fourteen. He said they feared that as the oldest child, he would have a negative influence on his younger siblings. Some Amish are widely known for effectively working with a succession of difficult children and teens over the years, acting as surrogate guardians and disciplinarians.

Another practice is to send the resistant teenager to a church- or faith-related rehabilitation center that specializes in working with rebellious or deviant youngsters. These organizations are generally run by more progressive Anabaptist affiliations such as the Beachy Amish. Typically, the daily regimen is highly structured and disciplined, and Christian teaching and prayer are important components in the treatment. Although most Amish approve of the strict discipline in such centers, they worry about these non-Amish influences on their child. "When you have an organization run by former Amish, what is this saying to our son about where the leaders' hearts really are?" asked a father. Leaders in another settlement who initially sent some troubled youth to a Christian rehabilitation center in Alabama decided to withdraw from the program because of concerns about the distance from home and questions about the theology and leadership of those in charge. A relatively new placement alternative that began in the late 1990s and continued to expand in the first decade of the twenty-first century has been the growth of Amish-run or horse-and-buggy Mennonite-run mental health facilities in or near the three largest plain communities. Places such as Green Pasture in Lebanon County, Pennsylvania, and Whispering Hope in Franklin County, Pennsylvania, have provided treatment options not only for adults but for troubled or difficult youth.

More frequently, parents who believe that their children's peers are having a negative impact on the core values of faith, hard work, simplicity, and frugality may move the entire family to an adult-oriented community where the young people are "in order" and there is "more control." One parent wrote in the "Letters to the Editor" section in *Family Life:* "If you don't want your children to grow up where they are out on Saturday night, play ball on Sundays, or date at age sixteen, then I think you had better move to a community where they don't do those things. And do it while your children are still in the lower grades at school. If you stay where you are, it is quite possible that your children will not heed your convictions. We found out that it is really hard on children to stay in the rules and convictions of their parents, because if all the others do it they will get very weak."[35] Parents who wish to move because of concerns with the youth typically try to relocate before their oldest child turns sixteen and begins "going with the young folk."

Leaders in some of the settlements that have formed to provide a "more decent" environment for their youth have resorted to writing their *Ordnung* and sending it to parents who are interested in their new settlement. In this way, they hope to attract only those families who will support their goals and distinctives. Most of these settlements seek to be repositories and guardians of plain living and values for years to come. A clear example of this is Parke County, Indiana, which originated in the early 1990s, mostly with families from Lancaster County, Pennsylvania. Although it is 650 miles away from Lancaster, it is a full-fledged Lancaster County daughter settlement. The people there, youth and adults, dress and drive carriages following the Lancaster *Ordnung.* However, the founders established rules that are considerably more conservative than those in the Pennsylvania mother settlement.[36] Several focused on practices that affect youth and their parents.

For example, singings were to be held only every other week and were to be monitored by adults. Organized sports, such as league softball, were forbidden. In fact, softball was forbidden for everyone except school children. Mid-week youth activities were discouraged unless planned ahead and approved. Currently, none of the young men own cars, and youth report that they are not aware of any of their peers who smoke, drink, or party. "In a small settlement like this," a seventeen-year-old boy explained, "it's pretty hard to do those things without everyone knowing it." Volleyball is permitted when visitors come, but never on Sunday. After the singings, the youth get together for a time to play games.

Not all parents applaud the migration to a new settlement, especially if it is related to moral rather than economic concerns. An Amish parent whose daughter was considering a move to Parke County criticized those who went there for being really more like Mennonites than Amish: "They are goodie-goodies, thinking they are better than we are back home." Actually, the majority of the migrants came from the most conservative southern part of Lancaster County.[37] Whatever the motivation for a new settlement, families often move away from loved ones, friends, and occupation at significant financial or emotional cost.

Staying the Course

Despite the complexities of parenting, most Amish parents do not dread their children's teenage years. For one thing, many parents and grandparents take comfort in knowing that though they themselves dabbled with worldliness and disobedience in their "running around" years, they became responsible, loyal Amish because of their parents' patience and love. They look at many leaders and "pillars of the church" who also had crossed boundaries and broke rules, yet their parents and grandparents did not lose heart or give up on them.

Through their confidence in the grace of God and the support of a united community, they approach their children's adolescent years with hope and confidence. They believe that they have laid a firm foundation by rearing their children "in the nurture and admonition of the Lord" (Ephesians 6:4). They trust that they will reap what they have sown—responsible sons and daughters who will in due season choose to be instructed in the ways of the church and be baptized into the faith. These beliefs provide strength and sustenance for parents as they cope with the foolishness and vagaries of youth.

Amish youth learn to work hard, but they also have lots of fun.
Photo by Lucian Niemeyer.

Teen Culture

Working Hard and Having Fun

*Letting children go unsupervised to watch the trash
that comes over the TV every day has to be
the greatest form of child abuse.*
—Amish father

Work as Virtue

When asked about the most important values for his children, a young Amish father said, "To become hard workers." Although hard work is not part of the *Ordnung*, all Amish parents want their children to be diligent workers. This virtue is a cultural distinctive as much as plain clothes and horse-drawn transportation. The Amish regard work as a privilege and an obligation to the family, to the community, and to God. They gain esteem and satisfaction, not from high status or high-paying positions, but from meeting the financial needs of the family and working industriously and intelligently.

The Amish understand work to be a vocation or calling, a fulfilling end in itself, one that glorifies God and brings joy to the worker and to the community. Parents not only model hard work but also tirelessly instruct their offspring to develop a rigorous work ethic. As children and young people learn to work hard and take pride in their accomplishments, they not only contribute to the family, but they confirm their Amish identity and strengthen their ties with the community and culture as well.

Parents expect all children and teenagers, whatever their ages and abilities, to make significant contributions to the family. Hostetler (1977, 358) writes, "The Amish ideal of work is not to get rid of it, but to utilize it in giving every member an opportunity to develop his faculties." Children as young as three or four may begin learning how to work by "helping" their older siblings and parents. Rather than telling their three-year-olds that they are too young to help, parents encourage them to help pick strawberries, water the chicks, and feed the calves. "One of my earliest memories," a middle-aged Amishman recalled, "was having to dust down the stairs with a feather duster when I was three."

A commercial orchard owner from Lancaster County, Pennsylvania, reports that when Amish families come to pick fruit, the contrast between their children and non-Amish children is dramatic. "Amish children usually keep to the task till the parents are satisfied that the work is done or else excuse the children," he said. "English children, on the other hand, may enthusiastically pick cherries for five to ten minutes till they get bored and end up in cherry fights, tree climbing, or sulking."

For Amish children, work and play often merge into one. For example, preschoolers milk imaginary cows or rig up rope harnesses on stick horses to plow imaginary fields. Two young children reported to a visitor their delight that morning in secretly sweeping the sidewalk and the porch to surprise their mother. When Hostetler and Huntington (1992, 99) asked a sample of elementary- and junior-high-aged Amish and mainstream children to draw a picture of a happy time, many of the Amish drawings related to activities such as child care, yard work, cooking, and farm chores. Not a single picture from the mainstream culture was work-related. The cover of an issue of *The Diary* featured a poem written by a nine-year-old Amish child entitled "Work is Fun":

In the morning when I get up
I make my bed so neat
Then quickly go downstairs
And put stockings on my feet.

I like to work with Mother
And do the dirty dishes.
I also like to set the table
And clean the house as she wishes.
I take good care of the baby
And rock her to sleep
Or just show her a book
Which tells about a baby sheep.

I like to sweep the kitchen
And put the toys away
So we don't have to fall
And spoil this happy day![1]

Planting the Seeds

One reason Amish children learn to work at an early age is that most parents are skilled in assigning age-appropriate tasks to meet the emerging abilities and interests of their growing children. Tourists who stop at Amish roadside businesses often express amazement at how young children can tend the produce stand, make change, and assume responsibilities. Observers marvel that ten-year-old girls regularly cook, bake, and clean, and that boys that age milk cows, help with the haying, and even disk the fields by themselves. If the family owns a cottage industry, such as a chair or broom shop, children will often work there for several hours daily when school is not in session.

When the children finish school at fourteen or fifteen, they commonly work full-time around the house or farm. Until state law permits their full-time paid employment, they may "hire out" for a couple of days each week to do housecleaning or general farm work for nearby neighbors or relatives. A sixteen-year-old said he could manage the family dairy farm for several weeks, if necessary. "I know just what needs to be done, how to do it, and how to organize my younger brothers to get the work done," he announced. Few Amish would find his assertion surprising, since the community expects such competencies for boys this age.

A father related that when he, his wife, and their younger children went to visit relatives for a weekend, he left the care of the farm and its forty milking cows in charge of their thirteen- and eleven-year-old sons. Another father reported that when he was away from home for several weeks helping a relative, his boys, under the direction of their seventeen-year-old brother, successfully ran their large dairy operation. A grandfather recalled that right after World War II he was given foreman responsibilities on a relief ship transporting seven hundred horses to Poland as part of reconstruction efforts in Europe. As a sixteen-year-old "sea-going cowboy," he was not only in charge of part of the herd but was also responsible for overseeing several older non-Amish volunteers.[2] The supervisors chose him, not simply because of his knowledge of horses, but because of his Amish work ethic. In communities where Amish work in factories, employers actively seek Amish and ex-Amish youth because they are hardworking and responsible employees.

This does not mean that each family is an Amish paradise where the children and teenagers work without complaint.[3] Monday mornings may be difficult if the youth have been out until the early hours. Given the choice, most Amish eighteen-year-olds getting home at 2:00 a.m. from their courting would undoubtedly prefer to sleep in rather than get up before dawn for the 4:30 milking. Nevertheless, most manage to show up in the barn or at the job, with or without prodding. After breakfast, the father generally outlines the day's tasks for the boys, while the mother assigns tasks for the daughters.

The Perks of Work

One reason work is so highly valued is that most Amish parents suspect that too much idle time impedes moral and spiritual development. After all, "An idle mind is the devil's workshop," and "Satan finds some mischief still for idle hands to do." A letter from a parent to the editor of Pathway publications expressed the concern of many parents: "We need to make work at home to keep the young boys and girls out of town after they're out of school."[4] Amish parents see work as the ideal solution for idleness and the God-given preventive for mischief-making.

When Amish parents look at neighboring English families, they are appalled that their children idle away the summer in trivial or questionable pastimes. They cringe at the notion of sleeping until noon before spending the rest of the day scrapping over who will operate the remote control on the television. "Talk about child abuse," said an Amish father. "Letting children go unsupervised to watch the trash that comes over the TV every day has to be the greatest form of child abuse."

Although farm families need not invent meaningless chores for their children, they want sufficient work to keep all of them busy. Horses used for farming and transportation require year-round care. Growing produce and grain for the family and the market provides not only food but an abundance of field and garden work at just the right time for children who are out of school for the summer. And of course dairy farming requires morning and evening chores every day of the year. As a *Die Botschaft* scribe wrote, "[Dairy farming] is a great thing as it gives the children work . . . and keeps us from getting rich," she added ruefully.[5] A minister admitted that one reason their church opposed piping milk directly through plastic tubing from the cows to the bulk storage tank was that it would eliminate the children's main jobs of carrying and "dumping" the milk into the tank by hand.

In recent years large numbers of Lancaster County Amish families have abandoned the cultivation of tobacco for health or moral reasons. Some parents lamented most the loss of labor-intensive work opportunities for their children. For a people who value hard work, tobacco-growing must have seemed like a gift from heaven. Transplanting the seedlings from the tobacco beds began shortly after school closed in May, and from then on, the plants needed almost constant attention. The children were mainly responsible to hoe around each plant and eventually break off the stems to promote better growth and curing. With nearly six thousand plants per acre, the tobacco demanded incessant care through the long, hot days of summer.

In the humid days of August, all of the family joined in the sweaty, sticky job of cutting the leaves, spearing them on four-foot lath sticks for drying, and hanging them in the curing sheds. After Christmas, the cured tobacco had to be cut from the stalks or stripped, an intensive indoor job that could last through February. Stripping rooms were often cold, drafty, and invariably filled with acrid tobacco dust. Eventually, the family stripped the stalks and baled the entire leaf crop for the tobacco auction.[6] To outsiders, such long, tedious work together may seem like a breeding place for family dissension. Yet many Amish recall these hours together as wonderful times of conversation, song, and storytelling among the generations.

Work and leisure are less compartmentalized for Amish young people than for their non-Amish counterparts. Most mainstream teenagers work almost exclusively to obtain the possessions and experiences they could not otherwise afford.[7] Their work is generally an unpleasant but necessary means to that end. By contrast, when a customer asked a seventeen-year-old worker in an Amish bakery what she did for fun, she appeared to be puzzled by the question. Her co-worker answered that they had fun baking and waiting on customers, and this on a frightfully hot August day with no air conditioning or fans. Similarly, a twenty-year-old explained that on his annual seven-day vacation from the outdoor furniture shop where he worked fifty hours weekly, he helped his family on the farm or worked with a neighbor filling silos.

In Amish society, work often combines recreation and socializing, as manifested in various frolics or work bees, sewings, quiltings, and still, in some communities, corn huskings.[8] Even today, if someone is disabled or alone and needs help husking corn or cutting firewood, community members often "pitch in to help out." Such a need also provides local youth with an excuse to get together on a designated afternoon or evening. They typically work together for several hours, after which they may eat, sing, play games, or dance, depending on the community.

In the plainest groups, this may be the only social event for the youth other than the Sunday singing. Work, service, and recreation combine too for the Ohio New Order youth, who plant and care for potato or peanut patches in their districts as fund-raisers for charity. After they plant the plots, the young people continue to gather on a weekly basis throughout the summer to tend them and then play volleyball and socialize. When they finally dig the potatoes, the youth celebrate with a huge supper featuring, among other things, mashed potatoes prepared from the culls. In both New Order and Old Order settlements, young people may meet on a Saturday to plant or weed a garden, paint or roof a shed, or do a massive cleaning project for a widow or shut-in.

Certainly, the most exciting shared-work project is the community barn raising. Here the young men from miles around assist the adults in constructing the barn, and the young women help their mothers in preparing and serving meals for everyone. Sometimes young men join their fathers to travel with the Mennonite Disaster Service or other relief groups in volunteer cleanup and rebuilding projects in the aftermath of natural disasters. A group of eleven young men from one of the gangs in the Pennsylvania Amish valleys hired a van to take them to Arcadia, Florida, to help in relief efforts following the three hurricanes that hit Florida in the fall of 2004. Similar groups of young men went south again to help survivors of Hurricane Katrina the following year. Part of the attraction is the opportunity to travel and work with Amish from other settlements.

Sometimes the work ethic of the Amish has put parents in conflict with local, state, or federal OSHA regulations. In some areas of central Pennsylvania, parents allowed their thirteen- and fourteen-year-old sons to stack lumber all day in Amish-run saw mills. "When visitors or outsiders came to our mill, us boys ran and hid until they left," a nineteen-year-old recalled. Upon hearing such stories, several members of Congress sought legislation to curtail all involvement with dangerous machinery until the youth were eighteen. Supporters of the Amish countered by saying that non-Amish youth were allowed to operate very dangerous machines at age sixteen when they received their driving permits. Finally, the issue was resolved early in 2004, when George W. Bush signed into a law a bill exempting Amish youth from a number of restrictions of the Child Labor Law.[9]

Take Me Out of the Ball Game

Although Amish adults want their children and teenagers to learn how to work hard, many are still ambivalent about play. One parent commented, "Young folk have a lot of energy, but I still think hoeing . . . for charity is a better way to work it off than softball or volleyball. But even hoeing gatherings can get too frequent until the young people are not contented to stay at home." Many more parents express concern if their sons are involved in organized sports.

Through the years, a number of Amish young men in the large settlements have formed softball teams and joined summer softball leagues. They frequently play under the lights, against each other and against non-Amish teams. In Lancaster County, various youth groups field their own teams, with names like Warriors, Rebels, and Bandits. The level of play and competition is considerably higher than at picnic pickup games. A Lancaster County team, the Routers, competed in California for the national title.[10]

To the amazement of their English neighbors, the bishops continue to oppose their youth's participation in a local softball league. They explain their opposition in light of the Amish values of hard work, frugality, simplicity, and separation from the rest of the world. Their objections mirror those of the editor of *Young Companion*:

> What if the players are no longer children, but young adults (or even adults that are not so very young)? What if the motive is no longer relaxation and diversion, but a spirit of competition? What if our plain clothes are left in the closet and the players don uniforms? What if these teams compete in tournaments and win the state championship in their class, and then go on to the nationals? . . . How unfortunate that so many people who claim the Christian name do not follow his [the Apostle Paul's] example, nor grow up and put away childish things. It is even more unfortunate when batting and catching a ball becomes more than play—when it becomes serious competition between opposing teams, when it requires many hours of precious time, and when there is a great outlay of money for equipment, uniforms, and travel.[11]

In another issue of the same magazine, "A Fellow Pilgrim" wrote, "The greater the pleasure the world gets out of sports, the greater is the sin for us as Christians to follow or practice sports."[12] A bishop who moved from a large settlement to Canada declared, "Worldliness is creeping in through sports." Many adults worry that the players look anything but Amish with their barber haircuts, high fives, and form-fitting uniforms. Moreover, teams have to pay for lights, umpires, and the use of playing fields, all of which run counter to traditional Amish frugality. Besides that, a team in Indiana was actually sponsored by a local bar, Duke's Tavern, a sponsorship that offended many Amish. Stories occasionally surface about drinking and fighting among players on rival teams caught up in the heat of competition.

One bishop likened these events to the circuses and games of the decadent Roman Empire. Parents also worry because away games require the use of motorized vehicles. On some game nights virtually no Amish carriages can be found in the ball field parking lots. The adults are also unhappy that triple headers sometimes last till midnight, though their children must rise early for work. An even greater concern is that league play-offs often occur on Sundays, thus competing with church and family gatherings. Perhaps the final straw in the Lancaster settlement was a rumor that males and females were using the same restroom at one of the ball fields.

Subsequently, the Lancaster bishops convened an unprecedented special meeting to deal with the softball issue. They decided that they would no longer permit church members to play or even attend league games. Also, church authorities would discipline any mothers who washed their sons' softball uniforms. The most controversial edict, however, was that all future softball games could be played only at school and under the supervision of a teacher.

Sunday afternoon games and picnic pickups were officially out. Following the ruling, some young men delayed church membership so that they could continue to play. An exasperated bishop stated, "If softball playing is more important than following church guidelines, it is better that they go elsewhere." Despite the official ruling, a team captain reported that at least twenty Amish teams continued to compete in the local softball leagues. Another ten to fifteen organized teams, all made up of youthful nonmembers, played regularly on summer evenings or Sunday afternoons.[13] However, church members who had been playing immediately dropped out, and Amish adults who had been spectators stopped attending.[14]

Parental reactions to the bishops' decision reveal the differing attitudes toward organized sports in some Amish communities. Some Lancaster County parents complained to each other about the bishops' edict. "At least we know where our children are and what they're doing," said a parent of a player. "I would rather have my son playing softball than partying with his friends," a mother admitted. "It might help keep him out of trouble." A father declared, "If I would have had to give up softball as a sixteen-year-old or else leave home, I would have left home. The bishops don't understand how important sports are to these young boys."

Most Amish parents from smaller communities, however, express relief that they do not have to worry about their teenage children being away from the family evening after evening, playing or watching softball. An article in *Family Life* summarized some of the unease that many feel concerning organized sports: "Sports belong to the world. . . . Games promote a genera-tion gap. . . . Sports break down our separation [from the world]. . . . Sports detract from worthwhile things."[15]

Despite negative attitudes toward sponsored sports, most Amish have accepted informal local sports and recreation as legitimate. Traditionally, softball has been the most popular game at school. Children learn to play during their recesses and lunch hours, and both boys and girls participate and seem to equally enjoy the sport. Although Amish youth like to win, most games are social occasions characterized by good-natured camarade-rie rather than cutthroat competitiveness. Players rarely criticize each other for ineptness or poor judgment, and most young people seem to win or lose equally well.

According to Thomas Meyers, a sociologist who has taught in an Amish school, this cooperative behavior stems from the core values of caring and friendship that the entire community reinforces. He relates his firsthand observations: "Children play games with great gusto, but place little em-phasis on winning or singling out the individual. I have been a teacher in an Amish school, and I was amazed that when we played softball in the fall or spring there was never an argument about who was out or safe at a base. Instead there was a quiet agreement on such matters and the game went on. The game was enjoyed as a communal activity, with frequent rota-tion of positions" (1994, 393). In the summer, children and youth will also play softball with siblings and neighbors in the evening after the chores are done, on holidays, and when visiting with friends.

However, the most popular warm-weather game among the youth is volleyball. One reason is that both sexes can play and socialize, whatever their skill level. Many families have their own volleyball net poles permanently fixed in concrete-filled tires. If young people decide to play at a creek-side park or in somebody's newly mown field, they have been known to stretch the net between the upright shafts of two parked buggies. At a summer singing, boys will sometimes hang lanterns or use generators to power electric lights so that the games can continue well past dark. In one of the large youth groups in Lancaster County, the players had erected six nets to accommodate everyone. When Amish youth go to Florida during the winter, at least two volleyball games run simultaneously under the lights of the local park until closing time at 10:00 p.m. Many players have obviously become highly skilled in serving, setting, digging, and spiking. Just as with recess or pick-up softball, however, the players generally focus on having fun together more than on winning.

Amish "March Madness"

In the past, volleyball was relatively unknown among the Amish. Next to softball, the most popular sport in Lancaster County was cornerball, or *eck bulle*, in the dialect. It was the plain peoples' equivalent of NCAA March Madness. This sports phenomenon is the Amish version of dodge ball, often played in barns in cold weather. With the advent of warmer weather, games moved from indoors to the fenced-in manure pen outside the barn, one of the first signs of spring to the rural southeastern Pennsylvania German people. Cornerball was a staple of farm sales and auctions held in late February and March.[16] Farm sales announcements from the first half of the twentieth century often included the line "Ball players invited."

Until the 1950s, cornerball flourished among most of the Pennsylvania Dutch communities, both plain and fancy.[17] Although the "fancy" or "church Dutch" eventually abandoned the game, it still thrives among the plainest Amish groups and the horse-and-buggy Mennonites in Lancaster County. Unlike organized league sports, cornerball is the quintessential plain game, requiring nothing but a small ball, an empty cow pen or lot, and a dozen willing players.

The game calls for two teams of six players, who try to eliminate each opponent by hitting him with a leather-covered ball. In the past, these were often homemade by wrapping a quarter-sized steel nut in twine and covering it with black tire tape. Balls today resemble a slightly oversized hacky-sack firmly packed with leather scraps and sand. Participants prefer playing in barnyards where the winter manure accumulation has softened in the sun. They scatter a thick layer of straw on the area, known as the *mosch*. It provides them a soft surface to duck, dive, and roll as they seek to avoid being hit.

A game consists of three rounds or innings in which a team takes its first turn by throwing at members of the other team and then takes its turn at being the targets for their opponents. The starting four players of the throwing team position themselves at each corner of a square about the size of a volleyball court, hence the name cornerball. Their first two opponents, who are their targets, crouch in the middle of the *mosch,* as far from the thrower as possible.

Players must throw only from the corners. They hurl the ball to their teammates from corner to corner, watching their opponents for a slip or momentary lapse in concentration. Each throw into the center is critical, since someone will be eliminated. Every time a corner player fires at an opponent, one or the other of them will be out, either the errant thrower or the hit target. A teammate replaces an eliminated player until all six players on one side have made an out. Teams then switch positions to finish the round. The winner of each round, and ultimately of the game, is the team that has the most surviving players and accumulated points.

Experienced corner men are adept at faking throws and looking at one opponent while throwing at the other. Meanwhile, their most skilled opponents dash about and leap into the air with amazing agility and contortions. The best players combine speed, throwing accuracy, faking, and strategic ability. Some are widely known and applauded for their aerial acrobatics. They sometimes leap horizontally into the air like a high jumper, presenting only the soles of their boots as a target.

Occasionally, depending on the speed of the throw, the hardness of the ball, or the point of impact, players injure their opponents. One young player recounted how the cartilage in his outer ear crumpled from a direct hit. In another game, an older player was rushed to the hospital with a shattered cheekbone from an errant throw.

In some locales, teams play for hours on end at auctions or farm sales. Hundreds of plain-clad spectators may pack the perimeters, cheering for their groups or for the underdogs. At a benefit auction for the local fire department near Gordonville, Pennsylvania, three games ran concurrently, one in the outside cow pen and two in barns. Black-garbed players, many wearing traditional hats and even glasses, kicked straw and chaff high into the air with their running and leaping.

Traditionally, Old Order Mennonite teams compete against the Amish, or the married men challenge the unmarried. Cornerball players are typically from either the more conservative settlements or the Lancaster County "buggy gangs." Boys from "higher" gangs tend to regard cornerball with some disdain and have reportedly mocked the players with exaggerated motions and derogatory shouts. Nevertheless, such behavior is the exception, and even in the closest contests, players and fans alike relish the occasion and the fun. One observer stated, "Cornerball is the only place I have ever seen Amish grandfathers so excited they literally had to grab ahold of their hats when they cheered." However, few outsiders witness a cornerball contest today. Even in Lancaster County, the historic heartland of cornerball, the game has dwindled in most areas, having become all but a quaint memory and relic of earlier times.

Other Leisure Activities

While participation in organized, highly competitive, or Sunday games cause concern among adults in some communities, virtually all nature-related or outdoors activities are acceptable. Hunting of all kinds is the most popular fall and winter outdoor activity for males in most settlements, large or small. Almost everywhere, boys as young as twelve begin hunting under the supervision of older family members. Many youth progress beyond conventional firearms to bow and arrows and black powder rifles. In some communities, criticisms occasionally surface when adults and youth travel to distant hunting camps or take expensive trips out west to hunt elk, antelope, or mule deer.[18] Moreover, hunters in some of the plainest communities have had problems with game wardens for their refusal to wear day-glow orange hunting clothes, which they regard as "too worldly."

Fishing is another popular outdoor activity, especially with families. Some youth have their own rowboats or canoes, and occasionally a national news service will feature a photo of an Amish carriage with a small boat tied to the top. Sometimes boys in the large settlements push the limits by owning or renting powerboats for fishing or water skiing. In one Pennsylvania settlement, dating couples traditionally go fishing on Ascension Day holiday, forty days after Easter. Amish teenagers and adults from the eastern states will sometimes charter boats to fish the Atlantic or Chesapeake Bay. Fishing on the Great Lakes is popular with youth and adults among many Ohio and Midwestern Amish.

A newer pastime among youth, especially males, in many Amish communities is bird-watching, or birding, as it is known by the dedicated hobbyists. Typically these rural people notice and appreciate birds around their houses, gardens, and fields as evidenced by the abundance of bird feeders, bluebird boxes, and purple martin houses. However, venturing out for the express purpose of identifying and listing birds is a relatively recent phenomenon. Now avid birders—adults, teenagers, and children—can be found in many communities, especially in Ohio and the Midwest.[19] *The Diary* features a monthly column, "The Birdwatchers Diary," written by a well-known Amish birder and author.

Many families post their annual listing of all bird species in a prominent place in the kitchen. Even teenagers record their "life lists" of all the birds they have ever seen. Several Amish circle letters have been formed by birders who take turns writing about their bird sightings and observations noted since the last time the packet of letters arrived. Some birding circle letters are composed entirely of youth. In a smaller settlement in Pennsylvania, a fifteen-year-old claimed, "Every boy in our school is interested in birds"; and in some places, teachers will invite local birders to lead half-day bird hikes for their students.[20]

Except for the Lancaster County affiliation and a few conservative settlements where it is prohibited, bicycling is universally popular, both for recreation and for transportation. In the summer of 2006, two single Amishmen from southern Indiana rode their recumbent bicycles through British Columbia and the Yukon Territory to Alaska. Since the mid-1990s, roller-blading has quickly caught on for both recreation and local travel, at least in the large settlements.[21] A young man reported that he routinely skated fifty miles round trip to see his girlfriend and that it took him only two hours each direction. "It's faster than a horse, and it's fun. You just feel free," he claimed. He also wore a flasher for coming home in the dark. With shoes in one hand and a lunch pail in the other, some Amish youth will skate several miles to work, weather permitting.

The sales manager at Roller Derby Skate Company just outside of Lancaster County said he had sold "a few thousand pairs of skates" to Amish customers for up to $180 per pair.[22] A Web site devoted exclusively to in-line skating has a section on the Amish and rollerblading.[23] When the weather is too cold and snowy for in-line skates, ice skating and sledding become the recreation of choice in most northern settlements. Many young men become adept at ice hockey, a sport that has been popular for generations in the large settlements.[24]

In the summer, some youth swim in nearby farm ponds and creeks, and young people will sometimes travel together to the ocean. But in a society that values modesty, males and females are not supposed to swim together. Consequently, at the beach the more conservative youth may be seen wading close to the shore, fully garbed, shoes in hand, a stark contrast to the nearby English bathers. Their more daring Amish counterparts are virtually indistinguishable from the other swimmers except that most of the boys wear boxer trunks and most of the girls wear one-piece bathing suits and gather their long hair in the back.

Visiting as Recreation

In all communities, visiting friends and relatives within one's church district and settlement has always been a favorite pastime for Amish of all ages. In the past, travel between settlements was generally limited to special occasions such as weddings and funerals. Now families increasingly hire local drivers with vans to "haul them" to visit relatives and friends in distant settlements. In addition, many families will travel by chauffeured van,

Greyhound, or Amtrak on sightseeing excursions to national parks. They also visit Amish settlements in scenic or recreational areas, such as in Rexford, Montana; Dover, Delaware; or Sarasota, Florida.[25]

As a result, many youth have also expanded their own travels to visit young friends or relatives in settlements hundreds of miles away. Often two or three young people will organize a group to share the expenses of hiring a "taxi," the common name for these locally owned vans.[26] Often accompanied by a married couple or other Amish adults, the youth will visit one or more settlements where they have relatives or friends. Thus, youth or adults from a Swartzentruber group from Stark County, Ohio, may visit a sister group in nearby Medina County, Ohio, or settlements as far away as St. Lawrence County, New York, or Harmony, Minnesota. They may also visit members of the conservative "Nebraska" group in Mifflin County, Pennsylvania. Ohio New Order youth routinely travel to other New Order settlements in North Carolina, Kentucky, Michigan, and elsewhere.

In all communities, both hosts and guests anticipate these visits. They provide a change from the daily routine, a chance to visit again with distant relatives and friends, and an opportunity to socialize with potentially new friends and mates. Host communities will often organize special singings and activities while their young guests are there. Some observers believe that these inter-settlement contacts have strengthened the holding power that Amish communities have shown in recent years.

Sun and Fun in Florida

One place where many Amish parents discourage their teenagers from visiting is Pinecraft, on the outskirts of Sarasota, Florida. Pinecraft has been a winter destination for many Amish and members of other Anabaptist groups since the late 1920s. After starting out as a celery farm, the owners later subdivided their land into many small building lots. Originally, the majority of winter residents were older people from the North, beset with cold-aggravated illnesses and discomfort. They found that the sunshine and warmth of the Florida west coast seemed to boost their spirits, if not lessen their ailments. As time passed, more and more winter-weary Amish and Mennonites found their way to Pinecraft. Some came for health reasons, but many simply came for the warmth of the sun, the relaxation of leisure activities, and the enjoyment of pleasant conversation.

Today, Pinecraft literally bursts with people and activity from November through March. After New Years, special weekly busses loaded with plain-garbed passengers seeking refuge from the ravages of northern winters run straight through from Pennsylvania, Ohio, and Indiana. The majority of bus travelers are older adults who come to enjoy fellowship and recreation with other like-minded visitors. Many of the youth who come to Pinecraft drive down in their own cars or hitch a ride with friends who drive. Sometimes entire families will join their parents and grandparents during the Christmas break. During January and February, the peak months, local residents estimate that as many as two thousand visitors per week squeeze into all available rooms in Pinecraft's one square mile.

In the large communities, most parents do not object to their entire family taking a Pinecraft vacation. However, they are decidedly wary about their teenage children going to Pinecraft alone or with other youth. They worry about the lack of supervision and accountability and about the kinds of peers their children may encounter. They hear rumors of alleged drug use and of occasional police raids made to investigate complaints of underage drinking, loitering, or disturbing the peace. These complaints generally center around the small city park in Pinecraft that is the hub of the local nighttime activity, although longtime residents say that conditions improved greatly when the city banned alcohol at the park and set a closing time.

Now, rather than being the party center, it is the venue for dozens of youth to play volleyball at two lighted courts. A lone security officer turns the lights out promptly at 10:00 p.m., gets back into his vehicle with lights flashing, and herds the scores of youth out of the park before locking the gate behind them. "In my eighteen months on this job, I have only had guff from one girl—the one in the red car over there," he reported. "She doesn't mouth off at me. She just won't move on when I tell her."

Not a few Pinecraft residents with rooms or apartments to rent avoid unmarried youth as tenants. Although landlords rarely use the word "trashed," at times it appears to be an apt description for their vacated properties. "One of the girls was skating around the kitchen with her rollerblades on," complained a housekeeper. "They left a terrible mess."

Another reason Pinecraft is suspect is that people often view it as a refuge for alienated youth and even adults who have abandoned their moral and spiritual values. For some dissatisfied Old Order church members, it serves as a temporary stop on the way out of the Amish fold. "They can go to Pinecraft an Old Order member, transfer to the local Amish church for a while, and finally move on to a conservative Mennonite church. That way they avoid being shunned when they join a more liberal Anabaptist church," an Old Order member explained.

Some plain people relate stories of teenage family members or friends who came to Pinecraft, allegedly to waitress in a restaurant or work in construction for the winter, only to abandon all semblances of faith. They reportedly live outside of any Christian fellowship and are involved with drugs, sex, or divorce. More commonly, however, people who leave the Amish and remain in Sarasota simply transfer their membership into a relatively plain Anabaptist group and may eventually move up to a more progressive Mennonite church. Ex-Amish form a significant minority in many of the dozen or more Mennonite churches in the Sarasota area.[27]

Because of these circumstances, bishops in some conservative Amish districts forbid their members to visit Pinecraft for any reason, including health concerns. Even in progressive Lancaster County, according to one resident, "some bishops have decided to discourage people from going." A newly ordained minister there had to sell his house in Pinecraft. Some bishops will reluctantly allow older people to spend the winter months there if their physician or chiropractor recommends a change of climate or if the members offer convincing health reasons.

One stumbling block had been that many Old Order communities viewed Pinecraft as part of the technologically progressive New Order Amish. Members ride two- or three-wheel bicycles instead of horses and carriages, and they worship in a meetinghouse instead of members' homes. More significantly, these "liberal" Amish have electricity and telephones in their Florida homes, and most have air conditioning and microwaves. And if that isn't enough, many men, single and married, routinely stroll or bicycle around Pinecraft without a hat, an omission that in most communities would at least raise eyebrows, if not prompt severe criticism.

Bishops fear that exposure to such luxuries, conveniences, and examples may cause not only young people but baptized members to return home dissatisfied with kerosene lanterns and antiquated ways. Finally, the bishops ask, how will young people ever learn to develop a respect for hard work, simplicity, and self-denial when they daily observe Amish elders wasting time at shuffleboard, checkers, and even golf? What kind of example is that, they wonder.

When the *Philadelphia Inquirer* and the *Boston Globe* ran front-page articles in 1999 on Pinecraft as the ultimate Amish vacation destination, they focused on the shuffleboard generation.[28] However, an eighty-year-old who has been wintering in Pinecraft for years complained, "Too many young people are coming down here and spoiling it for everyone. In the past, people came for health reasons." Whether his assessment is accurate or not, everyone agrees that many youth, especially from the large settlements, find their way to Pinecraft each winter. A mother from Pennsylvania reported that ten boys and four girls from their settlement went to Pinecraft for two weeks and played volleyball on the beach every day.

Besides the lure of the climate, the beach, bay fishing, sports, and other young people, some youth seek distance from the accountability of home. A young Amishman who came to visit soon decided to stay permanently. He confessed, "My parents aren't real happy that I'm down here. And I admit that this can be a dangerous place for young people, without supervision and all." Although most long-term winter residents believe that youthful behavior is much better now than it used to be, a young man from Daviess County, Indiana, said that a person could easily locate the late-night party by the large number of vehicles parked at the party site. He also indicated that drugs were easily available to anyone with money. Back home, a mother in a large settlement expressed relief that her seventeen-year-old was going to Pinecraft with a "good bunch of youth, not like some of them who come from other settlements. It's too easy for the youth to get out of control down there."

According to Hostetler (1993, 358–60), parents in the past worried not only about what their children did in Pinecraft but about the "Florida Reunion," the back-home weekend bash held each summer by youth who had been to Sarasota. Typically, the reunion rotated among Pennsylvania, Ohio, or Indiana sites, and hundreds of young people attended. It was, in essence, the same as a Lancaster County band hop or an Indiana party, held at an upscale campground, country club, or resort.

According to informants, the atmosphere was decidedly laid-back, if not hedonistic. Attenders drank, danced, listened to live bands, and reminisced about the good times they had together in Florida. Each participant paid an admission to cover the expenses for the site rental, musicians, food, and drink. Hostetler reported that the nature of the reunion often resulted in strong sanctions on any church member who participated. Although the adults of Pinecraft believe the reunion is a thing of the past, a young man who lives year-round in Pinecraft says that the annual party is alive and well.

Cutting Capers Back Home

Parents in large settlements worry more about the kinds of youth bashes that take place right around home than what happens in Florida or at some distant "Florida Reunion." The get-togethers are called "hops," or "band hops" in some locales, and simply "parties" in others. They may be planned and sponsored by a gang or simply develop spontaneously at an opportune time, for example, when someone's parents go away for the weekend. They may be best described as weekend drinking and dancing parties. In one settlement, these events occur most often during the warm months. Organizers prefer the main summer holiday weekends of Memorial Day, Fourth of July, and Labor Day rather than in the weeks before spring and fall baptism or during winter.

In the past, news of the parties could be found at the local convenience store, ball field, hitching rack, or even a specially designated mailbox reserved for such announcements. Increasingly in large settlements, youth call each other on their cell phones. These events may attract as many as a thousand youth and have also attracted the attention of non-Amish neighbors, law enforcement officials, and the press. Local papers near the large communities frequently feature front-page coverage of parties, police raids, and arrests involving Amish youth.[29]

A lesser-known form of recreation, known as scouting, tomcatting, or *Rowda,* depending on the community, has been common in some settlements in Ohio and Pennsylvania for many years. In Lancaster County, scouting has been most common among the conservative open buggy gangs. It centers around hassling courting couples. Several youth, usually males, travel to the houses of girls who are entertaining suitors on Saturday nights or after the Sunday night singings.

Where scouting is still practiced, it consists of playing pranks on the male, such as hiding his horse or dismantling the harness or the carriage. One suitor climbed into his buggy, only to find it sagging under the weight of a massive anvil that scouters had managed to hoist into it. Another young suitor was startled, when he went to untie his horse in the dark, only to find that some intrepid scouters had hitched the farmer's bull to his buggy.

One young man related a scouting incident from his community. "It happened one time that a boy and girl were sharing a room in a courting way. Their window was forced open from the outside and a chicken was flung inside, followed by a goose, a cat, a sheep, and a calf." He continued, "I was too little to be a ringleader, but mind, I lent a spirited helping hand, and I got knocked around somewhat [by the boyfriend]. It is only because he lacked the main strength that I am not as bald as a peach today. As it was, he took a painful fistful of my hair. Perhaps he wanted them to paste in his scrapbook, I don't know—there is no way to find out; he never speaks to me much."

In the same community, he related, "a newly-courting couple was a prime target for scouting. The hapless young man who tied his rig by the barn on a Sunday night and accompanied his beloved into the house there to spend some quality time with her might come out again to find his horse gone and a harnessed cow in its stead and his carriage parked on a shed roof. Or, what was worse, sometimes the harness was dismantled, and the pieces scattered hither and yon, and the carriage parked in the creek, with the seats balanced atop the chimney."[30] Most scouters claim that such activities are carried out and accepted in a spirit of fun, or at least resignation.

Despite occasional forays into objectionable leisure or trifling activities, the Amish youth's work ethic and daily habits of self-discipline are more likely to define them over time than parties, sports, or scouting. They learn to work hard at a young age and will continue to work hard until after they retire. For some youth in the large, peer-oriented settlements, the activities of their "running around" years are simply a brief interlude in a culture of responsibility. Virtually all who return to be baptized into the faith will end their deviance. They will assume roles as faithful church members and responsible adults, for which their parents and grandparents will offer sincere praise to God. Their return is also a testimony to the effectiveness of the early socialization by their parents and the entire community. As one Amish father explained, "Chickens come home to roost."

Although most of them will eventually come home to the roost, some of them will take months or years to finally return. For some teens, at least, these are the vulnerable, "betwixt and between" years. They have much more freedom to explore and experiment, and they spend more time with their peers. The most important venue for socializing in almost all communities is the Sunday night singing, to which we now turn.

Volleyball is one of the most popular sports among Amish teens.
Photo by Keith Baum.

CHAPTER SEVEN

Singings

Socializing and Stepping Out

We all count the days till our sixteenth birthday.
—A teenager

Far More than Tunes

Although very few outsiders are ever invited to an Amish youth singing, those who are may initially wonder what the big attraction is. A typical American teenager would likely be bored attending a similar social activity—sitting on hard wooden benches around long tables, singing hymns for two hours in a language used only in church, and having limited spontaneous interaction with their friends. Few outsiders would recognize that this event is fraught with great significance for both the adolescents and for the parents. For the first time in their lives, these young people are interacting in a setting that is not predominately adult-centered.

When a young person reaches the "right age," which is sixteen in most settlements, *Rumspringa* provides the venue for youth to shift their focus from family to peers. *Rumspringa,* the topic of the next chapter, literally means "running around" in Pennsylvania German. Kraybill says, "It is the key moment that ritually signals a rite of passage. . . . Youth are betwixt and between home and the church."[1] Such a transfer may explain the ambivalent feelings that many Amish parents express as they release their children to the company of their peers. Intuitively, parents know that singings are much more than a religious or social event. They provide a testing ground to see if the values espoused by the adult community will be accepted or rejected by their children. Little wonder, then, that both adults and teens take a keen interest in this important tradition, even though their reasons differ.

Ever since anyone can remember, the singing has been a weekly or bi-weekly event in which the unmarried youth in a church district meet at a member's house on a Sunday evening to sing German hymns.[2] It appears to have been part of Amish culture since their arrival in North America. Although much has been written about Amish worship services, little has been published about Sunday night singings. One reason is that in many communities, singings are off-limits to observers. Outsiders may be invited to Sunday worship, weddings, and funerals, but few ever attend singings. In some communities, not even Amish adults are invited to attend. More than any other area of Amish society, singings have been the domain of the young. Having musical talent or enjoying music matters less than socializing with other youth in a setting with minimal adult control. The singings offer increased independence and an arena for developing relationships that will shape the youth for the rest of their lives. This is especially true in male-female relationships.

Gateway to *Rumspringa*

It is not surprising, then, to find that singings have been held in virtually every settlement.[3] Traditionally, youth attend until they marry—or until they and everyone else conclude that marriage is unlikely (by age thirty), at which time they drop out.[4] Nobody apparently knows why sixteen is the right age to begin "going with the young folk." But in most settlements it is an important milestone, universally regarded by both adults and youth as a watershed event. Undoubtedly, it is more important than obtaining one's driver's license or even graduating from high school in mainstream society because the change of status for Amish youth is so abrupt. In some settlements, teens move from highly regulated lives to exhilarating freedom in a single day.

Most of them anticipate their new status, although a few fifteen-year-olds experience some anxiety as their birthday approaches. For the first time, they must establish their standing among their peers of both sexes. Such anxiety occasionally leads a young person to stay home on Sunday evenings instead of immediately joining the group. Referring to his granddaughter, who had recently turned sixteen, an Amishman explained, "Sally is family oriented and hasn't been exposed to all that excitement." She concurred: "I'll miss my brothers and sisters at home." A fifteen-year-old boy who had not fully matured physically expressed doubts that he would join the youth when he reached his next birthday.

In a few settlements, "going with the youth" happens gradually, and some youth may routinely delay their entry for several weeks or months. "We begin somewhere around sixteen and a half or seventeen—whenever we feel like starting," explained a seventeen-year-old.[5] More typical, however, is the response of a seventeen-year-old from a large settlement who was asked what would happen if some new sixteen-year-olds might not feel quite ready to start the social whirl. "It would never even happen," he grinned. "We all count the days till our sixteenth birthday."

Stepping Out in Style

In recognition of this rite of transition, parents in most places customarily give each son his own carriage and horse.[6] In many communities, a young man's carriage is easily discernible from the family carriage. For example, in certain conservative Lancaster County gangs, unmarried youth still drive open buggies year-round. Until the 1970s, all young couples traveled in these "courting buggies," completely exposed to the elements and to the eyes of the curious.

A father who was a teenager at that time thought that the move to the closed carriages began when non-Amish youth began hassling courting couples by jumping in the back of the buggies as they passed. "Also it was ridiculous riding around in an open buggy in the freezing winter," he added. When church districts began to permit closed carriages for the youth, some elders predicted a surge in sexual immorality. Others complained that it would be easier to hide radios or other forbidden things. Nevertheless, people soon accepted the change when they failed to detect any discernible moral decline.

Amish teenagers do not alter the basic contours and configurations of the approved community carriages. For example, they do not custom paint them, change the color, or embellish the wheels with chrome spokes.[7] However, a young person's carriage often has its own accouterments that a knowledgeable outsider can quickly identify. In many places, the young owners "customize" them by adding auxiliary features to conform to the latest fads of their peers. In Lancaster County, young men's carriages may sport two dozen or more red reflectors around the rear perimeter as compared to the three or four reflectors on the family carriage. In addition, the more daring youth now fasten on the back of the carriage a strip of blinking LED lights, which serve to attract the attention of passing motorists and the young drivers' peers.

Frequently, boys dress up their slow-moving-vehicle triangle with a decal from the National Rifle Association or the NASCAR racing logo, and one carriage sported a Great Adventures Amusement Park bumper sticker. An article in the *Lancaster Sunday News* on carriage accouterments reported that boys' carriages sported a variety of decals and bumper sticker messages, including "Single and Ready to Mingle" and "Get High on Milk: Our Cows are on Grass."[8] Another visual clue to young men's transportation in Lancaster County is that many youth employ white or blue harness guides and keepers rather than the traditional black accessories that characterize adult carriages.[9]

In Central Pennsylvania's Big Valley, the Nebraska youth drive simple white-topped, open-front buggies constructed at home or a neighbor's shop for half the cost of buggies belonging to boys in the Renno or Byler churches. The design is a simple brown wooden riding box with friction foot brakes and two hard benches. It also features a kerosene lantern and a blanket for the benches to protect the passengers from blowing horse hair, dirt, or cold air. Meanwhile, some Byler youth living just across the valley sport shiny yellow-topped carriages, custom-made in Lancaster County and selling for as much as $6,000 at the turn of the twenty-first century. They will pay another $800 to have fiberglass wheels instead of wooden wheels or $1,000 more for aluminum.

Riding in Style

Marvin, a personable nineteen-year-old, expressed obvious pride as he showed off his new purchase, an incongruous juxtaposition of plain and fancy. "I went down to Lancaster County to buy this one because their carriages are a lot nicer than the ones sold here in the Big Valley. One thing, their buggies have nicer switch boxes made out of oak with this glossy finish and they have this ignition switch so that nobody can mess with my battery-operated lights," Marvin explained. "They also put these nice burnt edges on the trim with acetylene torches," he pointed out. The switch box also featured a toggle for his running lights (flashing lights used at night for safety) and another switch to control the two interior floor lights. Finally he showed us the cigarette lighter, "for my spotlight," he quickly added.

One observer described this kind of interior decor as "neo-Vegas" (Goldstein 1997, 40). Everything in Marvin's carriage was color-coordinated in maroon, from the swirled, velvet-covered walls, ceilings, and carpets to the wine-dyed sheepskin on the front seat and the rabbit foot hanging from one of the switches. Even the two theatre-style inside lights glowed red. Artificial roses and apple blossoms decorated each corner, and a wreath of roses encircled the overhead dome light.

A pair of fluffy dice, a car air-freshener, and a mini-flashlight inscribed with the name of the carriage shop dangled from the switch box. On the box itself, a decidedly non-Amish decal of a bald eagle clutched an American flag in its talons. Two more eagles graced both ends of a glossy shelf where he kept his *Liedersammlung,* the thin songbook used at their Sunday night singings. "Indian feathers" hung from a tack in the ceiling, and more feathers intertwined with the roses in the wreath. A small stuffed teddy bear completed the soft decor. In the glove box he stashed a bottle of musk cologne, and the polished dash featured a clock and a battery gauge. A second air-freshener dangled in the rear. Under the back seat he stored his horse blanket.

Marvin purchased the most luxurious carriage available. Unlike the Nebraska buggies, it boasted fiberglass shafts and hydraulic brakes. He had battery-operated yellow safety lights mounted on the front and red flashers, reflector tape, and six reflectors on the rear. "Dad and Mom gave me $2,500 towards the carriage. I had to pay the rest from what I saved from my job working for an English neighbor," he explained.

A few conservative communities will permit their youth to individualize their carriages. In Mercer County, Pennsylvania, a relatively plain settlement, young people call their carriages "cozy-cabs," and the owners lovingly "fancy them up" with plush carpets and velvet. Nevertheless, most do not buy CBs, clocks, and speedometers, nor do they hide radios, boom boxes or VCRs behind a curtain in the back as do some of their large settlement counterparts. Even young men from the more sedate New Order Amish occasionally succumb to carriage fads. A few years ago, according to one teenage girl, the current style was to sport a cracked windshield. To the consternation of their parents, her brothers and some of their peers reputedly cracked the glass in their own windshields to make the appropriate fashion statement.

Top-of-the-Line Horsepower

Besides having a fine carriage, most young men seem to prefer fast, high-stepping horses, ones that can awe or intimidate their sisters or girlfriends. "I always hated to be stuck with the family horse," recalled one Amishman, "some old plug which my sisters had wore out going to town shopping Saturday morning. I wanted my own horse, fresh and raring to go, to head out on a date." "It's like in your society," explained an eighteen-year-old, "young guys want to drive around in a sports car, not the family station wagon."

A spirited and well-proportioned horse adds status to its owner as he seeks to impress his peers, both male and female. In Lancaster County, boys usually prefer saddlebreds, but some like standardbreds best. Marvin, from the Byler group in the Big Valley of Pennsylvania, chose a saddlebred horse to go with his yellow carriage. "Saddlebreds look good when you drive them," he explained. "They hold their heads up high and are also high steppers. They may not be as fast as standardbreds, but they are stronger in the long haul. The Nebraska boys' horses look so tired because the church won't let them use the rein that holds their head up. And some of their horses aren't very well cared for," he added.

He continued, "Sometimes our boys will race our horses after the singing. One horse will break out of line and try to pass the horses in front. One time I went over the crest of a hill at night because my horse couldn't get past the others. But these back roads are pretty quiet around 11:00 when we race. Another time I let my horse run like that, and he passed about fourteen carriages when I couldn't hold him back. Horses like to run once they get into it. But it's hard on the horses. I sprained one of our horses' legs six months ago, and it's still bad. You learn not to do that," he grinned.

Obviously, for Marvin and many Amish boys, receiving their horse and carriage, a quintessential symbol of Amish culture, is one of the first of several steps into a full-fledged Amish adulthood. However, some boys, mostly in the large settlements, put their horses out to pasture or leave them in the stable for most of their teenage years. Instead they opt for car keys and a driver's license and travel to singings and elsewhere with varying degrees of convenience and horsepower. A father complained, "I have to take Raymond's horse out every once in a while or he would never get exercise. Now that he is running around, he neglects his horse."

A Glimpse from the Past

The image of a group of young people singing church songs in German fails to portray the underlying excitement and color of this major institution in the life of Amish youth. In a rare look at the past, Joseph W. Yoder, who grew up Amish in the Big Valley of Mifflin County, Pennsylvania, captured the vitality of a traditional singing in the late nineteenth century in his book, *Rosanna of the Amish:*

> At a singing two or three tables are set end to end along one side of the living room for the singers. The girls sit back of the table along the wall while the boys sit on the other side. . . . During the singing of any hymn all persons present are supposed to join in the singing or abstain from conversation. Sometimes it happens that boys forget and annoy the singers by talking too loudly whereupon the man of the house says, "Let us have order . . . "

When the tables were filled, as others came they stood back of the young men, both boys and girls, until there were well onto a hundred voices sing-ing. . . .

There is no part singing; all voices sing in unison. Since the Amish do not have these chorales set to music, they must be passed on from generation to generation by rote. Consequently only boys and girls with a keen sense of pitch and sound can ever learn to sing them and many can never learn them well enough to "lead" singing. Little Crist and Ben Sharp wanted to learn to lead so they followed with great care. Yost turned to Little Crist and said, "Now, Cristly, you lead the next verse and if you 'stall,' I'll help you out." . . . After they had sung several of the slow chorales, one of the girls announced, *Wo ist Jesus mein Verlangen,* to the tune of, "What a Friend We Have in Jesus." The "fast" tunes are easily sung, but the chorales must be learned for preach-ing services; no fast tunes are ever sung there. (1995 [1940], 114–17)

Singings Today

Although Yoder's passage depicted life in the late 1800s, his description still accurately portrays what parents in scores of settlements call "decent" singings. In the adult-centered end of the settlements, New Order singings open and close with prayer and feature a small sermon or devotional in the middle. At the other end, many singings in peer-centered communi-ties bear faint resemblance to the traditional event and may actually involve little or no singing. In some places, singings and parties have become syn-onymous.

Depending on the size of the young person's gang or church district and whether or not they welcome youth from other districts, a dozen to two hundred young people may come to the singing. In the past, as many as four to five hundred have attended these Sunday night events. In those settlements where singings occur within the boundaries of a single church district, they almost always take place at the same home that hosted the district's house church that morning. This is a practical custom, since the church benches and songbooks are already there.

In many settlements, the host family traditionally prepares a substantial pre-singing supper for the young people and for the dozen or two relatives and invited neighbors who will later "help sing." In Lancaster County, where singings are large, the supper will typically take place at a different location from the singing. So that the host family for the "supper gang" does not have to provide food for large numbers, a few older girls usually assign various youth to bring food items such as chips, salads, and main dishes. Other girls will clean up and wash the dishes before they leave for the singing. In Somerset County, Pennsylvania, no evening meal is provided, and only youth who attended the morning church service are permitted to go to the singing that evening.

Although the basic format of singings in most settlements is similar to the one described in *Rosanna of the Amish,* other aspects vary. Today in the four or five largest settlements, many youth arrive at their singings in cars or pickups instead of carriages. For some unknown reason, in Lancaster County singings are rarely held outdoors, even on the longest June evening.[10] Shortly before the singing is to begin, males and females gather in separate groups, just as they do for the morning church service. At the appointed hour, they file into the house, barn, or shop and seat themselves on benches along the row of tables, boys on one side, girls on the other, as in Rosanna's days.[11] The singings may begin as early as 7:00 p.m. or as late as 9:00 p.m., depending on the time of year and the available light for outdoor activities. In various settlements, getting the youth to break off their games or socializing to start the singing can be a challenge to the host family. Youth report that sometimes singings have started an hour and a half late. To combat this late start and subsequent late finish, an adult leader in a supervised group promised the children of the host family that they could quit fifteen minutes early if they started on time, a challenge they readily accepted. This helped the host family teenagers and the more mature young to form the lines and proceed inside. In some settlements, girls always go first, and the boys file in only after the singing has started. In settlements where parents, relatives, and children are invited, they take their seats in the back or periphery, usually before the youth enter.

Despite these efforts, some couples and cliques scattered around the premises may continue their socializing or game-playing. Some of the younger members may have drifted out behind the barn, or others may be involved in a spirited volleyball game. Even after most of the young people have already entered the barn, shop, or house, a sizable number—more often the sixteen- and seventeen-year-old boys—may linger outside or gather in other parts of the building, coming in twenty minutes late. Others may stay out until the last few minutes of the singing or never come in at all. In certain singings in one large settlement, most of the sixteen-year-olds customarily stay outside or elsewhere in the house until the last ten or fifteen minutes. "They usually sit in their buggies and listen to music on their boom boxes, and then show up for the last few minutes so they can tell their parents they actually attended," reported an eighteen-year-old.

A parent commented on those who entered late in his letter to *Die Botschaft:* "Along Hershey Church Road they had a Pine Cone youth singing. Oh! it was so wonderful about the first thirty boys wore a kinda satisfied and happy look on their faces, Oh! so respectful, those boys gave us pappys a hearty handshake, my feelings were give each boy a deserved pat on the back. Of course those fellows helped sing even lead some slow tunes from the [thick] book. Then came the last 20 or 30 boys when the singing was almost over and [a] few of those were under influence of strong drink, Oh! what were the feelings of us pappys now??"[12]

Plain Repertoire

Once the youth are seated, well-worn songbooks—generally the German *Ausbund* or *Unpartheyisches Gesang-Buch*—are passed out to each person, just as in the Sunday morning church service. The singing is now ready to begin. Typically, no one welcomes the group, leads in an invocation, or takes charge. Yet everyone from the newest sixteen-year-old to the oldest visiting grandparent knows the exact script for their community. The tempo of events varies from settlement to settlement. In some places, the youth leaf through the hymnal for a couple of minutes even though the songs are well known. Finally someone breaks the ice and calls out the number of a hymn. "They don't want to appear too forward in getting their song sung," explained an Amish adult. Throughout the evening, youth may wait two or three minutes before calling out the name or number of the next song.

In contrast to the morning church services, where only designated male *Vorsingers,* or song leaders, begin songs, the boy or girl who chooses the hymn starts it. In many Lancaster County districts, the singing begins without hesitation, since a teenager from the host family is expected to choose and lead the first selection. There, unlike in most other settlements, nobody calls out page numbers of their requests, but a person simply begins singing his or her chosen song. Frequently, two people will start different hymns simultaneously. "In our gang, it was a competition to sing," one father remembered. The other singers quickly join in singing the selected song while turning to the appropriate place in the book since they know virtually all of the page numbers by heart.

Although each settlement has its own repertoire of songs and tunes, the first songs usually consist of the "slow tunes." In some settlements, both plain and progressive, all of the first hymns come from the traditional *Ausbund*. Many of these songs recount the persecution of the Anabaptist martyrs. In a Sunday morning worship service, the *Vorsinger* lines, or sings alone, the first few notes of each line before the group joins in. This still happens in some of the most conservative singings, but in most places no lining is done, and the andante tempo of the songs is similar to that of Protestant hymns like "A Mighty Fortress Is Our God" or "Rock of Ages."

In many settlements, the youth never sing from the *Ausbund*. In Indiana, youth in some of the Amish settlements of Swiss extraction use the *Schwartzs' Song Book* (1980), a compilation of German hymns, gospel songs in English, secular folk songs, and even country and western songs [13] The book also includes several Swiss and English yodeling songs, a favorite among some of the Indiana Swiss Amish people.

Just as in the morning church services, the young people sing all melodies from memory since there are no musical notations. Because nobody uses a pitch pipe, the person starting the hymn sometimes begins the melody too low or, more frequently, too high. At this point, the singers with a better musical ear immediately "take over and get the tune on track." In the plainest groups, such as the Swartzentrubers and Nebraskas, all songs at the singings are in German; and in the most conservative, they are all from the *Ausbund*. In most settlements, the youth still sing in unison, since part or harmony singing is regarded as showy and worldly.[14] However, in the more progressive areas, part singing is no longer uncommon or forbidden at singings.

Over the years, songs from the outside have occasionally slipped into the singing repertoire. The country gospel song "We Need a Whole Lot More of Jesus" from the 1960s became popular at that time in several singings in Lancaster County:

> *Well, you can read it in the morning papers,*
> *Hear it on the radio,*
> *Crime is sweeping the nation,*
> *This world is about to go;*
> *We need a good old case of salvation,*
> *To put the love of God in our souls;*
> *We need a whole lot more of Jesus,*
> *And a lot less rock and roll.*[15]

Occasionally some groups add a secular English chorus to German religious verses. For example, since the early 1950s, scattered youth groups in Illinois, Indiana, Ohio, and Pennsylvania juxtaposed the chorus from "Bluebird on Your Window Sill" to the end of a German hymn.[16] A sixty-year-old recalled, "From the first time I heard the song, I liked the thought." A middle-aged Amish father from Holmes County, Ohio, reminisced, "When I was young, it was the top song on country station WWVA in Wheeling, West Virginia, where they had the Saturday night Wheeling Jamboree." Many Amish youth in Ohio and Pennsylvania listened to the Jamboree on clandestine battery-powered radios in their buggies or at their Saturday night gatherings. More than a few of them traveled to Wheeling for the live concerts. "Maybe that's how it caught on," the grandfather said. Another Amishman stated, "Back then, it took only a week for a song that reached the Hit Parade [a popular weekly radio program] to get into the Amish community."

Picking up the Tempo

About midway through many singings, the traditional songbooks are collected and different ones are distributed. From here on, the tempo of the music quickens noticeably. Most songs are sung to approximations of gospel tunes, such as "Amazing Grace," "When the Roll Is Called Up Yonder," and "Sweet Hour of Prayer," depending on the group. Outsiders who have attended singings have noted that many tunes seem to be pitched uncomfortably high on the scale, and some have described the singing style as nasal or even "hillbilly."[17]

Another custom that has persisted through the years in many settlements is that near the midway point of the singing, family members (usually young teenage girls) suddenly appear bearing water pitchers and glasses, reputedly to fortify the singers for the duration. When youth from an old settlement in Pennsylvania visited a singing at one of the most traditional groups in that state, they were startled to find that their young people customarily drank directly from the pitchers. "Since we also watched everyone drink from the pitchers at the noon meal, we had already decided that we were not thirsty!" the visitors reported. In Lancaster County, hosts always place filled water pitchers and glasses on each table.

In Ohio, one of the plainest groups still serves small dishes of salt on the tables "because it helps the youth to sing better by opening their throats." Grandparents from Pennsylvania and Indiana recall that fifty years ago, the hosts would always place salt shakers on the tables for the same purpose. This tradition persists in a few scattered settlements even today, but in most places mints or throat lozenges have replaced salt.

In the last half of the singings, some groups, especially New Order youth, regularly sing gospel songs in English from mimeographed sheets, standard hymnbooks, or custom-printed settlement song books consisting of songs the community has selected and approved.[18] Surprisingly, some parents and grandparents from various Old Order districts scattered throughout the larger settlements report that forty or fifty years ago all songs were in English. A recent trend in some Old Order groups, however, has been to print High German translations of English gospel songs learned in Amish private schools.[19] This practice has resulted in a significant increase in the number of new songs used in the weekly or bi-weekly singings and even in the traditional afternoon or evening singings at wedding receptions. Teenagers in a large settlement reported that one of these songs became so popular that it was sung at every wedding reception they attended in the previous fall.

In some settlements, among both Old and New Orders, the actual sing-ing part is regarded as the females' domain. "My brother doesn't sing be-cause he wants to be cool," explained his teenage sister. The girls there as-sumed the responsibility of requesting and singing, while most of the boys, according to a visiting teenager at the youth-only singing, "cut up." "Some of their boys were throwing popcorn or corn curls at other singers, and some of them were actually smoking during the singing," he reported.

A woman from a large settlement remembers, "When I was a teenager, it was often only three of us girls who would be inside singing. The rest of the youth were outside doing whatever." A bishop's wife in a rural Pennsylvania settlement declared, "It's hard to take church [at your place] when you know the young folks will descend on you and bring drinks and music. Often not much singing is done. Sometimes as many as half a barrel of bottles will be picked up."[20]

In contrast to the peer-centered communities, the Ohio New Order Amish generally regard the singing as a religious or worship service much more than as a social event. A minister, relative, or even a young man designated by the host family leads a short Bible study at the midpoint. Predictably, the behavior at their singings is more church-like. Usually everyone sings, little if any conversing takes place between songs, and most attenders, both male and female, request their favorite songs.

In a few communities, some plain and some progressive, parents and other adults are not expected or welcomed by the youth to the singings. A visiting Amish parent from Somerset County, Pennsylvania, who asked to attend a singing with his teenagers at one of those settlements was told by his host, "We have never done it that way around here. Only the young folk go to the singings." "I was not surprised," the father reported later, "to find out why their singings had more of a reputation for rowdiness than for good singing."

In some Indiana settlements, the youth reportedly try to keep the loca-tion of their "crowd" a secret from the adults. An informant from that group claimed that youth often smoked, drank, and played the card game Rook instead of singing. However, according to those from another youth-only singing, the absence of adults does not automatically equate with teenage rowdiness. "Except for some teasing and talking between songs, our sing-ings are decent," they reported.

Observers report that boys typically tire of singing more quickly than girls. A minister and his wife recalled that at their singings fifty years ago, some boys would occasionally try to lighten up the evening by singing their own version of the "Loblied," the only hymn sung in every Sunday worship service by Amish everywhere. "They sang it to the tune of 'Yankee Doodle,'" reported the couple ruefully, "and they could make the words fit!"

A ploy to get out early centered on the traditional farewell and blessing song signaling the end of the music. Parents complained that when some boys tired of the singing, one would prematurely start their farewell song, such as "Ich sage gut Nacht" (I Say Goodnight), and as the final note died, would leap to their feet and file out, effectively ending the singing. One mother reported, however, that when the boys tried that in her group back in the 1970s, the girls would interrupt them with shouts of, "Be quiet, it ain't over yet!" and would continue to sing till the appropriate ending time arrived.

Closing Customs

Today, as soon as the farewell song is sung, host family members in many settlements typically appear with light refreshments such as chips, pop-corn, pretzels, apples, and cheese, and seasonal beverages of mint tea, cider, or hot chocolate. In most places, coffee or soft drinks are not served, but at least one Swiss settlement reportedly provides a glass of wine to all youth who attend. In Mifflin County, Pennsylvania, host families customarily set out bean soup and other leftovers from the shared noon meal, plus the traditional half-moon pies, baked crescent-shaped turnovers made of pie dough and filled with stewed apple *Schnitz* (dried apples). Some singings, such as in Mercer County, Pennsylvania, serve no refreshments at all.

A unique custom has developed at some singings in Lancaster County. Near the end, host family singers and some of their friends leave the room to return shortly, bearing trays of the locally popular figure-eight hard pret-zels. This signals to everyone that the current song is to be the last of the evening. Next, the singers break into a traditional "Thank-you-for-having-the-singing" song—origin unknown. Then everyone sings "Happy Birthday" in English for those celebrating a birthday within the next week.

During the song, the singers pelt all those being "honored" with a barrage of pretzels. One boy admitted, "It's not always fun. Getting hit with hard pretzels in the face and head really stings." In some groups, this pretzel shower is also directed at youth whose boyfriend's or girlfriend's parents have attended the singing that night. Elam explained, "You know how hard it is to meet your girlfriend's parents when your friends are around. Well, everybody sings the song, 'Cheer up, Elam; cheer up, Elam; don't be sad, don't be sad . . .' (sung to the tune of *Frère Jacques*) while they bombard you with pretzels."

A *Die Botschaft* scribe who had recently hosted a singing expressed her sentiments on pretzel showers: "Pretzel throwing at the 'Birthday ones' was new to us. What a waste! Pretzels are not cheap. Next time you young folks are tempted to throw food think of the poor children who go to bed 'hungry' daily."[21] A mother claimed that such a barrage wasted at least three bags of pretzels a night and wished "the adults could find a way to end such waste!"

Another *Die Botschaft* scribe expressed her displeasure for some of the youthful antics at a singing she had recently attended: "I was quite disappointed and ashamed with the behavior of many of the young girls and boys at the singing at Mike Lapps. Young folks, WHERE is our RESPECT for others?? Especially to those who give us a place for our gatherings? The girls seemed to be quite fussy [rowdy] and much water was being splashed at the time they should've been singing. Also, I wonder to whom we sing? Singings should always be quiet like at church and the songs should be sung *onstlich* [in earnest], so that we would not be mocking God, who sees and hears all."[22]

Postlude Activities

In most settlements, as soon as the singing officially ends, courting couples exit immediately for the girl's house for refreshments and privacy. In some places, all of the non-courting youth remain for another hour or more to socialize, sometimes in same-sex groups, but often with the sexes mixing.

If people fail to join in or leave the main group, they are usually the sixteen-year-olds, who tend to arrive or leave en masse. In one community, sixteen-year-old boys brought whiskey to their singing and dumped it into the chickens' water supply to see the effects of alcohol on thirsty birds. During the summer in a large Midwestern settlement, most of the youth reportedly leave as soon as the singing ends to go to the local drive-in movie theater outside of town.

However, after-singing activities vary considerably, depending on the settlement or group. If youth become rowdy in the peer-centered communities, they usually do so after the adults leave. In communities where tobacco is tolerated, some boys may immediately begin smoking. Girls, on the other hand, are much less likely to smoke.[23] If drinking occurs on the premises, it is most commonly a minority of males who stay outside or "drink behind the barn." However, in some of the peer-centered gangs or settlements, observers report that as many as half of the youth participate in drinking and partying. Such behavior is rare in many Old Order circles and is almost never found in the New Order youth groups.

In some settlements the non-courting youth stay in the house or barn to play table games such as Rook, Uno, checkers, chess, Dutch Blitz, Old Maid, Parcheesi, or Monopoly. In most places, games that use traditional playing cards are forbidden, although a conservative boy visiting a large settlement expressed surprise that their teenagers openly played poker. In the plainer settlements, they more often play their traditional "barn games," active games such as Six Old Maids, Swat, and Steal the Bacon.[24] In other areas, some games reputedly include kissing and hugging. One mother recalls from the 1940s playing Spin the Plate, apparently an Amish version of the kissing game, Spin the Bottle.

In other settlements, generally the larger ones, the youth traditionally clear away the benches or move to a nearby location for a dance following the singing. In some places the youth may dance for as little as a half hour, whereas in others, dancing will go into the early hours of the morning. In Lancaster County, this Sunday night activity is generally called a hoedown. The style of music and dancing depends on the nature of the group. The "fast" groups generally dance to taped or live music, whereas the more conservative ones have traditionally danced to the accompaniment of a harmonica or simply danced to the unaccompanied singing of the young people or to a caller.

In one of the most conservative settlements, this kind of activity has been called four-square dancing. In the most conservative Lancaster County gangs, it is called *ring spiele,* a kind of prescribed square dance with no musical accompaniment of any kind. One seventeen-year-old exclaimed, "You should see it, dancing outside together under the stars. It's wonderful!" For him, at least, music was incidental to the excitement of being together with his peers.

At times, drinking becomes the main activity in certain gangs or areas as the night goes on. Neighbors may call local law-enforcement officers to complain of excessive noise, reckless driving, or presumed underage drinking. Sometimes host families have even been known to call the police when they felt that the activities were "getting out of control."[25] However, this has usually been the choice of last resort. "There's a lot of pressure from our children not to do anything. And there's even pressure from some of the other parents to look away," reported a frustrated father. "We might get bad publicity in the news. So we're just supposed to let it go and clean up the next day."

Some families report spending half of Monday morning loading trash bags with bottles, cans, broken glass, and trash scattered about from the previous night. Amish parents in these settlements frequently express their frustration and helplessness: "What can we do?" asked a father. "How do you stop something like this that has been going on for years? You can't do it alone."[26]

Actually, many parents, grandparents, and even ministers with similar complaints behaved in the same way during and after the singings that they attended with their peers in the past. An Amish writer sent this anonymous letter to *Family Life* in 1969:

> Not all our youth are involved in these [rowdy] happenings. No, not half. But too many are. Sometimes such parties bring in young people from different states and communities. When I actually saw what took place, I was shocked.

There is still a vivid picture in my mind of a boy and girl walking hand in hand down the lane, the girl carrying a beer bottle and talking boisterously. It made me think, "And this is a Christian community known far and wide for its plain people." Yes, it happened at one of their farms.

As another car approached, the couple slipped over the grassy bank. I stood watching them. Paris hairdo, miniskirt, sheer hose, college haircut, checkered shirt—surely it had to be a dream. It was hard to believe that only hours before the couple had attended a plain church.

Knowing nothing of the planned party, some friends and I had spent that evening in a nearby home. Since we had tied our horse where later they parked their cars, we suddenly found ourselves in the center of the activity. As the shadows lengthened over the scene, cars were lining up, one after the other, five, ten, fifteen, up to a total of twenty-five cars. Dirty talk filled the evening air. The roar of stationary racing motors became louder as dusk shed its blanket over this shame. At the very moment, Mom and Dad were probably lighting a lamp.

Some people will be saying, "Such things are not for the public to know about." I wish, too, the public didn't know, but in this case, they knew all too well. A local paper had a write-up on these doings. . . . With cigarettes in one hand and beer in the other, these young people could hardly be imagined as the future church. Now and then, religion was heard mentioned—in mockery.[27]

In response to rowdy singings in their settlement, a group of eight bishops and eleven ministers in Geauga County, Ohio, gathered to answer the question, How we can change ways that our young folks have their gatherings? They agreed to the following rules:

1. Singing to start around 8:00 and end around 10:00.
2. *Youngie* will be expected to leave soon after the singing is over.
3. No alcoholic beverages on the premises.
4. No music and no dancing at any time.
5. No smoking in house.
6. Late arrivals not welcome unless good reason.
7. Singing every Sunday night.

8. Home owner should not open shop or other buildings for *youngie* after singing.

9. Unruly *youngie* to be reported to church and parents.

They also discussed the possibility of changing the starting age to seventeen, of considering smaller allowances to teach them the value of money, of keeping the singing at a "reasonable size," and of having more singings in other districts on the same night if the crowds get too big. The person recording the minutes included a plaintive note: "Hopefully after singings boys and girls will go home, as many parents lie awake worrying where their children are."[28] Although it is not known if this effort to change was successful, it was one of the first adult initiatives to intentionally reform youth gatherings.

Some non-Amish residents, especially those who lived in communities with large Amish populations, have not hesitated to extend advice to Amish parents about improving the behavior of their teenage children. In the Letters section of the local newspaper, a disturbed resident offered a number of suggestions in a "Letter to Amish Parents," after learning that a local convenience store had to hire a security guard on weekends to reduce shoplifting and "harassment of customers" and that four Amish youth were apprehended by police for "public drunkenness."

> May I suggest you as a group care for your young people by giving them something constructive to do with their time on the weekends. They dress in English clothes, drive cars and drink beer as if to pretend they are not Amish. Give them pride. . . .The young people need a place to gather. I'm talking about baseball games, volleyball games, home-made ice cream parties, picnics, chicken barbecues or even a well-chaperoned hoe-down.
>
> Parents could sit in the barn with the kids and show them they will tolerate clean fun only. Open your homes to the kids. It is extra work and bother, but wouldn't it be worth the effort? . . .
>
> Please take time to find a way. Haven't you turned your backs long enough? Someone will be killed again. How many highway deaths involving Amish does it take in this area to get your attention? . . .

At this point, I only say at least I tried.

—An Intercourse Resident[29]

If adults rarely talk to their children about their behavior during or after the singing, it is even less likely that they would talk to their children about their own youthful antics. It is hard to picture any of these scrubbed boys and demure-looking girls partying into the night. It is even harder picturing their staid and serious-miened parents or grandparents, some of whom are now pillars of the church, swinging with their partners or drinking beer with their peers. "I hate to say it," admitted a minister, "but I gave my parents a much harder time than my children give me. Truthfully, my wife and I have a lot to be thankful for." Allowing the young such freedom of choice always involves the danger of excesses.

The fact is that singings, whether commended or criticized, supervised or free, remain at the center of social life for Amish youth in the strongest communities or church districts. The singing of religious songs in German helps strengthen and reinforce the culture's religious and cultural distinctives. Thus, this often low-key event provides far more than a setting for social interactions and mate selection. Even for the rowdiest of youth, this venue provides a safe haven that discourages social interactions and intimate relationships with non-Amish youth. It is little wonder that adults hope and pray that their *Youngie's* singings will be "upbuilding." By blending increased freedom with songs of the church, Sunday night singings can help affirm the Amish heritage and may even reduce some of the excesses that often accompany the *rumspringa* experience, to which we now turn.

During Rumspringa *some Amish teens own and drive cars.*
Photo by Dennis Hughes.

Rumspringa
The Running-Around Years

*We don't give our young folks leave to go out and sin just to get it
out of their system. We give them a little space so they can be
with people their own age and find a life partner.*
—An Amish minister

A New Stage

Until two young men from Lancaster County, Pennsylvania, were
charged by federal agents in the summer of 1998 with trafficking
in cocaine, the word *Rumspringa* was known only to Pennsylvania German
speakers and to a few academics who studied the Amish. Since then, it has
been cropping up on talk shows, television advertisements, and tee shirts
(the logo reads, "What happens in Rumspringa stays in Rumspringa"). An
alternative music group calls itself Rumspringa, and an art rock group from
Holland, Nits, recorded a song entitled "Rumspringa." UPN's reality series
Amish in the City used the word in every episode, and British filmmaker
Lucy Walker filmed *Devil's Playground,* a widely acclaimed documentary
dedicated to the subject. Likewise, at least two American television series,
ER and *Judging Amy,* featured an Amish *Rumspringa*-based plot. Even Oprah

Winfrey devoted a program featuring the *Rumspringa* of young adults who grew up in Amish families.

The word *Rumspringa* comes from German and literally translated means "running around." The Amish use this term to describe the period between the time when young people reach their sixteenth birthday and the time when they are baptized and join the church. Outsiders whose understanding of the word comes primarily from watching *Amish in the City* or *Devil's Playground* or from reading the many reviews of these media productions cannot be blamed if they have a distorted understanding of the typical *Rumspringa* experience. According to the UPN Web site, *Rumspringa* is "running wild." One reviewer wrote, "Rumspringa is an Amish version of spring break and Mardi Gras rolled into one."[1] Another writer, using the contemporary German spelling, described *Rumschpringe* as "the Amish equivalent of teenage rebellion." Another reviewer concluded, "During *Rumspringa*, the Amish are . . . encouraged to experience the world of the 'English' to expose themselves to temptations before they make an adult commitment."[2]

The idea that most Amish youth "go wild" likely emerged first from the spate of stories covering the 1998 drug busts. An unidentified writer coined the term "time out period" to describe the *Rumspringa* as an opportunity the community granted its young people to experience worldly pursuits. Other writers quickly adopted the phrase. However, Lucy Walker's documenting two years in the lives of five youth brought up Amish in northern Indiana in *Devil's Playground* reinforces the belief that *Rumspringa* and wildness are synonymous. From the DVD's jarring cover image of a young Amish girl in plain attire lighting up a cigarette in the back seat of a car, to a scene with four girls drinking beer at a party, to a shot of boys huddled around a bong smoking pot, the message is clear: these teens have cast aside their plain inhibitions for unbridled hedonism. Indeed, amidst scenes of rural tranquility, Walker juxtaposes drunkenness, coupling up, and serious drug use.

The main focus of her film is Faron Yoder, a young man who has spent time in reform school. He says his idol is gangster rapper Tupac Shakur. Faron, the son of an Amish bishop, is a likeable eighteen-year-old who deals drugs to support a $100-a-day crank habit. For fear of his life, he goes into hiding after allowing law enforcement authorities to wire him to obtain incriminating evidence on other local drug dealers. Although not as deeply involved as Faron, the other main characters indulge in various self-destructive behaviors—or, at the least, atypical practices for Amish adolescents. One teenager bragged, "If I were living at home, then I couldn't have two hundred different channels of Direct TV, stereo, Nintendo, and a fridge full of beer."

Critics of *Devil's Playground* consistently praise Walker's careful work and objectivity in filming this previously undocumented aspect of Amish life. They express amazement that she was able to penetrate "the Amish community" in amassing over three hundred hours of highly unusual footage. What many fail to recognize, however, is that she is dealing with the extreme end of the behavioral spectrum, and that the experiences of Faron and the others are not the norm. Typical Amish adolescents, even in their *rumspringa* years, would not permit anyone to photograph them in the way that Walker did. Not only would day-to-day *rumspringa* behavior be unavailable to her and her crew, but most viewers would likely lose interest in the mundane world of weekly singings and Amish teenage friendships that would fill her documentary.

The partying and drug use that Walker captures occurs not only in the northern Indiana settlement but also takes place in the other large settlements such as Lancaster County, Pennsylvania, and Holmes County, Ohio. Drinking occurs in some small settlements, but other kinds of drug use would typically be very rare. However, the *Rumspringa* occurs everywhere. Parents routinely reduce control over their teenagers and grant them more freedom to choose their friends and activities. Although nobody knows when such a practice began, it likely relates to the Amish belief in adult choice and believer's baptism. *Devil's Playground* viewers learn that being born into an Amish family is not enough to qualify one for church membership. Only an adult, choosing freely, is qualified to become a full-fledged part of this believers' community.

A Mennonite writer who grew up Amish presents a much more nuanced and accurate portrayal of the *Rumspringa* years as it still occurs in parts of Ohio and elsewhere. Although his book, *Ben's Wayne* (1989), is listed as fiction, it is a thinly disguised picture of the running-around years that he and his family members experienced in Holmes County. In fact, the author, Levi Miller, portrayed life so realistically that some family members were offended and tried to persuade Miller not to publish his book. In it, one family member leaves the Amish, some of the *Bouve* (young men) drink and smoke, carloads of youth drive to nearby Wheeling, West Virginia, to attend the Saturday night Jamboree, and the protagonist, Wayne, experiences sexual temptations with his girlfriend and later with a nurse at a hospital where he works. However, nowhere do the main characters "hook up," do drugs, deliberately shame their parents, or disgrace their community. *Ben's Wayne* realistically portrays the *Rumspringa* for most Amish youth.

Life does change when sixteen-year-old boys like Wayne get their own wheels, usually buggy wheels, and then start attending the Sunday night singings. But until they begin Saturday night courting, life in most places consists primarily of work, chores at home, and family interactions—a continuation of life as they have known it since finishing school at age fourteen or fifteen.

Youth in Lancaster County, Pennsylvania, however, experience their *Rumspringa* a bit differently from their Ohio counterparts or from youth in most other settlements. Few outsiders knew about this difference until the national media reported that the two young men arrested for trafficking in cocaine belonged to an Amish gang. For most mainstream people, the word *gang* conveys images associated with drug dealing, the Pagans motorcycle gang, and other deviant activities.

In Lancaster County Amish parlance, however, a gang simply denotes a local youth group of 50 to 150 self-chosen peers.[3] At age sixteen, Lancaster youth choose to join one of about thirty gangs. In December 1993, many readers of the plain-community newspaper *Die Botschaft* learned about the gangs when a well-known Lancaster scribe listed the names and membership count for all fifteen gangs in the county.[4] For the most part, the names of the gangs appeared to be innocuous, if not quaint: Antiques, Bluebirds, Canaries, Cardinals, Crickets, Chickadees, Happy Jacks, Orioles, Pilgrims, Pinecones, Pioneers, and Souvenirs, among others.[5]

Today, Amish readers in other settlements are surprised when they learn that some of the gangs then had more than two hundred members. Their reactions range from disbelief to amazement. And they ponder what happens when large groups of youth spend long periods of unsupervised time together. Many Amish from distant settlements puzzle over how such a non-Amish phenomenon originated in Lancaster County, since the Amish traditionally value small, decentralized structures. When did all of this begin, and why would the ministers and parents let such a thing happen? Many Amish ask these questions.

As noted before, identifiable gangs in Lancaster were unheard of in the 1930s and the first half of the 1940s. Early in the twentieth century, when the Amish population was small and districts few, most Lancaster County families knew each other. Many youth were related and often attended school or church together. They socialized at a work frolic or at the fall weddings, and youth across the settlement got together at the Sunday night singings.

However, as the settlement grew, the youth population expanded. According to an Amish historian, increasing numbers of youth would converge in the town of Intercourse on a Sunday night instead of attending a singing or staying home on nights when there was none. To curb this practice, church leaders decided that any youth who were already church members and "found guilty of stopping in Intercourse on a Sunday evening would be asked to make a confession before the church council."[6] The ministers and elders continued to struggle with the problem of having many youth hanging out in town or driving around the back roads in large numbers. Neither option apparently pleased the adults.

A middle-aged Amishman related that, according to his father, a group of concerned parents in the late 1940s pushed for the formation of a new break-off group as an alternative to the single get-together. As a result, the one large group eventually broke into smaller groups. Some formed primarily on the basis of proximity. For example, youth from the densely populated Groffdale area in the center of the county formed a group who became the Groffies. Another group formed from those who lived mostly in the southern part of the settlement. However, young people were free to join the group of their choice, regardless of where they lived.

By 1950, at least three or four groups had emerged. According to Hostetler (1993), these original gangs were the Groffies, the Ammies, and the Trailers.[7] Elderly informants remember that the Groffies were the "fastest, wildest, and most liberal"; the Ammies were the moderates; and the Trailers were the most conservative. Young men in the Groffies were more likely to drive cars and party on the weekends. The Trailers, on the other hand, originated in the more sparsely populated and conservative southern part of the settlement. They drove buggies, dressed mostly like their parents, and generally avoided the party excesses of their faster cousins.

As time passed and the gangs grew to 150 or more members, they would divide, generally with the older youth splitting off from the younger, less-mature members to form a new gang. Thus, the three original groups split into six, then twelve. In 2007, more than thirty gangs reflected various positions on the traditional-progressive spectrum.

Amish adults from distant settlements inevitably asked, What actually goes on in these gangs when so many young people get together? Aren't they bound to have problems? Inquirers soon learned that typical behavior of the different groups today varied as much as the behavior in the early gangs of the 1950s. One church leader explained that of the approximately twenty-two hundred youth in Lancaster County in the mid-1990s, almost 10 percent belonged to the Antiques, a peer-centered gang in which all the males had cars and dressed English. This group had few singings, sponsored notorious drinking parties, and were later identified as the gang of the two young men convicted of selling cocaine.[8]

To a lesser extent, several other "fast" groups were similar to the Antiques in that most male members drank, drove, and owned their own cars or trucks.[9] The half-dozen smaller "buggy gangs," such as the Bluebirds, Canaries, Chickadees, and Pequea, were more adult and tradition-centered. They dressed plainly, rode in old-fashioned open buggies, and generally conformed to the dress and transportation standards of their elders. For example, girls in the buggy groups were the only ones in Lancaster County to wear the large black bonnets over their *Kapps* to singings. The middle groups reflected some aspects of both ends of the spectrum.

The Critical Choice

The majority of youth from small settlements unaffiliated with the Lancaster County settlement would likely feel most at home with one of the buggy gangs.[10] Because most teenagers from those small settlements attend singings exclusively with peers and friends from their home church district, they would be surprised to find a mixture of youth from all over the settlement. They might be more astounded to learn that some gang members come from adjacent and even distant counties.[11]

A few youth regularly travel up to two hundred miles on a weekend, and some young people whose families have moved to distant settlements regularly travel from as far away as western Pennsylvania, southern Virginia, or eastern Indiana to join their friends for the weekend activities.[12] Each person will pay more than one hundred dollars to hire a van for the weekend.

One result of self-selected gangs is that members from seven or eight different gangs may attend the same church, and brothers and sisters from the same family may belong to three or four different gangs. Non-Amish visitors to an Amish church service would likely be oblivious to this. When they observe the young men filing into worship, dressed in identical hats, white shirts, black vests, suspenders, and broadfall pants, these rows of youth probably look more or less like black and white facsimiles. Likewise the young women, with their long parted hair, organdy head coverings, plain-colored dresses, and dark stockings may appear to be cookie-cutter copies of modesty, humility, and sobriety, despite their membership in different gangs.

Although the nuances may be subtle to outsiders, Amish adults can quickly identify the kind of gang to which each young person belongs by the type of haircuts, the tilt of hat, suspender styles and color, and the kind of shirt buttons for boys, as well as by hem length, brightness of dress materials, use of straight pins or buttons, and thickness of the stockings for girls. Even without those indicators, the local youth, the ministers, and most of their parents know each youth's gang and where it fits into the larger constellation of gangs.

Long before they join, most preteens have learned from older siblings or friends about every gang and its place on the plain-to-wild continuum. When asked to describe the Lancaster County gangs, a ten-year-old girl promptly identified and described each of them in detail. Of course, the young people also know their parents' view of the various gangs. Many choose the gang that their parents approve. For some youth, choosing a "wild" group automatically brings them into conflict with their parents, especially if the adults were never rebellious. Many Amish adolescents are torn between not wanting to be a "goodie-goodie," and not wishing to disappoint their parents and grandparents or incur their displeasure.

By any measure, an Amish teenager's choice of gangs is as momentous as the important peer decisions that English youth might make—for example, selecting a college fraternity or sorority. The gang will influence how members spend their free time and money; how they dress and style their hair; their mode of transportation; their use or rejection of tobacco, alcohol, and drugs; how they relate to the other sex; and if and when they join the church. Finally, if they do join the church, their mate will most often come from the same gang.

Buddy Bunches and Sidekicks

In good Anabaptist fashion, gang members are not drafted or picked for desirable qualities like candidates for an exclusive fraternity. Anyone who shows up may join a gang. Within most Lancaster gangs, new members are automatically part of a smaller, more intimate unit known as a "buddy bunch."[13] This cohort consists of as many as fifteen to twenty age-mates who join the gang at about the same time. Another buddy bunch forms as soon as the next fifteen to twenty newcomers come along, and so on. Inside the buddy bunch, each person has a special friend or "sidekick." Thus, there is a two-tiered structure of friendships within each gang consisting of a sidekick and their buddy bunch.

When asked what determines the size of the particular buddy bunches in his gang, a seventeen-year-old explained, "We like each group to have at least eight boys and eight girls, just the right size to play volleyball." In some gangs, buddy bunches may consist of only eight to ten members with an unequal number of males and females, but a group rarely exceeds twenty members. Most teens interact with their buddies throughout their dating years and find their most intimate and enduring friendships in the bunch.[14]

In Lancaster County, the young people choose the name of their buddy bunch. A seventeen-year-old explained, "We are part of the Sparkies Gang, which broke away from the Diamonds a couple years ago. Our buddy bunch is the Ranchers." A sixteen-year-old girl explained, "Sometimes it's hard to come up with a name that everyone can agree with. Usually the boys decide and the girls go along with it. When we were choosing our name, some of the boys put their choice on signs, which they hung up everywhere at the singing. Their name won."[15]

On Sunday afternoons, buddy bunch members typically interact exclusively with each other. Depending on the season, they play volleyball, go sledding or ice skating, or play indoor games such as table tennis or board games. Softball is still a popular warm weather choice with some buddy bunches in Lancaster County even though the bishops tried to ban league play in 1996. All the buddy bunches in a gang meet together for a large "supper gang" before a combined evening singing, but even there, they socialize mostly with their own age-mates.

In many gangs, the girls in each buddy bunch wear identically colored dresses to singings and other events. They bring their changes of clothes to church in bags and switch to their matching attire right after the morning service. "The boys aren't very cooperative, and they don't really get into wearing the same colors. Besides, they don't have as many clothes as we do," explained one sixteen-year-old girl.[16] When a singing occurs at the home of a buddy bunch member, the buddies have the choice seats at the tables. Buddy bunch members in Lancaster County will also get together by themselves or join with the entire gang on appropriate holidays, such as Ascension Day in May, the Monday after Easter, or the Monday following Pentecost Sunday, for day trips, picnics, hikes, sports, or parties.

Nobody knows how Amish youth came up with the word *sidekick* to designate their best same-sex friend. "A sidekick is as plain or as rowdy as you are," explained a seventeen-year-old boy. Girls often write to their sidekick, especially if their only contact is on Sundays. These letters, notes, and cards provide an opportunity for developing and strengthening close friendships. Boys typically engage in the same activities and sports as their sidekick.

Because a sidekick provides moral support and a protection from being alone at the gang activities and singings, a sixteen-year-old who does not get a sidekick may feel isolated and vulnerable. "I still remember how painful it was when a girl who promised to be my sidekick changed her mind and dropped me. I didn't have anybody to be my special friend. Finally, my cousin and another girl agreed to let me be with them, but I always felt like the outsider—like they were saying, 'It's a privilege for you to be running with us.' Eventually, I just stopped going and dropped out of the gang for three years. I finally started with a different group."[17]

Because buddies and sidekicks "run around together" and are highly involved with each other, they often take membership instruction and join the church at the same time. Although the role of the buddy bunch and the sidekick declines somewhat when youth begin dating seriously, these ties usually remain strong through life. Even after members marry and move away, they keep in touch through visits, buddy get-togethers, and circle letters (a round-robin packet of letters written by each member in turn). Few high school or college classes in the larger society maintain such close ties over the years as do Amish "buddies."

Addition and Division

Occasionally teenagers do not like either the gang they originally chose or their particular buddy bunch. Anyone may change gangs, but switching is not common since friendship patterns in the new gang are already in place. Boys are more likely to change gangs than are girls, and the most common reason for a boy changing is that his girlfriend is in another gang. In general, however, individuals are reluctant to change gangs if none of their buddy members or their sidekick goes along with them.

Changes occur more frequently when a number of gang members—usually the older buddy groups—decide to form a new gang. This typically happens when a gang approaches 150 members or when the eighteen- or nineteen-year-olds increasingly find the behavior of the younger members irritating, immature, or morally objectionable. Such splits are common. For example, a gang split when thirty-five of the older Rangers broke away to form the more conservative Pinecones. A less common division occurred when the entire seventeen-year-old buddy bunch led a split from the Diamonds to form a new gang, the Sparkies. This too was a conservative split, but it was unusual in that it was initiated by younger rather than the oldest members. A bishop observed that splits occur under certain predictable conditions: "Most gangs naturally evolve from slow to fast in Lancaster County. Groups may start out with conservative ideals and practices, but they soon move toward behavior that is unacceptable and ungodly."

When asked why change moves from "slow to fast," a twenty-year-old explained, "When it's time for your younger brothers and sisters to join a gang, Mom and Dad want them to pick a slower group. Even if they agree to that, they will still want the same kind of fun and freedoms that their older brothers and sisters have, so they bring that desire right along with them to the gang. Usually the younger ones bring in the faster ways."

A minister offered another explanation: "Most parents appreciate a plain group and want their children to be in one. Because of parents' pressure, however, too many young folk who are 'pushing the fences' end up in a decent gang, and like bad apples, sooner or later spoil the barrel." He, along with others, believes that at the present, newly formed gangs in Lancaster typically lose their conservative orientation in less than three years. On the other hand, a bishop's wife noted that when a new gang formed because of some dissatisfaction with the conservative orientation of her children's gang, the singings improved noticeably.

Unless they are seriously dating, gang members in the most conservative, adult-centered groups typically stay at home on Saturday nights because their only approved social activity is the Sunday night singing. Young people at the peer-centered end of the spectrum meet frequently during the week and spend most of the weekend together. In some areas this is called an overnight gang, and teens routinely stay away from home from Saturday afternoon until the predawn hours of Monday morning.[18] Thus, on a typical Saturday night in Lancaster County, some youth interact with their families in ways reminiscent of small settlement life, whereas a mile or two away, their more liberal counterparts behave in ways similar to mainstream youth bent on having a good time.

Band Hops: The Extreme *Rumspringa* Experience

Someone driving along the back roads of Lancaster County on a summer Saturday night would never happen upon a hand-painted sign proclaiming, "Amish Party—next lane right" or "Amish Band Hop here tonight" at the end of a farm lane, private picnic grove, or gravel road leading to a reclaimed strip mine. Few outsiders would recognize that the growing crowd was actually an Amish youth gathering. Rather than seeing horses and buggies, the observer would likely encounter a line of high-performance cars or late-model pickup trucks. Many would sport mag wheels, CB antennas, and booming stereos. One might spot the occasional telltale buggy, but in most venues, partiers prefer motorized vehicles.

Over the normally quiet countryside, the twang of electric guitars and an electric bass tuning up pinpoint the location. Loudspeakers crackle and boom with the background rattle of drums, and somebody's voice tests a state-of-the-art sound system powered by a gasoline- or diesel-powered generator. A band hop is ready to begin, an event that can easily run all night until next morning's milking.

Although these gatherings have been part of Lancaster County and the other large communities as long as anyone can remember, their continued appeal is that they provide an exciting and totally unsupervised activity for these otherwise hardworking rural youth. Most band hops are spur-of-the-moment happenings, seized upon by opportunistic youthful gangs when parents or parents of friends leave town to visit distant relatives for a weekend or a few days.[19] News of the party travels quickly and widely over the Amish youth grapevine or cell phones.

Band hops usually take place these days in an Amish shop building, a local park, a rented picnic ground, or a reclaimed coal field. If the event is planned, organizers sometimes notify friends and relatives from neighboring states, and carloads of youth drive hundreds of miles to attend parties. In Lancaster County, the more rowdy gangs invariably sponsor the band hops. Five hundred youth may attend, although two hundred and fifty may be more typical. In Indiana, local newspapers have reported one thousand youth in attendance.[20]

Few outsiders attend band hops, but Amish youth will occasionally invite a friend.[21] The following observations were provided by a college student from Lancaster County who attended a summer hop with a group of Amish friends. Most males wore knit shirts, tight black jeans, and the white high-top Converse athletic shoes that were then in vogue. The majority of males left their suspenders and traditional hats behind. Haircuts were mostly uniform, roughly mirroring the hairstyles popular in mainstream culture at the time. Few if any young men at the hop had the traditional Dutch boy bowl cut that denotes membership in a plain gang. On the other hand, even the rowdiest partiers did not sport tattoos, earrings, or other piercings. The most extreme fashion statements for the males were baseball caps and moustaches. Virtually all females were identifiably Amish, both by cloth-ing and hairstyle.[22] Although the girls did not literally "let their hair down," the few who were smoking or drinking replaced their head coverings with baseball caps. Males outnumbered females five to one.

On the makeshift stage, two of the local "Amish bands," the Roamers and the Renegades, alternated playing Rolling Stones, Beatles, and other classic rock songs from the 1960s and 70s. During the 1980s, some Amish bands reportedly played heavy metal and even disco music. However, in the late 1990s and at the turn of the century, country and western music regained its earlier popularity, both at Saturday night hops and at Sunday night hoe-downs. Even when classic rock was played at gatherings, the Amish style of dancing was not exactly square dancing or round dancing. Guys and girls would face each other, bump hips, kick under the other's legs, and embrace from time to time.

The Roamers generally played with two six-string guitars (rhythm and lead), bass guitar, drums, and keyboard. The musicians, a group of self-taught Amish youth, performed with $1,000 electric instruments and, reputedly, a $14,000 Peavy sound system. Periodically, partiers rewarded their favorite musician with paper cups full of beer. At some point in the night, the musicians passed the hat to help pay expenses. One former band member from the Roamers reported that their group earned $16,000 in contributions over the four years they played.

Drinking was the major activity, and although a few brought coolers full of hard liquor and other alcohol, Coors Lite was the drink of choice. Most males carried two Coors cans stacked in one hand while drinking from the third can. Eventually, a number of boys became inebriated and passed out. The smell of urine permeated the area immediately adjacent to the shop as the celebrants continually went outside to relieve themselves.

Most of the boys were smoking Marlboros or Marlboro Lites rather than the traditional cigarette-sized Winchester cigars permitted in some settle-ments. "It is definitely not cool to be smoking anything other than ciga-rettes," a boy declared. Nevertheless, a knot of boys gathered outside around a bong for smoking marijuana, and the visiting student estimated that at least ten percent of the young men went outside to "smoke weed or snort cocaine," although somewhat secretively. Occasionally fights break out between individuals who have had too much to drink; however, none did at this event, and party-goers today say that rumbles are less frequent today than in the past.[23]

Conversations among males at the band hop centered on drinking, cars ("Camaros are definitely the best"), occasionally on drugs ("Think how easy it would be to grow marijuana in the cornfields"), and girls. At this particular band hop, some young men claimed that the local law enforcement officials were lax about under-aged drinking among the Amish compared with those in the next township. Nevertheless, as a precaution before they left, many celebrants bequeathed their unopened six packs to those who remained. The hop lasted to the early hours of the morning. The last to leave poured out the rest of the leftover beer.

Over the years, a few other outsiders occasionally attended parties. A young man in the 1960s went out of curiosity when he was invited to a barn party by an Amish friend who met him at the barn around 10:00 p.m. As he entered, the visitor saw cases of beer stacked high along a wall. Up front, an Amish band played on acoustic instruments. Most of the males were drinking, smoking, and playing cards for money.

The card players lounged around "tables" formed from hay bales that they had shoved together. Several times he heard players admonish each other to be careful of starting a barn fire with their cigarettes. After a couple hours, some card players left the games to be with their girlfriends. He reports that the couples scattered throughout the haymow to "make out," and although he observed caressing and kissing, he saw nothing more intimate. The band continued to play up front while some of the card players persisted in their games, apparently oblivious to the music or the couples.[24]

Amish adults who attended hops or parties in their youth say that the basic script remains remarkably stable. However, Cherokees, Chevy trucks, and Camaros have replaced buggies, and shops and picnic groves have replaced barns as preferred party sites. In most places, Amish youth still exclude non-Amish from these social events, occasionally by force, if reports are accurate. Although the names of the bands have changed and the songs are played on electric rather than acoustic instruments, accordions, or harmonicas, music still holds a prominent place at these gatherings. As one young man said, "All Amish youth like music, and they like it loud."

Amish parents who long ago put aside their musical instruments and loudspeakers for church hymnals may sometimes grin as they reminisce about the bands of their youth. "We had several bands in the sixties. Two of them were actually invited to come and play at the Grand Ole Opry, they were so good," an Amish grandfather recalled. "In 1967, some of us went to Sunset Park in Rising Sun, Maryland, to an Osborne Brothers concert. After it was over, we invited them to come back with us to Lancaster and play in one of our barns, and they accepted. Their big bus pulled into the farm about midnight. It was wonderful. Our banjo picker, who is now a minister, played right along with their lead picker, and they played for most of the night." For many of these gang members, behaving in ways that the adults would find unacceptable may have added an extra bit of excitement to the experience. For many parents, however, music was often the least of their concerns.

A New Kind of Gang

Disturbed by rowdy gang activity, a Lancaster County couple tried unsuccessfully to print the following notice in a national Amish publication in the late 1970s: "If there are any young folks in Lancaster County that are tired of the standards of the groups they are in and would like to start a group with better standards, we would very much like to help."[25] At that time, parents taking such a proactive stand to change something as entrenched as the gang structure was highly unusual, and the letter was never printed. The traditional way of dealing with dissatisfaction with the local youth scene was to move the family to a new or smaller settlement.

Twenty years later, some Lancaster County parents again decided to try for a change. Persistent rumors of excessive drinking and increased drug use among some of the youth prompted them to take steps to organize an alternative group. In mid-1997, six months before the drug bust, more than a dozen concerned couples began meeting to alert parents and ministers of alleged illegal and dangerous behaviors being reported among the young people. Several of the couples' sons were involved in the Antiques or other "fast" groups.

The parents decided to write a letter of concern to the bishops of Lancaster County and its daughter settlements in three other Pennsylvania counties. The letter described signs of drug use and abuse that parents should look for. At the leaders' request, many bishops agreed to read the letter in their church districts prior to the fall communion. In part, the letter said, "Parents, beware of evil changes which your children could or might be going through. There are drugs out there easily available to our young people in the form of marijuana, heroin, cocaine, and other types that can be smoked."

Beyond disseminating their warnings, the parents decided to form an alternative, adult-supervised gang with a no drinking, no drugs, zero tolerance policy. "We wanted a good Christian atmosphere, a wholesome place for our children to sing, and wholesome companions to socialize with," stated one of the founders.

From their efforts, a new group emerged and adopted the name of a former group, the Quakers. Most of the initial members in the new Quakers were boys, and many came from the notorious Antiques. The majority had reportedly been involved to some degree in the drinking and drug scene. A former Antiques member was interviewed later by a reporter for French television and stated that members had been involved with marijuana and cocaine.

Besides having explicit guidelines for behavior, the Quakers were different from typical youth gangs in several other respects. First, the parents were highly involved from the start. Most of them attended the singings along with their children. "When people learned that us parents were involved," a mother recalled, "they accused us of acting like the Mennonites. Some also said that we thought we were better than others." Although the parents were not required to directly intervene in the happenings, their presence provided accountability and a restraint on deviant activities.

Second, the organizers asked two young married couples to serve as advisors. Since neither couple had children, they attended almost all of the singings and activities with the youth. These advisors also helped plan weekly or weekend activities for the youth. "It's not enough to tell kids not to drink and use drugs," said one of the mothers. "We need to provide them with good, clean alternatives." Eventually, the leaders provided a written schedule of activities each month. These activities included skiing weekends, work projects, and a trip to the Bowery area of New York City.

From the beginning, this new group met with considerable resistance from more conservative leaders and parents in the Lancaster community. Some of the older people worried that they would become like the "Goodies," a group from the 1960s that originated in part from a revivalistic movement among the Amish and in part from indignation with some of the youthful behavior at that time. Among other things, the Goodies eschewed all drinking, partying, and any other forms of "ungodly behavior." They also had regular Bible studies but were criticized because they were not always led by a minister. Eventually, the majority of these youth left the Old Order to join the New Order Amish or some Amish-Mennonite churches that emerged in the split of 1966. Some of these new churches permitted members to drive cars, use tractors in the fields, install electricity and phones in the houses, and dress less plainly than their Old Order relatives.

Critics of the Quakers predicted that these young people would also defect from the Old Order Amish. Some also predicted that the Quakers would be a conduit into car churches like the Spring Garden congregation, a church that some Old Orders call a "pass-through" church for people on their way up to more liberal Mennonite circles. Critics believed that the adult Quaker leaders were taking a much too casual attitude toward vehicles, a mistake that would lead to mass defections. They also criticized the Quakers for their attire, especially the girls. "They look like Beachy Amish with their waved hair, shiny dresses, puffed sleeves, and short hems," said one observer.

Finally, one of the founders of the Quakers admitted that they had considered starting a Bible study with their new group but decided against it since "some were scared of what the church would think. A bishop warned us to be careful of going ahead because he said there's pride involved in Bible studies." Like the Catholics, most Amish are dubious about private interpretations of the Scriptures.

Despite criticisms, the Quakers were well established by the turn of the twenty-first century, with forty-five members and regularly attracting interested families and their teenagers. "Besides that," explained one father, "several girls and boys are planning to join the Old Order church this fall. The biggest percent of them will become Old Order." A year later the group had grown to more than sixty. Both supporters and detractors recognized that the future of the Quakers depended on whether they joined the Old Order church or eventually defected to more liberal churches. In 2006, parents were still meeting to discuss their Quaker children's future.

Supervised Gangs

Since the 1998 drug arrests, alternative groups, such as the Eagles, the Hummingbirds, the Parakeets, and the Falcons, have emerged in Lancaster County. All emphasized "decent, righteous behavior," and all adhered more closely to traditional Amish standards of dress and transportation than the Quakers. For example, many of these new gangs required all of the youth to wear church clothes rather than informal garb to the singings. "Youth are not permitted to carry on, laugh, or joke around during the singing itself, and boys with [sound] systems in their carriages will be talked to, even if they don't play them when they are with the gang," an eighteen-year-old reported.

Before launching the groups, the adult organizers met to decide what standards to expect and how to enforce them. They asked for advice and involvement from like-minded ministers and sympathetic bishops. Some of the Lancaster leaders also "sought counsel" from an out-of-state minister who helped found an early alternative singing movement in Ohio. "At the time," a father explained, "things out there were so bad that they had almost no singings left among the Old Order group in Holmes County. Nobody was willing to host them. Their new group in Ohio began with only five youth, and it took a few years to see the changes take place. Now they have several decent singings going. The decision to change may be rapid, but real change may take years to happen. We can take our time in Lancaster County," he concluded.

"But starting a new group is not easy," confided one of the leaders. "You have to go slow and get agreement from those who are interested. Of course, some people are always ready to criticize anything new. They ask, 'Why do we need another gang when we already have twenty-five to choose from? If parents want their child in a plain group, they can find them in the southern part of the county.' But we do what we have to do, not seeking to lead a cause or have a following, but just wanting to do the right thing."

The Eagles, one of the adult-supervised Lancaster groups, took the unprecedented step of soliciting fifteen-year-olds as charter members. "We wanted them to get started out right," one of the leaders explained. In these groups, written guidelines spelling out the requirements for the youth and the expectations for the parents were distributed to interested families. The groups required total abstinence from smoking, drinking, and drugs. Also, members had to agree to wear Amish clothing to group singings and activities, to refrain from Saturday night partying, and to drive only horses and carriages.

One group wanted the singing and the "supper gang" to be held at the same location. "Too much can happen from the time the *Youngie* leave from supper a few miles away till they arrive at the singing. It's much easier to get everybody together and start on time if they're already here," a parent explained. Initially, the groups prohibited Saturday night get-togethers, but one of the groups relented and permitted their youth to stay out till midnight. According to an observer, the same group lost several boys in the summer of 2000 "because they wanted to play softball." "If the *Youngie* don't wish to follow the rules that are set up, they should find another group," said one of the founders.

Not all parents who expressed an interest in the new movement found it to their liking. A couple who had attended one of these supervised groups with their fifteen-year-old daughter decided to look elsewhere for their child's group. "We were involved for a while with the new gang," reported the father, "but we kinda dropped out because the youth were being policed too much. When she's sixteen, our daughter will start with the new off-shoot from the Rangers, the Cherokees. Their attitude is simply, 'If you choose not to drink, take drugs, or have a vehicle, you are welcome.'"

After the 1998 drug arrests, many bishops repeated their concerns about the rowdier gangs. Although they warned the youth and their parents that a gang could be either a stepping stone or stumbling block to righteousness, some parents thought that many of the bishops were out of touch with how bad things really were. A mother who confessed to having used marijuana when she was young lamented, "There are seven gangs that are bad news. Some guys are doing heroin. It's only a matter of time till somebody overdoses. It blows my mind that we plain people have to deal with this. We are human. Our own people have more peer pressure than outsiders. And it was nothing when we were young compared to what it is today."

Lancaster County gangs continue to be a reality that church leaders, parents, and especially the youth must face. While most young people anticipate their new status and freedom, parents and ministers think and pray about the choices their sixteen-year-olds will be making. More parents are seeking to influence their children's peers by taking them to selected Sunday night singings well before their sixteenth birthday. "We want them to be exposed early to a good group and the right kind of young people," a father explained. "If the parents and the children have the right kind of relationship, the children will generally follow the parents' choice. We need prayer to provide a better way for our precious children." They are especially invested in their children's choices because it is likely that their future "special friend" and eventual spouse will come from within their close circle of friends. Next to baptism and church membership, Amish everywhere believe that their child's future mate choice is the most important decision that he or she will make. In most cases, the gang provides the members' future dates, acceptable standards of dating and courtship, and future mates. Sixteen-year-olds are making choices with lifetime consequences.

An open buggy is used for courtship in some communities.
Photo by Lucian Niemeyer.

Courtship

Finding a Mate

When Aaron asked to take me home after the next singing,
you can be sure that I went all out to impress him.
—Aaron's wife

Getting Together

M ate selection occurs naturally in every viable society, but in a separatist religious group both community and parents are especially
invested in their children's quest to find a mate. Not only do they hope that
their children will marry, but all Amish parents fervently desire that their
sons and daughters marry within the faith and establish committed lifetime
relationships. Parents realize that the future of the society depends on the
formation of stable family units within the faith.

Despite their high investment, however, these Anabaptist parents allow
their offspring the freedom to choose or reject potential dates and mates, in
contrast to traditional societies that arrange marriages in order to maintain
cultural separation.[1] Allowing such freedom carries risks, of course, but it
is consistent with their belief in adult choices.

On the other hand, the Amish realize that failing to place any limits on young peoples' dating and marriage choices could result in a loss of numbers or commitment. The community has resolved this tension by allowing their youth to choose whom they will marry as long as the person has been baptized into the Amish faith. They permit no exceptions to this practice that anthropologists call *endogamy*—marriage within one's group.

However much parents and leaders worry about these issues, typical sixteen-year-olds give little thought to the cultural complexities involved in mate selection. Rather, they are more elated with the new possibilities that are emerging and are absorbed in the jitters and joys of developing a "special friendship," as they call it. Many worry about their inexperience and whether they will find that "special friend" or be found. As they mature, they become increasingly aware that dating or courtship will eventually lead to a lifetime relationship.

To be Amish almost always means being married. Indeed, to remain unmarried is usually considered to be in an incomplete state. Community members often feel sorry for females who were "never asked" and worry about males who never marry. Singles sometimes feel that they lack the respect, status, and power that their married counterparts enjoy. Unmarried men will never be placed in the lot to be candidates for the ministry, and unmarried women are often called "girls" well into middle age and beyond.

Youth feel the pressure to join the church, settle down, and marry. "We have two sons in their twenties who aren't married yet," worried an Amish deacon. "We wish they'd hurry up and find a wife." Although teenagers may not be thinking about power, status, and cultural viability when they enter the dating arena, they see a clear connection between dating and marriage.

Courting Practices, Then and Now

In the past, virtually all dating and courting relations traditionally occurred in secret. Joseph Yoder's description of a Sunday night in central Pennsylvania during the late 1800s in *Rosanna of the Amish* (1995 [1940]) captures the traditional air of secrecy:

Soon after the early autumn sunset, the buggies began coming over the hill. The boys were bringing their sisters and maybe a sister's friend, but not their own girlfriends. Boys are rarely if ever seen driving in daytime with their own girlfriends. The greatest possible secrecy surrounds their social relations. The one time when prevarication is permissible is when a boy is charged with having a "girl" or when a girl is charged with having a beau. Both will deny the accusation to the last even though they know it is true, and that is why they are never seen together alone in daytime. They do not take their "girls" to singing, but they do take them home after singing. A boy never goes to his girl's home in daytime alone, and he does not enter the house in the evening when he calls on her till after her parents have retired. (109–10)

A little later, Rosanna's suitor, Crist, decides to visit her for the first time:

He had put a few grains of corn in his pocket, and when he reached the house he made sure that the parents were in bed. He then went to Rosanna's bedroom window, tossed a few grains of corn up against the window and waited. In a moment he heard the window raised very quietly and Rosanna whispered, "Who's there?" He whispered back, "Crist Yoder . . . " They sat in the kitchen by a very dim tallow candlelight, because the kitchen was farthest away from the bedroom where the old folks slept, and the old folks must not know. Secrecy was the important thing. (128–29)

In some smaller, more isolated settlements, or in conservative affiliations, present practices still resemble Yoder's description. There, courting couples still do not disclose information about their boyfriend or girlfriend, and parents often distance themselves from their children's romantic relationships. Although parents usually learn the identity of their child's "special friend" in these traditional communities, young people still try to keep their relationships a secret from family members, sometimes not revealing or mentioning the name of their boyfriend or girlfriend. Some couples reportedly have not told their parents their partner's name until they were ready to seek permission to marry.

Even today in parts of Pennsylvania, the girl's parents will retire early on a courting Saturday night so that the couple is assured of privacy. In a Swiss Amish settlement in Indiana, parents and siblings of the young woman also retire early on Wednesdays or Saturday evenings, the traditional court-ing nights in that community. However, instead of announcing his arrival with a handful of corn kernels, the young man more often signals his pres-ence by beaming his flashlight on the window.

But secrecy is now the exception in most communities. Although en-gagements may still be kept secret, dating itself has become characteristi-cally much more open today. Young couples routinely discuss their boy-friends or girlfriends with families and peers. Also, once the couple has established a "special friendship," the young man may appear for meals, conversation, and family activities, depending on the settlement's customs. In the Big Valley of Pennsylvania, a relatively conservative Amish area, a young man from the Byler affiliation claimed that almost everyone already knows about an upcoming wedding even before it is formally announced in church. "Nobody around here is surprised when a couple gets published," he asserted.

Waiting for Dating

Amish youth rarely, if ever, begin dating before age sixteen. Nobody seems to know how this has become the magic age. Perhaps it relates to Euro-pean or colonial American practices; perhaps parents have intuitively rec-ognized that early dating tends to result in premature commitments or in early sexual activity.[2] Whatever the reasons, young adolescents have few sanctioned opportunities to mingle with members of the other sex. They are always sex-segregated in church, and elsewhere they stay with their own sex to play or socialize. Age mates and older siblings would unmercifully tease any fourteen- or fifteen-year-old boy and girl who paired off. If social pressure were not sufficient, parents would directly intervene to stop the relationship.

However, since everyone in each community knows when dating is sup-posed to begin, early dating is never an issue. The actual age when youth be-gin pairing off varies by settlement and by sex. In some communities, boys are expected to postpone dating for six months to two years from the time they begin attending the singings, even if they receive their own carriages at sixteen. Elsewhere, all sixteen-year-olds may begin dating immediately if they wish. In other settlements, sixteen-year-old girls may accept a date with a seventeen- or eighteen-year-old, but sixteen-year-old males customarily delay their dating activities. A sixteen-year-old boy who would attempt to date in such a settlement would be regarded by everyone as presumptuous and "acting too high," according to an eighteen-year-old.[3]

Just as boys receive a carriage and horse from their families to denote the passage into a new stage in life, the girl's new status is often acknowledged with a gift from the family. In Mifflin County, Pennsylvania, a girl's parents may give her a corner cupboard when she starts attending the singings with the other *Youngie*. In other communities, parents give their daughters "hope chests." In Lancaster County, a father explained, "Every girl around here gets a bureau while running around. A girl is proud of things in her bureau. There are embroidered pillowcases, bed sheets, tablecloths, hand towels, wash clothes, dish clothes, [and] crocheted dresser doilies."[4] In some New Order settlements, her parents provide her with practical gifts such as quilts, cookware, and a treadle sewing machine. These tacitly acknowledge her new status and portend her future role as a housewife. If she marries, she will have a well-stocked trousseau and gifts from her family that she will take to her marriage.

Getting to Know You

Before the first date ever takes place, the young people have had ample opportunity to get to know their age mates in the surrounding area and form opinions about them. They have interacted with their immediate peers all their lives at church and school. In some larger settlements, their peer contacts expand rapidly when they turn sixteen and begin attending the singings. Elsewhere, they are able to interact with the other sex at work frolics and weddings. New Order Amish youth typically see each other weekly at their Wednesday night youth meetings and also at their work projects.

In some of the more conservative settlements, the boys and girls play Walk-a-Mile, a traditional game that their grandparents enjoyed when they were teenagers. After the singing, all of the unattached boys and girls stroll hand-in-hand or arm-in-arm along the back roads in the vicinity, with the boys walking closest to traffic. Invariably, the males do the choosing. The boy who is "it" chooses the girl he wishes to walk with by replacing the boy who is walking with her. He taps him on the shoulder and orders him to move forward or backward so many places in the line. That boy now becomes "it," and the activity continues. In some areas, girls also choose who they will walk with. Sometimes the activity will last an hour or more as boys and girls interact with many different young people in a nonthreatening environment.[5]

In certain parts of northern Indiana, teens get to know each other on Saturday nights when the boys go "cruising." Groups of five or six eligible girls will get together at one of their houses to await the arrival of different groups of boys who will drop in during the course of the evening. The boys will stay for an hour or two playing games such as Uno or Rook. The girls have prepared snacks of chips, pretzels, and sodas for their visitors. "This is the way our grandchildren who are with the youth folk get to know each other," a grandfather explained. Most parents believe that this is a better setting for their teenage children to meet other youth than what they experienced during their teenage years. All of these opportunities pave the way for their eventual pairing.

The First Date

With few exceptions, couples begin dating or courting in the context of the Sunday night singing, the most important event for Amish youth. They may first meet before the singing when the boy goes to pick up the girl he has asked out, or their meeting may occur afterward when he takes her home, depending on the local tradition. In all settlements, however, the boy takes the initiative in dating or courtship. He may show his interest by writing a letter or by going through a mutual friend instead of directly asking the girl for a date. She will typically respond through a third person. Having a mutual friend prepare the way or respond to the invitation reduces the likelihood of public rejection, shame, or teasing.[6]

The script for the first date varies considerably from settlement to settlement. In some plainer Lancaster groups, when a boy wants to establish a "special friendship" with a girl, he invites her to take a walk with him after a singing. Two boys may pair up for moral support, and each asks a girl to join them at a designated time and place, somewhere away from the crowd.

A young man in the conservative Lancaster County Pequea gang recalled his first experience. "A couple of my friends had walked with Ruth before, but she turned them down when they asked her to go steady. . . . I was nervous with Ruth—wow, was I ever—and had no idea what to say. You put your arms around each other and just walk for a while. Oh, we talked about the weather, small talk. After maybe ten minutes we were discovered, and a whole bunch of sixteen-year-olds chased after us, at least ten of them. I was completely red—you can't talk or visit at that point, you're so embarrassed."[7]

"When the boy asks the girl to walk a second or a third time, the other youth take special notice. If anyone sees her going to his buggy after the singing without his invitation, we all know that they have become special friends," explained a young man from a conservative group. "Then when they start down the lane together in our settlement," he continued, "everyone begins to whoop and scream and shine flashlights on them. Sometimes the guys even run alongside the buggy and rock it. I don't know how this got started, but it often happens."

Even if he has not personally contacted her before, a girl often knows through her friends or siblings of a boy's interest before he asks her to walk with him. In other groups, a boy shows his interest by inviting the girl to ride with him to or from the singing. In some places in Lancaster County, a girl will typically accept the boy's initial invitation but will demonstrate her level of interest in him by the amount of care she takes in preparing the customary after-singing snack. One newlywed recalled her first date with her future husband: "When Aaron asked to take me home after the next singing, you can be sure that I went all out to impress him. If I hadn't been interested, he would have gotten just the bare minimum."

At this point in most settlements, the couple begins seeing each other every other Saturday night on the weekend that the girl's district does not have church. Sylvan, a young man in a conservative Lancaster County gang, describes a typical date: "I might arrive at her house around 7, she'll come out and help me unharness my horse. We'll play Monopoly or Scrabble or cards with the brothers and sisters or other dating couples. Around 9, the boys will go out to the barn, have a smoke, feed the horse, take a leak. Ruth fixes a snack for everybody, a Sloppy Joe maybe, some applesauce. We're sort of intent on a clean courtship. Especially Ruth. She didn't really want to, but I have kissed her a few times."[8]

Even after couples begin dating steadily, personal contacts during the week have typically been limited, and telephone conversations are difficult to arrange. With the advent of mobile phones, the more daring youth in large settlements have their own cell phones and have much easier access to their special friends.

In the more conservative settlements, courting youth start and maintain their courtship through letter writing, even if they live only a mile or two away. Samuel, an eighteen-year-old from a conservative Lancaster County daughter settlement, explained: "Three weeks before I wanted to take Sarah home from the singing, I wrote her about my intentions. I wanted to give her a chance to think about being my special friend. Also I wanted her to talk to her parents to see how they felt. She wrote back, saying yes, I could take her home after the singing." Beyond getting acquainted, the small talk and descriptions of family events help confirm their status as special friends. They also provide a means of cementing relationships when their face-to-face contacts are limited. The arrival of the daily mail is often a time of great anticipation and teasing.

Different Dating Practices

Acceptable norms of dating behavior vary widely in different settlements. In all New Order groups and in several Old Order groups, such as Kalona, Iowa, and Somerset County, Pennsylvania, young people must either be church members or candidates for membership before they can date. In groups like these, dating and courtship are synonymous, so that when a young man and woman finally appear together publicly, everyone correctly assumes that they will marry. "Playing the field" is either discouraged or forbidden. Having to be a member first can inadvertently or directly act as an incentive to join the church.

Both Old Order and New Order members often criticize those settlements in which the youth "date around." "We believe that courting should be that time for a couple to be sure that it is the Lord's will for them to marry," an Old Order father explained. "Finding one's life mate should be a matter of prayer." A minister was incredulous when he heard that some young men in a neighboring state had dated as many as five different girls in the past year. He would have undoubtedly been shocked to learn that in some settlements, young men report having dated as many as forty different girls before settling down.

New Order churches, besides objecting to casual dating, discourage long courtships. Consequently, their young people generally do not even begin going out until they are eighteen or nineteen, and they must be church members before they begin dating. Because of these factors, New Order couples tend to marry at least a year later than do most of their Old Order neighbors. All New Order groups and many morally conservative Old Order groups consistently advocate "pure courtships" that preach totally "hands-off" behavior between the sexes. A well-known admonition to these youth is "Lips off, laps off, hands off." Most supervised singings in large settlements, organized by parents to reduce rowdiness and immorality, require prospective members to agree with these prohibitions before they may join the group.

Recognizing the danger of their children's establishing friendships with non-Amish youth, Amish communities and parents vigorously combat dating outsiders. When violations occur, Amish males are more likely than females to be involved. "Boys have more outside contacts and opportunities, and girls are more obedient," an Amish father explained. These separatist parents and elders universally regard dating outsiders as a violation of the New Testament teaching, "Be not unequally yoked together with unbelievers" (2 Corinthians 6:14). Based on this biblical admonition, they regard dating outsiders as entering into an unholy alliance with the world. A concerned father asked a non-Amish friend to pray for his nineteen-year-old son who he thought was attracted to English girls he met at a local grocery store and at a sales stable. Some parents force their children to either give up dating the non-Amish person or leave home. Others prefer to give their wayward son or daughter time: "Let the fire go out by itself. As they get to know each other, they will see how mismatched their ways are," a father explained.

If two young people from nonaffiliated groups (those which do not share the communion service and are not "in full fellowship") begin dating, the person who is from the more progressive affiliation will generally face fewer objections from his or her family and church than the person from the more conservative affiliation. In general, it is more acceptable to date someone who is more conservative than somebody who is more liberal. "In the Big Valley," a young Mifflin County man reported, "you're okay if you go with someone whose church still practices strict shunning."

Some members from conservative groups worry that marrying into a more liberal affiliation will introduce new ideas and dissatisfaction with the status quo or may influence the member to leave for the spouse's more liberal group. Either outcome threatens the integrity of the community. Thus, in these plainest groups, the adults keep a careful eye on budding relationships. In these communities, young church members who date someone from a more progressive settlement may be warned first and then excommunicated and shunned if they persist.

The Ideal Date

What constitutes the "ideal date" depends on the age, sex, and settlement of the Amish youth. The one common denominator is that the person must be Amish. Many progressive Amish believe that young men in plainer communities place more value on young women whose traits will be useful in their roles of housewife, helpmeet, and mother—traditional traits such as hard work, perseverance, and submissiveness. In fact, in one large settlement in Ohio, girls described as "plain-looking" reportedly have boosted their dating prospects by dropping from a "higher" to a more conservative group with its greater emphasis on role-fulfillment and lesser emphasis on physical attractiveness.

Family Life and *Young Companion* regularly feature articles and stories extolling character over appearance and substance over showiness. Nevertheless, in the progressive communities at least, many teenagers of both sexes admit that a girl's looks and personality are highly valued commodities in seeking a date and mate. And some more progressive Amish with contacts among the plainest groups believe that even their boys increasingly choose dates on the basis of "pretty."

In describing the traits girls wanted in boys, writers for Pathway Publications claimed that girls admired males who embodied traditional Amish values such as industry, strength, responsibility, and humility—in short, those that would help make good husbands, fathers, providers, and responsible church members. A nineteen-year-old in a small Amish community described the most popular boys as "kind, soft-spoken, neatly dressed as well as outgoing and friendly." However, a mother of five in her mid-thirties reported, "I always wanted a good-looking husband, and as you can see, I found one." So for at least some Amish youth, love is not always blind.

Sex, the Sacred Subject

As in virtually all morally conservative Christian groups, the Amish unequivocally advocate sexual abstinence before marriage. Because the Amish are very private, they rarely disclose anything about their sexual attitudes or behaviors to outsiders, researchers, or even to each other. Although parents know very little about this aspect of their children's lives, they are very concerned about the sexual temptations and possible activities of their youth. Despite these concerns, many adults report that their parents provided little or no sex education in either their childhood or adolescence.

A parent from Indiana may have expressed the sentiments of a sizeable number of adults in a letter to *Family Life:* "We remember when sex education was started in public schools with disastrous results. Parents need to be educated in this, but children don't need any suggestions. Maybe this would be a good time to recommend the 'Sacred Subjects' booklets, which can be parent-controlled."[9] This set is advertised as "a set of six booklets written by an Amish minister to help parents talk to their children about life, growing up, and keeping themselves pure."

The titles are "I Wish I Could Have Confided in My Parents," "Ignorance Is Not Bliss," "To a Girl of Eleven," "To a Boy of Twelve," "Before You Date," and "Before You Marry." The set has been discreetly advertised for several years and "is available to married couples." Many adults say they grew up with little or no overt teaching at home about sex. A mother from a very plain Amish settlement in western Pennsylvania believes that fewer than half the girls in that settlement had been told about menstruation. A middle-aged mother from another settlement said, "Our parents believed that with regard to sex, we would learn what we needed to know when the time came. I can't believe how little I knew."

To respond to this perceived omission, concerned ministers and laypersons from a New Order Amish affiliation in Ohio wrote and distributed a four-page brief entitled "Christian Courtship." Their stated purpose was to establish courtship practices based on scriptural principles. The brief consisted of twenty-five questions and answers. For example, question 15 asks, "Should body caresses be permitted?" The written answer advises the following:

> In the earliest stage of courtship a strict "hands off" is an ideal policy. Then as mutual affections continue to grow, an affectionate hand-clasp becomes in order, and in maturer courtships (especially after engagement) a hand resting on the shoulder should not be objectionable. The sacred "first kiss" should be strictly reserved for sealing the engagement, and from then on a farewell kiss with a moderate embrace may be sanctioned. However, caressing, such as embracing, hugging, necking, petting, or any bodily contact for the purpose of gaining any unchristian liberties, or that stimulate immoral thinking should never be permitted, before or after engagement. "Can a man take fire in his bosom and his clothes not burn? Can one go upon hot coals and his feet not be burned?" Proverbs 6:27–28.

In one large community, rumors sometimes surface about a number of girls being on the "woman's pill" or of boys carrying contraceptives in their carriages.[10] A bishop in a plain affiliation was so concerned about the youth in his church that he asked the local doctor if he was providing birth control pills for the girls in his district. The bishop was relieved when the physician assured him that their office was not providing those services to the single young women.

Rumors of youthful sexual behavior crop up more frequently for communities or affiliations outside one's own. Referring to a large community in another state, an older Amishman declared, "With the kind of things that go on there, either lots of the youth are using birth control or lots of girls are having abortions." He based his suspicions on the party reputation of the settlement coupled with a low premarital pregnancy rate. However, he was unable to support any of his allegations of premarital sex, abortion, or birth control use, and many adults in that large community report that they have never heard of abortions there. "If one Amish girl had an abortion," said a mother, "you can be sure it would be the best-kept secret in the world."

Although most settlements have relatively few premarital pregnancies, some have a reputation for "moral looseness" in their courtship. At least three settlements have this reputation among the Amish. Curious about whether the rumors of premarital pregnancies were true in two of these settlements, an Amish parent examined the wedding dates from the community directories to see on which day of the week couples were married. "Couples who have to get married are wed on Sunday instead of on the traditional weekday," he explained. Using Sunday weddings as his standard, the statistics revealed that over a three-year period between 20 and 30 percent of the weddings occurred on Sunday rather than the traditional days. However, an analysis of Sunday weddings and first births failed to confirm his suspicions. A former resident of one of those communities declared that Sunday ceremonies did not necessarily indicate premarital sexual relationships.

Elsewhere, an Amish minister alleged that in another settlement in his state, "at least half of the girls are pregnant on their wedding day." He had heard this from a Mennonite minister who lived in that community. Indeed, other Amish adults and youth in nearby settlements concurred with his assessment. A nineteen-year-old from a neighboring community declared, "I don't know why they have this problem. But they have always been different." However, checking the community directory to determine the relationship between wedding dates and birth dates for the first child revealed that premarital pregnancies accounted for 20 percent of those births rather than the alleged 50 percent.

In another community with a reputation for extensive premarital sexual activity, Amish informants claimed that out-of-wedlock pregnancies there dropped significantly in the two previous years: "The ministry finally decided to do something about it by pressuring the wayward youth—and also their parents." Many Amish regard these "problem settlements" to be among the plainest or most traditional, although not as plain as the Swartzentruber or Nebraska groups.

Donnermeyer and Cooksey (2004) did the best-documented study on the timing of marriages in relation to first births in Holmes County, Ohio. They analyzed the Amish directories, a listing of all of the Old Order and New Order groups in Holmes, Wayne, and Stark counties in Ohio, with the exception of the conservative Swartzentruber Amish, who refused to participate in directories. Analyzing data on women who were born between 1940 and 1969, they found that 10 percent of all couples gave birth to their first child within the first seven months of marriage. An additional 12 percent gave birth within the eighth or ninth months of pregnancy. "Our estimate of premarital conceptions is likely a conservative one," they concluded (2004, 21). They also compared early births among the New Order, Old Order, and Andy Weaver Amish, a very conservative group. They found that "the percent of premarital conceptions occurring among the New Order youth was less than half the level of the Old Order youth and less than one-third of the level of the Andy Weaver youth" (2004, 21). Many Amish and non-Amish await the results of their ongoing data analyses from those who were born in the 1970s and early 1980s.

Although the actual premarital pregnancy rate in any settlement turned out to be considerably lower than the alleged 50 percent, most Amish would consider settlements with a 20 percent premarital pregnancy rate to reflect serious moral problems. When individuals tried to explain why some places struggled with higher incidences of premarital sexual behavior, the reasons varied widely. A common explanation was, "Moral problems simply reflect problems and dissension in the church." Others speculated that parental laxness and example, alcohol use, and bed courtship were to blame.

Referring to the relatively high premarital pregnancy rates in those communities, some Amish reported, "These problems have existed there for generations. The youth have simply adopted the permissive attitudes from their parents and others." Additionally, a deacon explained, "If only the boys are drinking, the girls will likely keep things under control. But if both boys and girls are drinking, couples are much more apt to be involved in sex." "Yes, this was the problem in —— County," explained a father.

If an unmarried Amish girl becomes pregnant, the outcome is predictable. She almost always marries the baby's father, unless he is not Amish. In the Lancaster County settlements, where the prescribed wedding season runs from late October to early December, a first wedding announced for any time other than those months means that the couple "had to get married."[11] In Lancaster, these weddings will still be held on the traditional Tuesday or Thursday. However, couples are expected to restrict the guest list to relatives and close friends. Also, they are to curtail the afternoon and evening festivities.

An Amishman from western Pennsylvania describes a similar practice: "The wedding size is smaller and (the couple) usually have what is called a 'day only' wedding, meaning you are invited for the wedding ceremony and Dinner and expected to leave by 5 or 6 o'clock. Aunts, uncles, and other close relatives, table waiters and cooks are invited for supper and they will leave by 8 or 9 o'clock. The ceremony will be carried out in the usual manner." Festivities at emergency weddings among the Renno and Byler Amish must be over by 4:00 p.m.

A deacon in a large settlement reports that young women who are in the first trimester of pregnancy will occasionally slip by with a large wedding. "When the deacon and the bishop ask the couple whether they have had a pure courtship, they just lie just so they can have a big wedding," he complained. Several other informants made the same comment about couples lying. In some communities, urgent weddings are simply conducted at the close of the regular Sunday church service. And in at least one of the plainest communities, bishops have reportedly refused to perform the wedding ceremony for the erring couple. The couple was instructed to seek the services of a justice of the peace to be married.

Traditionally, when word gets out that an Amish couple has been sexually involved, the church expects them to marry as soon as possible, although an Indiana mother stated that the couple would not be pressured to marry if they were unwilling or unsuited for each other. Either way, the offending couple must immediately drop out of the Sunday singing socials and all other youth activities and begin sitting in church with the married men or women. If they already belong to the church, they are temporarily excommunicated—usually for six weeks—then married. If they are not church members but wish to be married, the ministers provide emergency membership instruction classes for them so that they can be baptized and "taken up" into the church.

The bishop may combine and condense the nine sessions or allow them to go to other churches for instruction on the off-Sundays so that the couple will not have to wait to complete the full eighteen-week instruction period. The wedding will occur shortly after the couple completes the membership classes and are baptized and taken into the church. When a scribe from *The Budget* reports that a person or a couple have been baptized and married on the same day, Amish readers assume that the bride was already pregnant.

In one of the large communities, some of the single members who have been sexually involved in any way during their dating or courtship relationships confess their misdeeds before the bishop and the church and ask to be placed in the ban for six weeks if they are planning to marry in the fall. When a deacon was asked why six weeks, he responded that since Peter denied the Lord three times, the offending party is to be excluded from membership for three consecutive Sunday services. Since church meets every other week, this means that they will attend church on the three Sundays but will not participate in any after-church members' meeting or stay to eat with the church members. At the end of the six weeks, they are restored into full fellowship with the church.[12]

Observers report that the entire community genuinely accepts the erring couple. They regard Christ's admonitions to forgive as applying to anyone who repents and changes. For most Amish, sins of the flesh are not considered worse than other transgressions. Thus, rather than being lost to the world, the transgressors are restored to the community.

An Old Courting Practice

A reason that has commonly been offered for premarital sex is *Uneheliche beischlof,* known as bed courtship, bedding, or bundling, depending on the locale. In Pennsylvania German, the term literally means "unmarried sleeping together." European emigrants apparently brought bundling with them to North America, and it existed among the Lutheran and Reformed Churches as well as the Amish.[13] The common explanation for its origins is that it stemmed from couples courting in unheated houses. Also, these early dwellings lacked privacy for the young woman to entertain her suitor.

Where youth still practice bed courtship today, they appear to follow the same script used by their parents, grandparents, and great grandparents. Typically, the couple retires to the girl's bedroom, where they lie down together. In the past, couples reputedly used a bundling board, a rough plank separating the partners. However, boards are no longer used. The Amish expect that when their courting youth "go to bed," they are to refrain from sexual activity of any kind.

In most places where bundling is still practiced, girls also wear a special night dress, the *Nacht rock,* for the occasions.[14] "In our settlement," a young man related, "my sister and her boyfriend had to delay because she had not yet finished sewing her dress." It often consists of fancier materials or attractive colors not allowed in public or in daily apparel. For example, in one of the plainest settlements, girls may use pink in their under-dresses, a color never acceptable in any other context. In another settlement, courting dresses are white, and in another plain settlement, girls may wear knee-length rather than full-length dresses.

Girls from the Swartzentruber Amish wear under-dresses and simply remove their outer dress. However, courting dresses are never sheer, low cut, or otherwise suggestive. Before lying down, boys typically take off their shoes and may also remove their shirts, depending on the weather. In some places, couples go to bed after the rest of the family have retired, and the boy may stay until 4:00 or 4:30 a.m., depending on when the family arises, the community's standards, and the strictness of the parents.

From the beginning, however, this practice was criticized, both from within and outside the Amish community. The rejection of bundling was one of the major issues that led to the formation of new settlements in Ontario, Indiana, Illinois, Kansas, and elsewhere. As early as 1837, the *Ordnung* of Somerset County, Pennsylvania, condemned any youth who slept or lay together before marriage. Evidently the custom persisted because, according to one historian, the practice of bundling in Somerset County in 1851 was one of the chief reasons for members leaving to establish a church in Johnson County, Iowa.[15] Two years later, George Jutzi, an Amish writer from Stark County, Ohio, condemned the practice; and in 1870 a highly respected Amish bishop from Holmes County, Ohio, David A. Troyer, wrote against the dangers of *uneheliche Zusammenliegen* (lying together without marriage).[16]

Almost a century later, opposition to bundling precipitated the New Order Amish breakaway in Ohio. They unequivocally equated bundling with immoral courtship practices. While many Old Order and all New Order leaders speak out against it on moral grounds today, scattered settlements in western and central Pennsylvania, Ohio, Minnesota, Wisconsin, Michigan, Indiana, and New York still condone bed courtship. Even in those communities, however, some parents refuse to allow their daughters to go to bed with suitors.

Despite the persistence of bundling in those places, it is not standard practice in most Amish settlements. The affiliations that still accept bundling are, with a few exceptions, generally those that are the plainest in dress and lifestyle. These groups typically seek to uphold traditional behavior in every aspect of life. Since these groups usually have a higher retention rate than the progressive groups, the more progressive Amish sometimes charge that these traditionalists hold on to bundling as an enticement to keep their young people.

In some settlements, the practice is regulated by the *Ordnung*. Community standards for bed courtship specify the frequency, place, and behavior permitted. For example, the couple may begin "going to bed" on the fifth date, it is allowed only in the girl's bedroom, the boy may remove only his shirt and shoes, dating must never occur on Saturday nights prior to church in the girl's district, the couple must always keep a light burning, and the boy must be gone before daylight.

The specifics vary from place to place. For example, in some settlements girls are permitted to remove their head covering, and in others they are not. A church leader where bundling is practiced admitted that it was not a good thing, but he thought it was impossible to eliminate it. "Our people would say, 'It's always been this way.' The only way I could see a change is if someone would start a new settlement and prohibit it like they did in Tennessee."

Scholars have criticized the accuracy of many early writings on bundling, but two books published in the latter part of the twentieth century provided a low-key but realistic description of bed courtship. The one described a six-teen-year-old girl's actual first bundling experience (Folsom 1994); and the second, a novel written by an author with an Amish background, portrayed a couple's bundling experiences from the young man's perspective (Miller 1989). Both writers described the couples as spending most of the night together, with the young men leaving just before the parents got up in the morning. Neither account portrayed any overt sexual involvement. Nevertheless, many Amish find the intimacy of the first account and the sexual thoughts of the protagonist in the novel to be offensive.[17]

Outsiders and critics often assume that a young man's furtive escape in the predawn hours reflects the couple's shame over questionable or immoral practices. However, members of these traditional communities explain these actions quite differently. They say that when couples try to keep their courting a secret, the discovery of a suitor's entering or leaving his girlfriend's house provides relatives and friends a splendid occasion for teasing and for entertaining relatives and friends with the story.

An older Amish adult recalled that during his courting days he once overslept at his girlfriend's house. Hearing her mother approaching the room early in the morning, he quickly sprang from bed, grabbed his shoes, climbed out of the bedroom window, and ran barefoot through the corn-fields to avoid discovery.

A middle-aged man from Pennsylvania laughingly described a similar incident. His best friend also fell asleep Sunday night, which necessitated an early-morning exit. However, he needed to cross a barley field to get home. Not wishing to muss his Sunday trousers, he decided to take them off and carry them through the field. Unfortunately, as the story goes, bull thistles were growing profusely among the barley, and by the time his friend reached the other side, the thistles scratched his bare legs raw.

Actually many middle-aged adults, both New Order and Old Order Amish opponents of the practice, concede that their going to bed together never resulted in sexual activity. Many assert that their bed courtship was "pure," that is, without any sexual involvement. One elder Amishman described his courtship experiences of "going to bed" with dozens of girls on Saturday or Sunday nights over half a century ago. He affirmed that although he hugged and kissed almost all of his dates, they never engaged in petting or intercourse. Since their community attached no shame or secrecy with bed courtship, he often greeted the girls' parents before the couple went up-stairs. If bedrooms were scarce, siblings would often "give up" a room for the couple, or if an older sister left home to teach or get married, the mother might help the next-in-line to move in and take over the vacated room.

At times friends would drop by to visit the courting couple as they re-clined together and would sit on the edge of the bed and talk. "Sometimes their friends drank and ate a snack in the couples' room," a visitor from a non-bundling settlement reported. "When I was there," he recalled, "the girl had a pumpkin pie and a bag of potato chips for the snack." On oc-casion, two couples would bundle together in the same bed, boys on the outside, girls in the middle. A grandfather recalled a time when he and his buddy bundled with their girlfriends in the same bed: "I was in the center with a girl on each side. The thing I remember most," he exclaimed, "is how hot it was with the four of us together in one bed!" A grandfather remem-bered as many as six youth crowded into the same bed. An Amishman from a non-bundling settlement recalled sitting on the bed in another settlement where his friend and his friend's girlfriend were lying. "I didn't know what to expect," he reported. His host asked him who he wanted to bundle with. "I can't," the young man exclaimed. "If our ministers found out, I'd be dis-ciplined. You'd be excommunicated with that!"

In many settlements that have since rejected the practice, going to bed together was regarded as the normal way to begin courting. In Lancaster County, a middle-aged father remembered his mother telling him, "You'll be too far away to return home tonight so you should plan to stay all night with her." She then gave him instructions on bundling etiquette. Another adult recalls that his mother's advice was short and plain: "There should be absolutely no touching. Don't act like a dog."

A grandfather related that he never felt that his parents wondered about whether his bed courtship involved any sexual activity. He admitted to temptation as his relationship with his wife-to-be deepened, but she would remind him of their need to remain chaste. "The more she said we had to wait," he recalled, "the more respect I had for her." Many Amish realize that moderns would find such descriptions difficult to believe. For example, a young man who left the Amish and joined the armed forces related that his barracks buddies roared in disbelief when he told them that the boys in his community went to bed with the girls but did not have sex. "But we didn't," he insisted.

Many Amish critics of bed courtship concede that relatively few girls become pregnant today in most of the plain settlements where bundling persists. A Swartzentruber Amish bishop could recall that in their settlement only five young women over a thirty-year span became pregnant before marriage. "Our group does better than those who don't go to bed together," he declared. "Our young people are taught self-discipline," he added.

A Mennonite physician who worked with that same affiliation for more than three decades reports that he has not encountered a single premarital pregnancy from that affiliation. A man from western Pennsylvania reported that in the sixty-year history of their settlement, he knew of only five couples "that had to get married."

"Because the plainest groups are so isolated from mainstream society," a New Order father speculated, "bed courtship might not have the same sexual meaning and temptations that it does for most Amish."[18] An Amishman who engaged in bundling before he joined the New Orders, however, recalls that bed courtship led to sexual temptation for him and his fiancée. Also, a minister who strongly opposes the custom today does so from his experience as a young man when a girl from a large community introduced him to the practice almost a half-century earlier. "It's not lying in bed together that is the problem," said a Midwestern minister. "It's when they start touching."

None of the light-hearted anecdotes or explanations satisfy the critics of bed courtship. They interpret a community's acceptance of bundling as evidence of "moral looseness and corruption." Their strongest argument comes from Romans 13:13, in which Paul condemns, among other things, "chambering and wantonness." Opponents of the practice equate chambering with bundling and bundling with sex. "And even if no sex is involved, it causes lustful thoughts and is a terrible witness to outsiders," they quickly point out.[19]

An Amish father who practiced bed courtship in his youth came to adamantly oppose the custom and eventually joined another Old Order affiliation that forbade the practice. He wrote, "You needn't worry about sensationalizing it. I've not yet read any accounts that truly capture the custom. If anything, most accounts make it sound rather innocent and quaint. It is not. . . . This custom may have been innocent enough when it started, but it has become a very immoral practice. As parents we shudder to think of our children falling into this."[20] An unmarried young man from a settlement in western Pennsylvania wrote, "[My girlfriend] and I have quit the practice of bed courtship in January. Since then we both feel we know each other, and can communicate better than we ever did in the previous 2 years we practiced bed courtship. I would not go back to practicing it again, as courtship now has a new and deeper meaning."[21]

A Waning Custom

One by one, groups have condemned and abandoned bed courtship, and churches discipline unmarried members caught in the practice. Even Swartzentruber settlements in Tennessee and Kentucky have rejected it. By best estimates, probably fewer than ten percent of Amish communities support or condone bundling today, far less than in the 1940s or 1950s, when bundling was apparently practiced in many settlements.[22] The decline in Pennsylvania, Ohio, Illinois, and even in horse-and-buggy Mennonite enclaves in Canada, generally occurred because one or two influential men spoke out against the practice. Eventually they gained a critical mass and garnered enough support to change their community's attitude and its *Ordnung*.

However, some middle-aged Amish in a large settlement believe that young couples actually initiated the move away from bed courtship. "The older folk thought that it was all right because it had always been done this way, but a lot of us realized that it was wrong. The young folk eventually brought about the change," insisted a grandfather. "And we wouldn't let any of our children go to bed either."

Nevertheless, reactions in many plain communities to the critics of bed courtship reveal how deeply ingrained the practice has been. A grandfather from a bundling community asked, "What would a couple do if they didn't go to bed? Often a boy is shy and they don't know what to say. They feel more at ease lying in bed." He also criticized the traditional courting custom of the girl sitting on the boy's lap in a rocking chair, which occurs in some of the plainer communities. "That's more of a temptation than going to bed together," he insisted.

A young husband agreed. "A lot worse things have happened sitting up on the couch than lying in bed. What's all the fuss about? Our ancestors have gone to bed for generations." Another proponent of bundling concurred, "We have always done it this way. If it was good enough for our grandparents and parents, it is good enough for us. If we're not careful, we are going to drift into liberalism." Those who hold on to the custom accuse the critics of being proud and divisive, whereas opponents to bed courtship claim to have been ostracized and treated as pariahs by the guardians of traditional practices.[23]

Many Old Order people believe that the influence of anti-bundling groups like the Mennonites or New Order Amish fostered the demise of bundling in some Old Order communities. One Amishman recalls that as early as the 1940s, his girlfriend's mother refused to let him and her daughter go to bed, explaining to her, "Your brother Aaron will be home tonight, and you know that since he has joined the Mennonites, he doesn't approve of the unmarrieds going to bed anymore."

Among the Amish, the most influential treatise against bed courtship, Ein Riss in der Mauer (A Break in the Wall) was written and published by an Ohio New Order Amish minister in the 1970s. In the opening pages, written in High German and in the Fraktur script, he claimed that up to half of the young women in some Amish communities were already pregnant on their wedding day. He attributed some of this to the corrupting contact with the outside world, to apathy and indifference on the part of parents and church leaders, to the influence of the automobile, and to the use of drugs. Most of all, however, he blamed the practice of bed courtship.

After tracing its history from early Europe to the present, this New Order author advocated a nonphysical courtship:

It may seem frigid to some but the best and most scriptural boy-girl conduct is a complete "hands-off" policy. Paul wrote Timothy to treat "the younger sisters with all purity." "With all purity" would mean to abstain from anything that gives illicit pleasure sensations and arouses the baser nature. Only after marriage is the "cleave to the wife" in its proper place. Sitting on separate chairs or a fair length couch would be in order to help maintain this. . . . Is it right for us to pray, "Lead us not into temptation," when we are not zealous in avoiding temptations whenever we can? How can parents pray the evening prayer on Saturday and Sunday evening and yet have open doors to rowdy, lusty boys or allow weekly boy-girl sleeping in the home? Jesus said, "Thou shalt not tempt the Lord thy God."[24]

Dozens of Amish bookstores sold the treatise, and many believe that this book, along with the influence of Pathway Publishers, was instrumental in bringing about change in many Amish communities.[25]

In 1999 Pathway Publishers picked up again on the courtship theme by reprinting an article that had originally appeared nearly thirty years earlier. It did not mention bed courtship by name, but it emphasized the danger of any kind of physical intimacy before marriage. In the same issue, the editor reiterated his concern over "impure courtship standards," warning youth and their parents about the ever-present lusts of the flesh.[26] This has been a recurrent theme for Pathway editors and writers since the inception of *Family Life* in 1968.

One issue that the editors have not felt a need to address is homosexuality. Although the Amish are well aware of homosexuality in mainstream society, most profess to know few, if any, youth or adults in their communities who are practicing homosexuals. Virtually all Amish regard homosexual behavior as aberrant, loathsome, and sinful. One ex-Amish writer (Burkholder 2005) describes, with great shame, bestiality and homosexual behavior among early adolescents in his community. In a rare case a homosexual pedophile who attempted to molest one of the boys in a settlement in western Pennsylvania committed suicide after he was discovered. Although outsiders may debate the reasons for so few reports of Amish homosexuals, the Amish themselves are confident that homosexuality in their communities is extremely rare. They simply do not consider it a pressing issue.

Although most communities do not practice bed courtship, adults in virtually all communities are concerned that their courting youth's need for emotional intimacy may combine with their emerging sexuality to draw them into what they call "carnal relations." Despite these concerns, however, most Amish believe that their youth are considerably less involved in sex than mainstream youth. One father asked rhetorically, "Are all Amish girls virgins when they marry? Is everybody absolutely innocent? No. But overall, I believe our youth do better than the society at large."

A French reporter flew to Lancaster County in the summer of 1998 after the story of the drug arrests broke. He wanted to research and write his own story, "Drugs, Rock and Roll, and Sex Among Amish Youth." "I found enough to write about the drugs and rock and roll part," he related, "but as hard as I tried, I just didn't find much evidence on sex. I still don't know what is really going on."[27] Amish parents often say the same. But most work hard to imbue their children and youth with traditional Christian values that will foster sexual integrity before they marry.[28] They also promote courtship practices that avoid entanglements with worldly youth, because the future of their society depends on it. Other than having their children receive baptism and join the church, nothing brings more joy to an Amish couple than having their children marry within the faith.

Weddings take place in Amish homes or shops. Hundreds attend the three-hour church service, followed by feasting and singing.
Photo by Lucian Niemeyer.

Weddings

High Times in Plain Places

*Marriage is really the time when Amish youth settle down once
and for all and leave their foolish, youthful ways behind.*
—A young bachelor

A Homespun High Time

*H*ochzeit, the German word for wedding, literally means "high time"
and reflects both the importance and the celebration that surround
this central event in Amish life. This quintessential Amish experience combines all the elements of life that they value most—faith, family, friends,
and community. Not only do weddings join two young people and their
families in a lifetime relationship, but they also reaffirm the health and
continuity of the culture.

A new family unit has been formed, children will soon follow, and another generation of Amish will be launched. In an important departure
from other ceremonies, the local community honors the couple and their
young friends by giving them the place of prominence throughout much
of the day's festivities. In the planning, execution, and follow-up, cultural

tradition uses the wedding ritual to sustain and strengthen the values of the Amish community.[1]

Because Amish families sometimes invite English friends to their weddings, more has been written in magazines and newspapers about this event than any other aspect of Amish life.[2] The traditional wedding ceremony itself is remarkably similar among settlements and affiliations, having changed little. However, pre- and post-wedding-day activities vary widely. For example, in many settlements couples marry at almost any time throughout the year except in the summer. In Geuaga County, Ohio, however, weddings are held in the summer. In Lancaster County, weddings typically occur only from late October to early December, on Tuesdays or Thursdays. The average age for a Holmes County, Ohio, Old Order Amish couple is twenty-one. New Order couples are generally a year older than their Old Order counterparts. In both, men are older than women (Donnermeyer and Cooksey 2004).

The marriage season is not specified in the *Ordnung* but likely derives from farming rhythms—coming after the fall harvest but before the onset of bad weather. However, limiting weddings to a narrow "wedding season" is not without problems, especially in large settlements. In Lancaster County, Pennsylvania, for example, 144 weddings took place in fifteen days, with seventeen occurring on a single day. A nineteen-year-old girl was invited to five weddings in one day, and a bishop was invited to twenty-five weddings in the six-week period. Families report high stress in trying to decide which weddings to attend and which to omit.[3] In contrast, in Holmes County May weddings are almost as common as October weddings.

In some places, both the wedding and the subsequent activities occur at the bride's home, whereas in other settlements, the two events are in different houses or even in a large shop belonging to the family or a neighbor. In some settlements, parents of the couples have no assigned duties on the wedding day, while in others, the parents traditionally prepare the wedding feast and miss the entire service, witnessing only the wedding vows.

In the plainest affiliations, the bride's parents are helping to prepare the dinner when the couple says their vows. The weddings in a particular church district are basically identical and minimize individuality, choice, and differences in wealth. Whatever the local customs, family, church, and community are invested in every aspect of this significant occasion.

Getting Published, Amish Style

Amish couples do not announce formal engagements as English couples typically do. In one settlement, a young man traditionally asks the girl to marry him when the strawberry blossoms are in bloom, usually in May. "By the time the strawberries are on the bushes and the girl hasn't been asked," a father observed, "she realizes that she'll probably have to wait for another year to get married."[4] Although parents and close friends know about the couple's intentions to marry, the rest of the community hears the official pronouncement at the close of a Sunday service. The deacon or bishop publicly announces a couple's wish to marry, typically from one to six weeks before the wedding day.

This custom originated in Europe with the Roman Catholic Council of Trent in the sixteenth century. Originally known as "the publishing of the banns," it was a formal announcement by a priest that a couple intended to marry. Later, the Anglicans and other Protestant groups adopted the practice and brought it to the British colonies. In the past, the banns were announced in three successive Sunday services or feast days before the wedding in order to permit church members or other citizens to disclose problems or irregularities, such as bigamy. Today Amish couples must still be published, and once the announcement is made on Sunday, they may marry as early as the following Tuesday but almost never more than six weeks later.[5]

Permission to Marry

Depending on community or family tradition, a young man may ask the girl's father for permission to marry his daughter. "I was close to my daughters. They were my little girls. They all knew that they would have to get Dad's approval for the boy they wanted to marry," a father explained. Other couples simply inform their parents of their plans to marry.

Because marriage and family play such a crucial role in their society, parents would never give their blessing to an Amish son or daughter contemplating marriage with a non–church member. Any youth intending to marry must be a church member in "good standing" and can marry only another church member in good standing. Before the wedding is announced, the ministers in both the bride and groom's home districts must certify that the young people are "in order" with their local congregations.

Today the young man goes privately to the deacon or bishop in his home district, states his intentions to marry, and discloses the name of his future wife and of her desire to marry him. He then requests a letter signed by the bishop and the rest of the ministry affirming that he is indeed a church member in good standing. The deacon or bishop asks him if he has been free of fornication, a sin that would result in immediate six-week excommunication. If he is "pushing the fences" in other ways—that is, dressing or behaving outside of the *Ordnung*—the minister asks the young man to come immediately into full compliance.

At this stage, however, admonitions are rarely necessary. For anyone who had been dabbling in the world, marriage is the final step into responsible adulthood. By now the wayward individual has almost certainly come into compliance with the church standards. In some settlements, the ministers prepare a letter of endorsement, sometimes written in the ornate German Fraktur script and signed by each one of them. Finally, the suitor delivers the letter, known as the *Zeugnis*, to the appropriate minister in the young woman's home district.[6]

In many settlements, the girl's deacon serves as the go-between to the family and the church after receiving this *Zeugnis*. First he confirms her desire to marry the young man. Then the deacon asks her if she is also free of fornication and has "remained pure" during their courtship. If she should say no, she and her suitor would be temporarily excommunicated and placed "under the ban" for six weeks. This not only necessitates a change in their wedding date but also changes the format of the wedding. For example, the bride would not be permitted to wear the white wedding cape and apron over her dress at the wedding. Also, the couple would be required to scale down their wedding, with no evening celebrations, as happens if a girl becomes pregnant before marriage. However, since couples rarely report sexual involvement, they routinely receive the church's blessing to marry.[7]

Following this conversation, the bride's deacon announces in church the couple's intentions to marry. In the same service, the girl's father invites members of the local congregation to the wedding.[8] In Lancaster County, the bride-to-be does not attend church when her wedding is published. If the young man is from the same district, he leaves either before the wedding announcements are made or else stays home and helps her prepare a meal for the family.[9] The same night that the wedding is published, the couple attends the youth singing for the final time and invites either all the youth or a select group of friends to the wedding, depending on their friendship and the space limitations at home.[10] Traditionally, the young man takes his carriage and drives to adjacent districts to invite special friends and relatives outside their church district. In the brief time period between the announcement and the wedding day, the couple appears together in public and begins to identify with the young married couples.

Festival Preparations

Some outside writers have emphasized that Amish couples do not have to worry about many of the wedding details that concern typical middle-class mainstream couples. For example, there are no rings, wedding gowns, tuxedo rentals, bridal bouquets, organists, soloists, photographers, or reception site rentals; no D.J.s or bands to hire; and no elaborate honeymoon plans to make. These are simply not part of the Amish "high time" in any settlement.

As one observer notes, the relative simplicity of their weddings reinforces Amish values of relationships, community, and faith, rather than calling attention to good taste, sophistication, and lavish expenditures typical of English weddings.[11] Simplicity is relative, since some couples invite as many as five hundred guests for the day and evening activities. In practice, however, the activities of the wedding and the wedding day are scripted in a way that minimizes ostentatious display in order to focus more on the meaning and importance of the new family unit.

Nevertheless, at least in the larger communities, planning a wedding is still a major undertaking, one that begins months before the couple is published. One reason is that with large families, scores of relatives and close friends, local church members, and co-workers, the couple will typically invite three hundred guests and may occasionally invite five hundred guests or more. English friends of a couple in St. Mary's County, Maryland, counted four chartered buses, ten vans, and dozens of buggies, wagons, and carts at the wedding site. In addition to the local Amish, relatives and friends traveled to Maryland from Indiana, New York, Ohio, Pennsylvania, Michigan, Virginia, and Wisconsin.

Because the Amish never employ outside caterers, preparing for this event and the hundreds of guests involves many of the same organizational and management skills required for a barn raising. Over the years, some communities have compiled a "wedding planner" notebook that outlines tasks to be done, the sequence of events, recipes and quantities of food needed, and who is responsible for what. This book is passed from family to family as the needs arise.

A Host of Helpers

By tradition, the bride's parents enlist many "wedding helpers" to assist in the preparations, serving, and cleanup. Local church members are often involved as helpers in food and site preparations ahead of time, and often with cleanup activities afterward. They routinely do this for the families of all the young women from the district when they get married.[12] In most places, parents choose a head couple to oversee all the activities, with the husband in charge of the men and the wife of the women. The cooks' tasks actually begin a day or two prior to the wedding. They and the waiters will work throughout the wedding day, cooking, serving, and cleaning up for hundreds of guests. Family members and the newlyweds customarily finish cleaning on the day after the wedding.

Long-term preparations vary, depending on the community and customs. In parts of Pennsylvania and Iowa, the bride's parents have typically bought and transplanted hundreds of celery plants into their garden in the late spring. They will not only be the base for the traditional hot creamed celery main dish ("cooked with pure cream," an Amish elder announced), but will also provide the edible centerpieces on each table—stalks of crisp, white celery hearts arranged in glasses, vases, or mason jars. Many families will also buy dozens of chicks months in advance to raise for the traditional roast or fried chicken.[13]

Changing Practices

Some wedding traditions, however, are giving way to the realities of modern life. For example, the method of inviting guests is changing. In the past, before distant daughter settlements sprang up and phones were so readily available, tradition called for the groom to personally invite most of the guests. In some places, the couple still send postcards to distant relatives and friends, often written with a single sentence simply saying, "Come to our wedding" with the day and place.[14] "After all," a young man explained, "if you have lots of invitations to send out, you don't have time to write anything else."

A more recent innovation, especially in larger settlements, is the use of printed invitations to the wedding and napkins embossed with the couple's names. An Amish businessman in Indiana who provides this service has been criticized for promoting formality and *Hochmut*—"high-mindedness," or pride. "Nowadays," said an Amish mother ruefully, "months before the couple is published we often have to invite distant friends and relatives so that they can reserve a van and driver. Otherwise, all the drivers are already hired out long before the wedding."

In parts of Holmes County, Ohio, another nontraditional arrangement made months ahead is to reserve the "wedding trailers." These are enclosed trailers built to refrigerate food, cook for large numbers of people, and provide the necessary accouterments for feeding hundreds of people.[15] Because some food preparation may start several days in advance, the trailers are equipped with a walk-in cooler, a "kitchen" section with three propane stoves, and a sink with hot running water. They are also stocked with folding tables and chairs, place settings, and linens. Providing this equipment and services for Amish weddings has sparked a growing business opportunity for nearly a dozen entrepreneurs, all Amish but one. Old Order Amish entrepreneurs hire pickup trucks to pull the wedding trailers to and from the sites. New Order businessmen pull their wagons with tractors.[16] They typically charge several hundred dollars for each rental unit.

In some settlements, such as Kalona, Iowa, the future groom lives with the family of the bride until the wedding day so that he can get to know the family better, help out around the home, and assist with the multitude of tasks required for such an event. At that time, he also begins growing his beard. A married couple in Pennsylvania reported that in the past, "one of the traditional tasks assigned to the future groom was to clean out the manure from his father-in-law's barn or horse stable before the wedding day."

Meanwhile, the bride-to-be assumes many of the last-minute tasks that spring up because of uncertain communication, changing guest lists, and the challenge of pairing up unequal numbers of unmarried male and female youth for the wedding supper. Arranging these details reminds the couple that weddings are a communal and familial as well as a personal event, one that provides an important and decisive entrance into full-blown Amish living and responsibility.

The immediate family, close relatives, and local church members hurry about with the many tasks associated with site and food preparations. Often the family must build an extension to the house or shop where the wedding will occur. It may be used as a cooking space or as a place to seat guests at the wedding. A crew of workers frames the extension, which may be 30 by 50 feet or more, with two-by-fours, plywood, particle board, and long rolls of heavy plastic to keep the temporary addition warm and dry. This building project may be the mini-version of the barn raising, because with adequate help, the crew will have the entire addition framed, roofed, floored, heated, and lighted in a single day.[17]

Preparing the Feast

Inside the house, shop, or partially finished addition, in most settlements the cooking crews are hard at work preparing for hundreds of guests. In Lancaster County, friends and relatives, often the grandparents and their cohorts, are dicing gallons of celery, choosing celery stalks for the centerpiece, and filling dozens of roasting pans with scores of chickens. Nearby, or even outside if the weather is clear, teams of men spread out and blend the ingredients on large plastic tarps for the bread stuffing that will be mixed with the roast chicken to make the Lancaster County *Roascht,* the centerpiece in the wedding feast.

Although the basic menu for both the wedding dinner at noon and the supper in the evening are traditional and unique to each community, food is universally abundant and lovingly prepared, timed to be served hot and fresh. In preparation for such massive feasts, relatives and neighbors in many settlements traditionally loan their stoves to the family for roasting the chickens, cooking the potatoes, and preparing the vegetables.[18]

For a typical large wedding in Lancaster County, three or four men join their wives to prepare the chickens, and three or four couples boil and mash the potatoes.[19] Additionally, pairs of local church women are often assigned to take care of various cooking details. For example, two women cook the creamed celery, two prepare the pickled cabbage, two make the gravy, and two will brew a constant supply of fresh coffee. These same women oversee the afternoon cleanup. Other couples are assigned to set the tables and serve the guests.

The *Vorgeher* (those who go before; ushers) are family members or relatives who are charged with the layout of the dining area and are responsible to supervise the setting up of the tables and benches immediately following the end of the service. For large weddings, the local church-bench wagon and one or two wagons from other nearby church districts are dropped off at the house. These horse-drawn wagons, approximately four by six by fourteen feet, carry the benches, hymnbooks, dishes, and a few folding chairs that are used for church services at the various houses.

The morning before the wedding, the ushers meet, survey the space available for the reception, and "draw up a map" to show the layout of the tables and benches. Each table consists of three church benches, the legs of which slip and clamp into slots on a pair of plywood "trusses," one at either end of the benches. The trusses elevate the three benches to table height and hold the tops flat and parallel with each other. All benches are marked with chalk so that they will be accounted for and easily assembled. Typically, the ushers assemble the tables and mark the floor in a trial run the day before, so that on the wedding day they will know exactly where every table belongs.

As soon as the service ends, each usher is responsible to make sure that volunteers place the three benches into their designated pair of trusses, place all tables in their pre-assigned spots, and set benches on both sides of every table. This transformation from church benches to wedding tables takes only a few minutes. As soon as they are in place, the servers place a white covering on each table. Ideally, volunteers are given only one job so that nobody will be overworked and everyone will have at least part of the day free for visiting. Virtually all the helpers consider it an honor to be asked to serve at a wedding.

Although the bride's family is ultimately in charge of wedding details, they need not worry about planning the menu for the wedding feast because it is prescribed by the community. For the noon meal in Lancaster, the three main dishes are roast chicken that has been removed from the bones and combined with *Roascht,* consisting of bread stuffing, celery, and spices; heaping bowls of mashed potatoes and chicken gravy; and the traditional celery dish. Additionally, the family serves pickled cabbage, homemade applesauce, bread, traditional sweets and sours, and for dessert, home-canned peaches or pears, tapioca pudding, cookies, and pies. Although side dishes and desserts vary from settlement to settlement, most places feature some form of chicken and mashed potatoes with gravy (Scott 1988, 35).

Participants say that working together to prepare and serve the meals is remarkably stress-free and energizing for the participants. After all, what could be better than having good fellowship while preparing good food to celebrate the union of a new couple and the formation of another Amish family? When they have finished their assigned duties, the volunteers and relatives enjoy the evening meal together. Distant guests stay for the night at nearby homes in order to be close and ready for tomorrow's activities.

The Wedding Day

The wedding day actually starts for the participants in the pre-dawn hours. If the bride lives on a farm, the family will want all the cows to be milked and chores completed long before the first horses and carriages come down the lane. The hostlers, often young teenage boys who are relatives of the bride, care for the dozens of horses and carriages.[20] In some settlements, such as in Kalona, Iowa, the wedding party will stay upstairs until the wedding begins. In the large Lancaster and Holmes County settlements, the bride and groom sit down together on benches or chairs, either inside or outside, depending on the weather and local custom, flanked by their attendants.[21] Guests file by the seated wedding party to shake hands and offer their greetings and well-wishes. Brides and grooms always wear new clothing but dress the same as they would for any regular church service. Also, their clothing is indistinguishable from the other four attendants' clothing.

Each community has its own customs for acceptable wedding apparel. The bride and her two attendants wear the same color dresses, sewed either by themselves or by their mothers. In Lancaster County, tradition calls for navy blue, teal blue, or purple for wedding dresses.[22] In some districts, the three women wear the black head covering denoting their singleness during the service, but shortly after the ceremony the bride will exchange her black *Kapp* for the traditional white covering worn by the married women. The groom and his two attendants also dress in their typical Sunday black and white. However, among the most conservative gangs, they, and sometimes the fathers of the bride and groom, wear black bow-ties, a curious anomaly for otherwise plain attire. For the ceremony, the bride and the groom also wear old-fashioned high-top shoes, normally worn only by older members and by ministers. Finally, for the first time, the groom wears the broader-brimmed black hat worn by the married men.[23] In the future, the couple will continue to wear their wedding clothes as normal Sunday garb, although in Lancaster County the bride puts away her new white cape and apron, which will be saved for her burial.

When the appointed time arrives, parents and grandparents typically enter the building first, followed by the ministers and other members of the *Freindschaft*, or extended family. The unmarried siblings of the groom lead the procession of the young people, followed by the newly married or soon-to-be-married friends. The ushers show the guests where to sit by age and sex.

Typically, these ushers are brothers or sisters of the couple and are regarded as important, not only in planning for seating, but for following protocol in seating the guests. Everyone except the very old and the wedding party sits through the three-and-a-half-hour service on the regular Sunday backless benches. English guests generally sit in the back on chairs.

The wedding service and ceremony are simple and have changed little over the years. Virtually everything is prescribed, and everyone knows the script. A description of an Amish wedding in the 1950s looks remarkably similar to a contemporary Amish wedding. A wedding rehearsal is never necessary or held. In all settlements, the actual wedding service is similar to a regular Sunday church service in both format and duration. The proceedings are always conducted in a mixture of old German and Pennsylvania German, and the songs and sermons pertain to marriage.

Unlike some mainstream weddings, where the church service and ceremony appear to be secondary to the conspicuous attention given the bride, groom, and the aesthetics of the setting, Amish weddings are solemn occasions, and as such, all couples comport themselves with restraint and reserve. The sacredness of the event takes precedence over the preferences and personalities of the individuals.[24]

Premarital Counseling

As the congregation begins to sing the first traditional wedding hymn in German, the participating ministers rise and leave the service, followed by the couple who accompany them into the adjoining basement or upstairs "counsel room" for the *Abroth,* a time of admonition and encouragement. Everyone sits down, with the bride and groom sitting together facing the ministers, who are in a semicircle. The couple is first asked by the bishop why they are there, if they are free from sexual relations with others, and finally if they are free of fornication with each other, the same question asked earlier when they first expressed their desire to be married.[25] Theoretically, if they should answer no, the bishop would immediately terminate the wedding. The ministers would discipline the couple by temporarily excommunicating and shunning them for six weeks. At the end of that time, they would be restored to fellowship and duly married. Both a deacon and a minister said that they had never heard of such a pre-wedding confession in their lifetimes. "I wouldn't want to say that a lot of couples lie," a minister said. "Let's just say they couldn't face up to telling the truth."

Then the ministers and bishops in attendance, sometimes numbering a dozen or more, give counsel and encouragement to the couple. A minister described the kinds of admonitions that couples receive in his affiliation: "Try and prevent the first argument, forgiveness, be helpful in church matters as well as in the neighborhood. The groom is admonished to make his wife's life easier during the pregnancy, etc. They are told that husband and wife need to be *best friends* as well as lovers. . . . This is considered a *serious* lifelong project."[26] At an Indiana wedding, the bishop counseled the couple to "choose a decent name for your children, not like Casper" (which was his name).

The couple is instructed that they may have marital relations at any time except during menstruation—the wife's "monthly sickness." Some ministers tell the couple that this is the time for the woman's body to cleanse itself. "Not having relations during that time of month comes from one of the books of Moses," a minister explained.[27]

Also, in many areas the couple is admonished to follow the example in the apocryphal book of Tobit in which Tobias and his bride, Sara, fasted and prayed on their wedding night instead of engaging immediately in conjugal relations.[28] When asked if ministers ever counsel couples about birth control, a bishop responded, "Seldom, if ever, because children and large families are considered a blessing." In some affiliations, bishops tell the couple that they should not attempt to prevent pregnancies. In almost all settlements, this twenty- to thirty-minute session with the ministers is the only formal premarital counseling that the couple receives, although in at least one area in northern Indiana, the couple and their parents counsel with the ministers three times before the wedding.[29]

Wedding Songs and Sermons

While the ministers meet with the couple, the congregants are singing the first selection from the *Ausbund*. In Lancaster County, this is a song that describes the church as Christ's bride.[30] They then turn to the "Loblied," the traditional praise hymn sung at all Amish worship services everywhere. Near the end of that song, which usually takes twenty minutes to sing, the bride and groom return from their instruction time and are rejoined and accompanied by their attendants to benches or chairs placed in front of the ministers. The groom, flanked by his two attendants, sits facing the bride, who is seated with her two attendants about four feet away.

In Lancaster County, the congregation sings another hymn emphasizing the relationship of the church as Christ's bride. Then the minister, sometimes a relative of the groom, delivers the first sermon, focusing on Old Testament examples of marriage, good and bad, from Adam and Eve, through Noah and his sons who found wives. This opening sermon may last a half-hour. After the first sermon, everyone kneels for silent prayer, then rises and stands for the reading from Matthew 19:1–12, a passage in which Jesus teaches about divorce. If young people leave the service to go to the bathroom or take a break to smoke, they almost always exit during this reading of the scriptures, the only time in the first two hours that the congregation stands.

Now the presiding bishop, frequently a relative of the bride or groom or the bride's home bishop, delivers the main sermon.[31] He resumes the biblical narrative with Abraham and the experience of the patriarchs as recorded in Genesis. The bishop recounts their relationships, strong or flawed, and also mentions Solomon and his disobedience in choosing many wives. Next he reads from the Apostle Paul's instruction on marriage in 1 Corinthians 7 and Ephesians 5:22–33.

Based on his understanding of these scriptures and his life experiences, the bishop instructs the couple on how to begin a godly home of their own and how to treat each other in love and respect. He admonishes them to be faithful members of the church and urges them to help others in need. Traditionally, he then moves to the story of Tobias and Sara from the intertestamental book of Tobit. The bishop emphasizes youthful Tobias's good works, the young couple's fasting and prayers, and the active intervention of Raphael, an angel sent from God, on their behalf.[32] The Tobias narrative precedes the wedding vows and typically lasts about forty-five minutes. In many settlements, the kitchen helpers leave their tasks and come in to hear at least part of the main sermon and witness the marriage ceremony.[33]

Tying the Lifetime Knot

As the bishop ends this part of the sermon, he says, "Now here are two in one faith" and gives their full names. He then asks those assembled to speak if they know of any scriptural reason why the two young people seated before them cannot be married: "You should let yourself be heard now," he intones. Some bishops have been known to pause as long as half a minute before proceeding.[34] He then invites the couple to stand before him, saying, "If it is still your desire to be married, you may in the name of the Lord come forth." The groom then rises, takes the bride's hand, and they stand before the bishop to take their vows.

He asks the following questions, calling each by name the first time he addresses them:

1. Do you believe and confess that it is scriptural order for one man and one woman to be one, and state that you have been led thus far?
2. Can you, brother, state that the Lord directs you to take this sister as your wife?
3. Can you, sister, state that the Lord directs you to take this brother as your husband?
4. Do you promise to support your wife when she is in weakness, sickness, what trials may befall you and stand as a Christian husband?
5. Do you promise to support your husband when he is in weakness, sickness, what trials may befall you and stand as a Christian wife?
6. Can you vow to remain together and have love, compassion, and patience for one another and not to part from one another until the beloved God shall part you in death? [35]

After the couple has assented to each of these questions, the bishop reads "A Prayer for Those About to Be Married" from the *Christenpflicht* prayer book. This prayer states the Amish understanding of marriage as "for the procreation of the human race and to avoid impurity."[36] Then the bishop, quoting from Tobit, joins the couple's right hands and holds them together in his own hands. He says, "So Raguel took the hand of his daughter, and placed it in Tobias' hand and said, 'May the God of Abraham, and the God of Isaac, and the God of Jacob be with you and help you together and give his blessings richly to you, and this through Jesus Christ, Amen.'" He concludes, "Go forth in the name of the Lord. You are now man and wife." With no show of emotion, the new couple returns to their seats. The bride and groom do not kiss, nor does the audience break the solemnity of the occasion with nods or affirming smiles. The Amish would regard such actions as frivolous and as a serious breach of decorum.

The bishop resumes his sermon, and for the next ten or fifteen minutes picks up on the theme of the day, often recounting the rest of the Tobit story. When he finally concludes, he then asks five or six ministers to comment on the message or add thoughts of their own. In many places, they will be the bride's bishop and the groom's bishop, if they did not preach, then minister relatives of the bride and of the groom, and in some places, such as Kalona and Lancaster, the groom's father and the bride's father. These *Zeugnis* (testimonies) usually add about twenty more minutes to the service.

To conclude, the congregation kneels while the presiding bishop reads again from the venerable *Christenpflicht* prayer book that includes this sober petition: "May they also enjoy the benefit of Thy divine comfort in all the affliction, suffering, and forthcoming troubles they meet in their married life." After the bishop recites the Lord's Prayer, the congregation rises from their knees and sits again to sing the final wedding song. Although the entire service might last more than three hours, the ceremony itself takes only three or four minutes.[37]

Center Stage in a Corner: The Festivities Begin

After the service, the mood quickly shifts from the solemnity of the marriage ceremony to the newlyweds and the invited youth. Depending on the custom of the settlement, the wedding dinner and reception will take place in the house of the bride or in a nearby neighbor's or relative's house. In parts of Indiana and Pennsylvania's Big Valley, "wedding church" is held in a neighbor's house, and the rest of the day's festivities take place at the bride's home. While the guests walk or ride in their own carriages, the bride and groom and their two attending couples are whisked back to the bride's house in three carriages, each driven by their own hostler. After the wedding, hostlers in Kalona also drive the three couples to the bride's house for the reception when an especially big crowd requires a larger venue for the actual wedding. Hostetler (1993, 196) reports that the Big Valley tradition was for the hostler to sit on the laps of the couple he was transporting.

As soon as the service is ended, the ushers and volunteers immediately begin turning the benches into tables and placing them end to end to form the long dining tables. The area that will be the central focus for all in attendance is called the *Eck* [corner], the special corner where two long rows of tables and benches converge to form an L. The bride and groom sit at the *Eck,* flanked by their attendants, peers, and relatives who are soon to be married. Nobody seems to know how this unusual seating arrangement started, but it is a fixture of virtually all Amish wedding receptions.

Most Amish believe that the Lancaster County people lavish more attention on wedding festivities and the *Eck* than do Amish in other settlements. In Lancaster, three married siblings or close relatives and their spouses meticulously decorate the tables in this corner and set out the new china, the groom's gift to the bride. They load the table with the wedding day gifts of candy-filled bowls called *Eck Schissle* or *Eck Sach.* Most gift bowls are covered with clear plastic wrap, bedecked with ribbons, and accompanied with a small card showing the givers' names and a message of congratulations and blessing.

When the servers indicate that the meal is ready, the wedding party enters the dining area first, followed by the single youth. As they enter, boys and girls divide at the ends of the tables with the boys filling in one side and the girls sitting across from them on the other. At this meal, unlike any other occasion, the servers attend to the youth first, while the adults converse and look on.

Once the youth are seated at the tables, the *Ecktender,* or wedding corner helpers, serve the rest of the young people. The *Ecktender* in Lancaster are often the aunts and uncles of the bride. They may treat the bride and groom to special snacks or their favorite foods.[38] In Lancaster, they often serve the couple rice or tapioca pudding in wine glasses. During the meal, the bride shares many of her gift packages of sweets from the *Eck,* sending them down the tables to close friends or relatives who sample from the contents. However, the dishes are gifts for the couple, and the bride will display and use many of them in her own home in years to come.

In the past, families served wine at most weddings in Lancaster County; and in some parts of Ohio, Indiana, and Pennsylvania, it is still served. "I think it has died out in most places because it was abused," said an Amish elder. Today in Lancaster County, single youth may wait on tables for the adults after the youth at the first setting are finished eating. Following the noon feast, the rest of the young guests have a few hours free for various activities while the adults eat, usually in two more shifts.[39] During that time, the *Ecktender* sit at the *Eck* on behalf of the bride and groom while the couple leaves the dining area to receive and open gifts. Usually unmarried sisters or cousins are appointed to record all gifts and those who visited.

Gift-Giving

Gift-giving traditions for invited guests vary among the settlements. In many places, guests take their gifts to the wedding, but in Lancaster County, only distant visitors and English guests take their gifts to the wedding. Closest friends and relatives bring only the bowl and dish treats on the wedding day. They wait until the newlyweds visit their homes in the winter months after the wedding to give their main gifts. In Holmes County, Ohio, and other places, all guests bring their gifts to the wedding. Later in the day, the bride and groom may open them, or in some places, designated friends or relatives open and display the gifts in another room or even outside, depending on the settlement and the time of year for weddings.

In typical Amish fashion, most gifts reflect the Amish values of practicality and simplicity. One English visitor described the gift display as a combination between a hardware store and a housewares department. Besides giving the traditional dishes, pots, pans, cutlery, canners, and roasters that the bride will use, guests may give push or power lawn mowers, chainsaws, weed whackers, garden hoses, hoes, rakes, sprinkling cans—tools appropriate for lawn and garden care in that particular settlement and affiliation.

Traditionally, male guests bring gifts for the husband, and females give to the wife. Gifts for the husband often involve carpentry tools or work-related equipment such as hammers, screwdrivers, tape measures, shovels, and wheelbarrows. A non-Amish visitor counted twenty super-size cans of the lubricant WD-40 and a pair of heavy-duty wire cutters among the wedding gifts.

In Lancaster County, women often give the bride gifts in her favorite color. Sometimes friends will give family gifts, such as a picnic table or lawn furniture, or even gifts that are simply for fun, such as a croquet set, jigsaw puzzles, and board games. "There's no competition or status symbols involved," a man declared, "but people do think about how these gifts compared to their own wedding."

In the past, parents of the bride traditionally provided a cow for the couple to help them get started. Today, in prosperous settlements, the bride's parents usually give the newlywed the essentials for housekeeping, and the groom's family provides a start toward housing—fixing up an adjacent building or preparing a separate part of the house for them. The gifts from the bride's family consist of the furniture, housewares, quilts, linens, and clothing that she brings to the marriage. This is likely a remnant from the early practice of providing a dowry, although few use the term today.[40]

A young housewife pointed out to visitors the things that her parents had given her when she was married. They included the dining room table and chairs, the corner cupboard, a dry sink, a china cupboard, a hutch, a bureau, their bedroom suite, a gas stove, a stainless steel cooking set, and a sewing machine. Her husband explained, "My dad helped us get on our farm by selling it to us at a very low price." A great-grandmother from southern Indiana received a farm from her family when she married during the Great Depression.

Festivities and Song

At about 2:30, when all the guests have finished eating and the tables have been cleared, chairs are set around the main dining area in preparation for the afternoon singing. One of the men from the couples in charge goes out to call in as many youth as will come back for the afternoon singing. In Lancaster, tradition dictates for the youth to return in couples at this time. "How many come back in depends pretty much on how fast a gang the couple was running with. The faster the gang, the fewer come in for the afternoon singing," a young Amishman explained.

Songbooks from the local church districts are then distributed. Traditionally, everyone knows what songs will be sung first in the afternoon singing. In some communities, adults do most of the singing, and the music serves mainly as a backdrop for youthful conversation and gaiety. The bride may send more of her gift packages of sweets down the tables for the couple's special friends and guests to sample. Ice cream is often served as an afternoon snack. From time to time, people will leave the singing to look at the gifts, the candy dishes, or the cakes. This singing lasts until late in the afternoon in parts of Pennsylvania or ends as early as 3:30 in Ohio New Order groups.

The young people in some settlements exit to the barn or shop for dancing, euphemistically called barn games or ring games. "It's really like square dancing, except the couples go in circles instead," a young man who attended weddings in a small settlement explained. "They would have ring games only at weddings. There would be as many as twenty couples involved. The girls would be singing as they skipped around. It was really beautiful. Then after the evening meal and the singing, the couples would get together after dark and play walk-a-mile," a game frequently played after singings.

In some large settlements, many of the young people, against the wishes of their parents, "will leave the wedding grounds" for a time and gather at a nearby house to be away from the adults and be with their peers. Some of them may play cards, either with regular playing cards or with Rook, depending on the settlement or gang. If youth are accustomed to drinking alcohol with their peers at weddings, it generally starts during this time.

In some areas, friends of the bride's mother have the responsibility of preparing a wedding supper. In most places, it is another full meal with its own menu. In the past it always featured more chicken over homemade biscuit-type wafers, boiled potatoes with parsley and butter, peas, tossed salad, and for dessert, fruit salad, cake, tapioca, or cornstarch pudding. The *Ecktender* traditionally serve the wedding party and their close friends ginger ale or punch laced with ginger ale.[41]

As early as the 1990s, many families were increasingly departing from the traditional Lancaster supper menu. Whatever the menu, however, the adults "eat at the first table," and the bride's parents sit at the honored place in the *Eck*.[42] In parts of Holmes County, youth who were not invited for the wedding dinner at noon are the featured guests for the wedding supper. In other Holmes County affiliations, the noon meal is the only one provided for the guests.

Pairing Off

In some settlements, the events surrounding the wedding supper and the evening singing are the most exciting part of the day. After the adults have eaten, the youth enter as couples and will eat and remain together for the evening singing. For many youth, especially the youngest teenagers, this is stressful as well as exciting. For them, this will be their first occasion to socialize with someone of the other sex. Sixteen-year-old boys especially worry about whether they will know the girl they get paired with or whether she is somebody they like. Until they gain enough courage, many of the younger boys will choose a cousin as their partner to avoid the stress. "At my age," a twenty-year-old explained, "you just learn to take it as it comes and don't get all excited or upset." Girls often have a different concern. In many settlements, single females outnumber single males, so the fear of "not being picked" and having to file in with other neglected peers may cast a pall on the day's festivities.

An English guest at a wedding at a Lancaster County daughter settlement in Maryland captures the excitement and mixed feelings that many of the youth experience prior to the pairings. "Emma and Raymond (the newlyweds) emerged from the house with a notebook and were immediately surrounded by young men. I asked Solly Jr. what that was all about . . . he said that if a young man has a steady date, they are paired to sit with each other at the evening meal. Those who do not have steady dates give their requests of whom they would LIKE to be paired with to the bride and groom. The bride and groom then turn the list over to the seaters, and they will be paired for the evening meal. He said a lot of young people are shy, and this is a good way to break the ice and get to sit with a girl you have your eye on."[43]

Typically, the bride has already worked on compiling the list of couples who will sit together at the evening meal.[44] If someone fails to show up, she must rearrange on the spot. "If the boys have a preference," a father in Lancaster County explained, "they tell the bride. The girls have no choice." The bride may try to accommodate the boys' wishes, but she has the final say.[45] "Her closest friends get their choices first, her family next, and the church youth get whoever is left over," a single male complained. "Together it takes about an hour till everybody has been assigned," he said.

A twenty-one-year-old single male from Pennsylvania's Big Valley complained, "Out here it may take more than two hours to get all of the couples together. Lots of youth don't want to go with the person that they were assigned to, so there's lots of requests and changes. Here the *Newehocke* (attendants) will help the bride arrange things."

The Grand Entrance

When the list is completed to the bride's satisfaction, all of the youth assemble outside, boys in one group, girls in the other. In an atmosphere charged with suspense, one of the groom's attendants begins reading off the names of each couple, calling out the boy's name first, then his partner's name. The two young people leave their respective group, join hands, and form a waiting line. Once everyone is paired, the bride, groom, and their attendants lead the procession into the dining room. Traditionally, they are followed by those couples who were recently married, then by those who will be married later in the fall, next by those who are seriously dating, and finally, by everyone else.

Where this is done, guests eagerly await the *Youngie*'s entrance to the wedding supper. In some places, curious adults, especially women, according to one report, crowd around both sides of the entrance. One Amishman declared that they are looking for potentially budding romances and hope to obtain grist for future gossip, speculation, and teasing. An Amish father even admitted, "It's interesting to see who's dating and who might marry sometime in the future."

Sometimes parents find out for the first time who their children are interested in. The visitor at the wedding in St. Mary's County, Maryland, reported the onlookers' reactions there: "One of my adult friends, Simeon, said that the adults ALL watch the entrance of the young folks . . . see who is sweet on who. And they do! When the young folks were called to the table, a hush fell over the crowds and everyone moved close to see who was paired with who. It was quite cute to watch these nervous young men walk in with their dinner dates . . . it had to be especially unnerving for them knowing ALL eyes were on them. The crowds were quiet except for whispers and giggles."[46] A New Order mother noted that at their weddings, "We try not to have 'gazing lines' watching the young people."

More Feasting and Festivities

The Amish do not have the cake-cutting tradition common at mainstream weddings. In Lancaster, for example, after the meal is finished, the servers cut and distribute dessert from the cakes on display at the *eck* table. Sometimes as many as twenty close friends and relatives bring in home-baked cakes as their special contributions to the festivities. In a settlement where the family is responsible for providing the cakes, one participant reported spending an entire day baking angel food cakes (Garrett 2004, 162). In Lancaster, many of the bakers decorate the cakes with themes commemorating events in the couple's lives together, their occupations, or a hobby. For example, if the bride was a teacher, the couple may get cakes with a schoolhouse or school bell theme; if they liked to ice skate, they may get skaters on a mirror pond, or if the groom was an avid softball player, the cake might be decorated like a baseball diamond. Cakes at New Order weddings are characteristically decorated only with icing flowers or a small Bible on top.

Cakes are displayed in the room along with the wedding gifts and are brought to the *Eck* to be cut and shared with the guests. In most Lancaster weddings, servers also provide ice cream for the guests, and young couples traditionally share from the same dish. In parts of the Big Valley, the bride traditionally sends plates of cake and sweets from the gift dishes as her thank-you to the cooks and helpers.

Meanwhile, the bride and groom preside at the *Eck* and receive the best wishes and farewells from early-departing guests. In the recent past in Lancaster County, the groom and his attendants passed out cigars to the men, but that custom has declined in most places. Now, the groom may pass out cigar-sized beef sticks for their guests, and the couple often gives away pens featuring their first names, wedding date, and an appropriate inscription on love or marriage.[47] In some places, the couples' names and the date of the wedding appear on the table napkins, but many settlements regard this as being "too high," especially since napkins are rarely used on other occasions.

More Singing and More Fun

Because the supper at large weddings may require up to three hours to serve all the guests, the evening singing might not even begin until 8:30 and may last until 11:00 p.m. or later. Guests may sing from a different book than they did in the afternoon singing, for example, the "thin book," the *Unpartheyisches Gesang-Buch*. Also it is not uncommon to use the "fast" tempos similar to that of hymns sung in Sunday morning worship services in mainline Protestant churches. In some locales, guests even sing gospel songs or choruses in English.

Sometimes uninvited young teenagers or children appear outside the windows near the *Eck*, hoping that the couple will open a window and send treats to them from the dishes. If the bride or groom fails to respond or ignores them, the beggars may make noise, rap on the windows, and engage in prank-playing. Traditionally, if the hostlers can catch the intruders, they will smear their faces with black shoe polish.

In many locales, the groom's unmarried peers still follow the old custom of capturing the groom and pitching him over a fence into the waiting arms of the young married men. This reportedly symbolizes his change of status. At the Maryland wedding mentioned earlier, the observer described a variation of this custom:

> Some of the young, newly-married men were horsin' around near the pasture. I am not sure what it is called that they were doing, but as Omer explained, he said, "There is an old saying that you are not truly married until you are thrown over the fence." ... So the young men were taking this year's newly married men—all except Raymond (the new groom)—and tossing them OVER the pasture fence. There were so many men on both sides of the fence it looked like they were playing volleyball with the young men. My husband said it looked like a rock concert. Every time they were successful at sending a newly married over the fence, you would hear the crowd yell out "YEAH."[48]

Likewise, the young women entice the bride to unwittingly step over a broom handle in her symbolic rite of passage into marriage. Among groups such as the Nebraska or Swartzentruber Amish, the youth may square dance, play games, or eat again until midnight or later.[49]

Wedding Pranks

In some settlements, young friends or family members try to play tricks on the newlyweds. Scott (1988, 35–36) recounts stories of celebrants putting rubber spiders in the couple's gravy or chewing gum in their food. In Lancaster County, some youth play pranks on the newlyweds at the end of the day's festivities. According to a parent, the first few couples in a buddy bunch to be married are the ones most likely to be the objects of pranksters. "If you're older, like we were, when you get married, nobody bothers playing tricks on you."

Pranksters have hoisted the groom's carriage onto the roof of an outbuilding or have powered up their chainsaws outside of the couple's bedroom window after they have retired. Sometimes they have scattered cornstarch, pepper, flour, and even doughnuts between the sheets. Some have set the alarm clock to go off in the middle of the night. Many pranks center on hiding or disassembling things—the horse's harness, the bedroom door, or even the bed. Some new couples have left the wedding festivities, only to find their bed in the middle of the cornfield or assembled on the top of the house. As a final touch, some pranksters even included a kerosene nightlight on a nightstand next to the purloined bed.

In Lancaster County, merrymakers try to remove the washing machine that the couple will need next day when they do the customary washing of the wedding-related linens and laundry. The Lancaster *Intelligencer Journal* featured a photo of an Amishman climbing a sixty-foot silo where the agitator from a washing machine had been tied by their young friends the night before.[50] In a similar incident, the following notice and letter appeared in *Die Botschaft* at the end of the wedding season: "To Whom It May Concern: If your boys were at the wedding at Aaron Ebersol's, will you ask them if they hid their washing machine. They cannot find it since the wedding. Please let them know. Thank you. Signed, A Neighbor."

The next week the following letter appeared in *Die Botschaft*: "Attention: To the people who were at the wedding at Aaron Ebersols. They had hidden their washing machine. It was found and hidden again at about 9:30 or 15 of 10:00. It was found in the evening and hid again and put in the haymow. They know who hid it there. Then it was removed from the haymow again and they haven't found it yet. Their wedding date was Nov. 13, this is now Dec. 10. Let's help them find it. If you had boys there at the wedding, would you please ask them if they helped remove it out of the haymow. And if they did would you please let Aaron know where it is. Thank you."[51] Because newlyweds are aware of these traditions, they take special efforts to hide the washing machine and their horse and carriage from potential pranksters.

Many adults complain that these pranks get out of hand. A *Die Botschaft* scribe complained, "There was mischief going on Tuesday evening with uninvited guests. It is such a shame to ruin someone's day by such dirty and unruly things. It is too bad when we as Amish must get the police out to keep things under control at an Amish wedding."[52]

Where adults have concluded that wedding pranks or partying have "gotten out of hand" over time, they have sometimes forbidden having the evening meal and nighttime festivities. For example, New Order Amish and even some Old Order groups now have instituted "day weddings," in which all activities are concluded before supper. A New Order father wrote, "Our bishops frequently remark that we have received great blessings by having 'day weddings.' This eliminated much of the questionable activity, 'belling' [noise-making], drinking, barn games, etc., which was common. . . . The youth seem not to want to come for the ceremony and noon meal and will show up only for the evening activity."[53]

An Amish Honeymoon

In Lancaster County, the couple usually spends their first night together at the bride's home place. The next morning, tradition calls for them to be up by 4:00 or 5:00 a.m. to have breakfast and then begin with the cleanup from the aftermath of the wedding. This may serve as a tacit reminder that although one may be entering the joy and excitement of young married love, dishes and clothes must still be washed, houses cleaned, and duties performed.

After breakfast, their first task is to scrub the floors and wash the table-

cloths and linens from the previous day (if they can find the washing machine). The bride's parents, siblings, and nearby aunts also show up to help
load the benches, pack the dishes and songbooks away, and even send back
the portable toilets, a practical addition in recent years.

Although weddings are officially celebrated for only a single day rather
than two weeks as in the days of Tobias and Sara, some settlements celebrate the couple's new status for several weeks until they move into their
own place in late winter or early spring. During the week, the new couple
may stay with the bride's parents. However, on weekends they routinely
visit all of their local relatives, followed by Amish friends who attended their
wedding, and even some who were not invited.

Typically, they first call on the parents of the groom, followed by both
sets of grandparents. After those immediate family visits are completed, the
couple may join two or three other couples, either cousins or close friends,
and travel together on successive weekends to see uncles, aunts, and other
wedding guests, "as it suits best," explained a mother. Not only do they enjoy traveling with each other and help reduce the number of separate visits
that the host families must prepare for, but it helps establish the couple's
new identity as "young marrieds."

The touring generally begins on Friday night and runs through the weekend. With careful planning, couples can stop at nine or ten homes in one
weekend. A young man described the well-planned itinerary: "Friday evening they can go to supper at one house, stay for a couple hours, and then
go for an overnight at a different place. Next morning they can have breakfast at a third home, dinner at someone else's, supper at a different place,
and if they do it right, get in two more families that night." All the while,
they are being assimilated as a married couple into the adult community.

Making the Rounds

Only if they must travel extensive distances do couples rent vans for these
visits. Families anticipate the visits from these new couples and like to see
them arrive in their carriages. They are prepared, not only with their wedding gifts, but with ample supplies of snacks or a full meal, depending
on the time of their guests' arrival. Sometimes host families will lend a

horse and carriage to the couple if they had to come in a van. In Lancaster, the groom traditionally prepares a game, story, prank, or riddles to entertain the host family. The children especially look forward to these *Yung-g'heierditricks,* as they are called.

An Amish grandfather described a prank from his generation where the host father was asked to put his fingers through the crack in an open door and then grasp a raw egg that was placed in his fingers. Of course, everyone understood his predicament since any true Amishman "dare not" drop and break a perfectly good egg. So he would be trapped in that dilemma until he figured a way out or broke the egg.

In other cases, the groom might do sleight of hand tricks or use scissors to cut folded paper in unexpected ways. Or he might ask the children a perennial riddle, such as, "Where was Moses when the light went out?" (Answer: In the dark.) Host families may also offer entertainment, such as mini-shuffle board and other table games. Sometimes the father will provide tricks or riddles of his own for the visiting newlyweds.

A father chuckled as he recalled a prank that he and his newlywed peers played on their host families. Sometime during the conversation, games, or festivities, "one of the visiting young married couples would prowl around the house of the host and hide the gifts which the host intended to present to them at their departure. . . . When we would be ready to leave, the hosts would be frantically searching for the gifts to give." Of course, the newlyweds enjoyed seeing how long it took their hosts to figure out what had happened. Even if many of the activities are well known, these visits are highly anticipated and later provide wonderful stories for regaling family and friends, both old and young.

After visiting two or three hours at one home, the couple or couples move on to the next home, where they are similarly greeted and feted. "It's easy to gain weight during those visiting weeks," one young Amishman reported. "Everyone wants to give you food." Newlyweds stay over at their last place on Saturday night and either go to church with their host family in the morning or continue their rounds with families who have an off-Sunday. Finally, they return home with a carriage or van laden with gifts and treats. An exhausted bride and groom, on their way home from visiting distant relatives in late January, concluded that they would have to be satisfied with the fifty visits that they had already completed. "We still have a hundred families to go, but it's just too much. We have too much to do getting our house fixed up."

Securing the Bonds

Finally, several weeks after a Lancaster County wedding, the family of the groom sponsors the traditional last official event for the couple, the *Infair*.[54] Before the couple moves into their new dwelling, the newlyweds and the bride's family are invited to the home of the groom on a winter Saturday. Traditionally, the visitors arrive at about nine in the morning and talk, play games, and feast until mid-afternoon. Hostetler (1993, 198) states that the purpose of this occasion is to acknowledge that two kinship systems have joined to form a new, lifetime union. If one were to plan an effective transition strategy to incorporate and establish newlyweds as full participants into the adult community, it would probably look very much like what happens every January and February in the Lancaster settlement.

However, Amish newlyweds everywhere appear to adjust to marriage and adult responsibilities and expectations equally well in communities that do not have the post-wedding tradition of extended visiting and the *Infair*. The ability of the new couples to quickly assume their adult and matrimonial responsibilities is a testimony to the strength of the parents and community in preparing the couple for their lifetime commitment. From childhood, they have learned the importance of working hard, "giving themselves up" for the sake of others, and obeying God's commandments instead of following their own will or whims. All their lives they have been taught and have observed the distinct roles of husbands and wives, fathers and mothers. They have realistic expectations of what constitutes marriage and parenthood in the Amish community. It is little wonder that they adjust so quickly.

Except for ordinations or baptisms, weddings are the most important events in the life of the Amish community. The Amish regard the union between a man and woman to be as sacred and permanent as the union between an Amish individual and the church. Marriage is never an experiment as it often is in mainstream culture, because divorce is not an option.

The Amish point out that Christ sanctioned marriage and compared himself to a bridegroom and the church to his bride, thus validating both the importance of the church and of marriage.

The sanctity of marriage and the lifetime union that is required demand the constant attention of the entire society. Thus, the church service, the ceremony, and the activities of the wedding day must be under the sponsorship and control of the church. The stakes are too important to allow for the personal whims, desires, or shortcomings of any couple or family. A strong union culminates from the harmonious working of every aspect of the community. The community not only celebrates the union of two of their beloved *Youngie* but recognizes that each wedding bodes well for the future of Amish society. No wonder it is such a high time.

*The Amish will survive as long as they capture the hearts
and minds of their youth.*
Photo by Blair Seitz.

CHAPTER ELEVEN

The Future

Keeping Faith and Coming Home

If they still take us back after being on television,
they'll take us back no matter what we do.
—Mose Gingerich from UPN's *Amish in the City*

An Unpredictable Future

F ew Amish, old or young, likely spend much time ruminating about
the abstractions of successful identity formation or cultural viability.
Young people are more focused on the upcoming weekend than on abstract
speculations about the future of Amish society. Riding with one's friends
to a Saturday night get-together or deciding who to take home after the
Sunday night singing fills the minds of Amish youth. But their parents and
grandparents intuitively know that the battle for their society's survival will
ultimately be won or lost to the degree that their youth absorb an authentic
Amish identity.

   In their formative years, some youth will naturally move into Amish
adulthood, others will be tempted to leave for the more expressive or liberal
churches and lifestyles, and some, in fact, will succumb to the temptations

of the world.[1] Either most of the youth will embrace the Amish way, or the strands that form the fabric of their society will unravel.

The last Amish community in Europe succumbed in the 1930s, and the history of the Amish in North America recounts scores of failed settlements (Luthy 1986). Some collapsed under the weight of economic hardships or natural disasters, and some because of church disunity. On some occasions, entire congregations abandoned their Amish heritage for a more comfortable, "progressive," or evangelical vision of Anabaptist Christianity. The Amish mark these failures as a constant warning that their future is tenuous.

Few among them predict a sudden demise, but many wonder how long they can maintain traditional Amish values and practices in the face of modern society. Some elders in a large settlement worry that creeping change will destroy the essential core of Amish life. Furthermore, they fear that the "true Amish" are migrating out to the smaller settlements, leaving behind those who look the part but have lost their core of simplicity, community, and faithfulness.

"How much of our tradition can we give up and still be Amish?" an elder wondered. "When will we have become worldly on the inside and simply look Amish on the outside?" Leaders struggle with knowing how much and when to change. Amish at either end of the conservative-progressive spectrum agree that change, whether motivated by economic or by moral issues, inevitably happens. They know that it can contribute to either the survival or the destruction of their culture.

As we have already seen, an overriding concern among some Amish is the growing number of families who cannot make a living farming or raise their children on the farm. Too much available farmland is either already under cultivation or is turning into shopping malls, industrial developments, or housing tracts. Many Amish fear that the loss of a farm livelihood or home will diminish their future viability. Until the mid-twentieth century, Amish and farming were practically synonymous. Although the Amish never declared that farming was next to godliness, they certainly equated the two. In the past, most children learned to be Amish in the context of the farm. Farming reinforced the core values of hard work, simplicity, and separation from the world. "Besides," said an Amish farmer, "cities are dangerous and destructive. After Cain killed Abel, the Bible says that he went and founded a city. The country is the place to live and raise a family." "Time will tell how we Amish will do as a society," said a young business owner. "This generation is the first in which most of the children and youth have grown up off the farm." Kraybill contends that the occupational shift to business poses the most serious challenge to historic Amish values and viability.[2] Despite these concerns, many nonfarming Amish are successfully transmitting their heritage and rearing their children as faithful Amish adults. Farming may not be the most crucial ingredient for socialization. Results from research are contradictory. Greska and Korbin (2002) found that 23 percent of nonfarming families in Geauga County, Ohio, had at least one child who was no longer Amish, versus only 15 percent of farming families. Meyers (1994) found no differences in loss between farming and nonfarming families, but Eriksen et al. (1980) found that nonfarm families were nearly six times more likely to have at least one non-Amish child than farming families.[3]

Some Amish think that a more critical factor is the presence of fathers at home.[4] Amish fathers who work on construction crews or in factories are away from home far more than fathers who farm. Researchers have yet to study the influence of father-absence on Amish children, but its negative impact is well documented in mainstream society.[5]

Besides paying attention to their children's behavior and attitudes, parents worry about the influences that affect their children as they decide whether to follow Amish traditions. "Will our *Youngie* remain true, or will they walk or fall away?" parents wonder.

Of great encouragement to many Old Order Amish parents and leaders in the large settlements has been the movement toward the supervised singings that started in the 1990s in Holmes County. They rejoice that youth and their parents now have a choice for a "decent *Rumspringa*," one that resembles the lifestyle and values espoused by the church. They see this movement, initially suspect and stigmatized, now receiving widespread acceptance by parents and ministers. The one area that was troublesome and "out of control" for years is increasingly becoming an intrinsic part of a

seamless society. Few Amish express concern that the youth are being chan-
neled so carefully that they lack real choice. Rather, they believe that the new
groups are strengthening moral behavior and church values.

Over time, Amish leaders have watched the evolution and change being played out in other less-conservative groups around them, such as
the Beachy Amish and the New Order Amish. Ostensibly, the New Order
churches started out with concerns for the spiritual and moral well-being
of their youth and their society in general. Now the Old Orders note the
New Order's growing acceptance of telephones and electricity in the homes.
Members in some "electric" New Order settlements own microwaves and
hair dryers. In other settlements, members routinely drive to town or go on
picnics on their tractors and wagons.

Their Old Order neighbors wonder if televisions and cars will come next.
Furthermore, in two or three settlements, the New Order leaders regularly
conduct the church services in English, and church members no longer
need to learn Pennsylvania German.[6] In Lancaster County, the horse and
carriage New Order churches had declined precipitously in the latter decades of the last century. In 2001, an Old Order minister reported, "Of their
two districts around here, all of the youth in the one have left. The other one
is struggling to keep their few young people who are still there. Almost all of
their youth have moved into the Beachy church or other more progressive
Anabaptist groups. Once they move up, they rarely come back." His observations proved to be prophetic, because by 2006, the original New Order
church had virtually disappeared in Lancaster County.

Predictors of Defection

Those who study the Amish or the transmission of culture also examine the
factors that relate to retention and defection of the young. Two studies of
Indiana youth found that the fewer contacts one had with the outsiders the
more likely they were to remain Amish. "If we want our children to remain
pure, we have to reduce the dangers of the secular, corrupt world," say the
parents. In most settlements, they intentionally seek to limit close contact
between their children and "worldly youth" with their liberal ideas, wayward
pastimes, and alluring gadgets. One reason that Amish do not actively seek

converts may be their fear that seekers might infect the church and the youth with deeply ingrained worldly influences, attitudes, and habits.

Meyers' study (1994) suggests that the simple fact of rural isolation relates to retention and attrition. He examined family records from the Amish directory in northern Indiana and found that the highest level of defection occurred in families residing closest to towns.[7] If these results are typical of other settlements, they confirm the Amish suspicion that "going to town" is where they encounter worldly contacts, activities, and temptations that are inherently dangerous for youth.

Similarly, Meyers also found that children who attended public schools were almost twice as likely to defect as children who attended Amish private schools. In the area of Indiana where Reiling (2002) conducted her study on the Amish, 80 percent of the children attended public school. She also reports that their attrition rate to be 20–25 percent, a higher rate than is reported in most other Old Order communities. Hostetler and Huntington conclude, "For an individual to become Amish, the person must be kept within the Amish community, physically and emotionally, during the crucial adolescent years" (1992, 30).

The degree of isolation may explain why the most conservative affiliations, such as the Nebraska Amish of Pennsylvania and the Andy Weaver or Swartzentruber groups of Ohio, have higher retention rates than their more progressive counterparts in the Old and New Orders. Most Amish informants believe that the ultraconservative groups lose fewer than 5 percent of their youth, one-third the loss reported for many Old Order groups. In the greater Holmes County, Ohio, area, only 3.7 percent of the conservative Andy Weaver group chose not to be baptized, compared to 15.3 percent of the Old Order Youth (Friedrich and Donnermeyer 2003).

On the other hand, the more progressive New Order churches, by virtually everyone's estimations, have the highest defection rate of all. Some districts reportedly lose 50 percent or more of their youth to less-conservative Anabaptist groups, especially to the Beachy Amish. Again, Friedrich and Donnermeyer (2003) found that 43 percent of New Order youth chose not to be baptized into the Amish Church. "We are like mules," declared a New Order elder ruefully. "We work hard in our generation, but we don't reproduce."[8] According to Iannaccone's research (1994), religious groups that are more conservative, separatist, and demanding retain adherents better than more accommodating religious groups.[9]

A New Order father, seeking to understand this loss of their youth to more liberal Anabaptist groups, speculated, "Our emphasis on evangelical teaching, such as the new birth, personal holiness, and sharing our faith puts less importance on keeping traditional forms. It also makes our people more congenial and comfortable with the religious activities and services of liberal Anabaptists, such as Beachy Amish and conservative Mennonites."

Many New Order Amish admit to feeling a kinship with "higher" Anabaptist groups that emphasize adult baptism, nonresistance, assurance of salvation, evangelism, and foreign missions. Although the gap between typical Old Order Amish and Beachy Amish remains large, by allowing car ownership, worshiping in a meeting house, and holding church services in English, the step from New Order Amish to Beachy Amish is smaller. "After all," said an Old Order man, "New Order Amish are basically Beachy Amish without the cars."

Some Old Order people claim that the problem lies more in the example set by the New Order parents. As one Old Order deacon commented, "It's because the parents and their churches are change-minded and compromising. When the youth see the parents taking steps away from their traditions, they figure, 'If Dad and Mom can make a change, so can I.' But, of course, they keep going further." A New Order member mused that the youth leave primarily when they observe adults living by a list of rules rather than by a deeply held conviction.

In his study of Old Order Amish defection, Meyers (1994) found birth order to be another predictive family variable for leaving. He reported that defection among the first three children occurred much more frequently than among the rest of the siblings. Compared to the first two children's leaving, the likelihood of later-born children's leaving declined almost linearly. Meyers wrote, "Those most likely to reject the values of their parents appear to be in early sibling positions, and those who conserve the tradition come later in the family" (1994, 383). He does not speculate about why the oldest child is more likely to defect. On the other hand, Greska and Korbin (2002) found that in Geauga County, Ohio, the fourth largest Amish settlement, if the oldest child leaves the church, a younger sibling is four times more likely to leave than in families where the first-born joins the church and stays Amish.

In both Old Order and New Order settlements, males are most likely to leave. Ministers' reports and Amish community directories both reveal that women typically outnumber men beyond the expected male-female birth ratio.[10] This tendency, of course, is not limited to the Amish. It reflects the fact that in religious groups in Western society generally, females tend to be more faithful and committed to their religious beliefs and practices.[11] When asked why this might be so among the Amish, one young man remarked, "Boys find it harder to be obedient and submissive to the rules than girls." His father added, "Boys generally have more contact with the world, have more opportunities, and are more confident that they can make it out there than the girls," further evidence of the importance of separation.

Meyers' summary of defections in northern Indiana likely reflects the tendencies in other Amish settlements: "The profile of likely defectors would include males who are in early sibling positions, did not attend an Amish school, grew up in communities that to some extent have relaxed the *Ordnung,* and/or were in close proximity to urban areas and hence in more frequent contact with the dominant culture during the childhood years. Furthermore, if these males remain single and opt to leave the farm and begin their occupational lives in industry, they may have a tendency to become even more involved in 'English' society" (1994, 385). Youth in the small settlements generally remain more isolated from the surrounding society, and if Myers is correct, less likely to defect.

The Ties That Bind

Another factor that affects retention in the collectivist society of the Amish is that the young people do not simply leave a church. Instead, they abandon an all-pervasive way of life, one reinforced by the entire community and especially by their parents. As a young Amishman struggling with the decision of whether to leave related, "The thing that keeps many of us from leaving is knowing that we will deeply hurt our parents if we go. Most Amish youth have great respect for their parents." On the other hand, some Amish believe that a disproportionate number of defectors experienced some kind of abuse in their families, although no systematic studies have been done in this area.[12]

Since parents fear for their wayward children's salvation and eternal destiny, most youth are reluctant to provoke this kind of heartbreak and pain. In addition, many youth believe that if they join the church but later break their membership vows and leave, they will go to hell when they die. An Amishman explained, "We're taught that if we leave, if you don't stay with what you were raised in, and honor your parents, which they say is doing exactly as I tell you to, if you're not honoring me, then you'll go to Hell."[13] Reiling reports that in her sample of the twenty ex-Amish she interviewed, "almost every one of the defected coethnics [former Amish] reported still fearing for their salvation, even though they had subsequently joined a Christian church that did accept John 3:16 as the plan of salvation" (2002, 159). In another state, a young man who left the church for theological reasons found his confidence in his decision profoundly shaken two years later, after hearing the Amish bishop at an Old Order funeral announce that this former member was going to hell for breaking his membership vows. So for some, if not many, fear of damnation likely motivates them to "stay with the church."

Not only will some young people remain Amish out of fear, but the community is structured in ways that tangibly benefit those who choose to join and stay. Young couples receive financial support from their families when establishing their own homes. Also, children who become members often receive part of their family inheritance even before the parents die. As a further enticement, some have reportedly promised their girls new clothes and their boys state-of-the-art carriages or other possessions when they join the church. In more extreme cases, parents have offered a wayward child a house or a farm if he would return to the fold.

A more immediate enticement for remaining is that in some Old and New Order settlements, youth must first become church members before they are permitted to court, and all settlements require church membership as a condition for marriage. Not a few Amishmen admit that an Amish sweetheart was a powerful motivator in bringing them into the fold. For example, an Amishman widely known for his independent tendencies was asked why, despite serious reservations as a young man, he decided to join the church. "I had found this cute little thing at a singing, and she wanted to be Amish," he acknowledged. "I ended up marrying her at twenty-two since I was afraid somebody else would get her."

Since girls generally join the church at an earlier age than do the boys, her status as a member provides an additional incentive for the young man to eventually join. An Amish woman whose future husband lived a worldly life for more than ten years before joining the church explained, "If the boy is leading a very worldly life, the girl will be more conservative and he won't be able talk her into leaving." Her own experience convinced her that an Amish boy will be more likely to join too rather than persuade his girlfriend to break her membership vows.

Another possible reason for young men joining or staying relates to their status as conscientious objectors. Historically, only Amish church members in good standing have been automatically exempted from military service. To the embarrassment of church leaders and the satisfaction of critics of the Amish, baptisms and church membership among young males increase disproportionately during times of national conscription or military action. One writer reported that in his community in the summer of 1942, "Many joined during that period because the country had entered World War II, and it was hard to get a nonresistant status if you did not belong to a church" (Renno 1993, 69). An Amish grandfather recounts that he joined the church in the 1950s to avoid the draft. This membership surge also occurred during the Vietnam War.

Some young people reputedly stay Amish because they fear they are neither educationally nor emotionally prepared for life in the outside world. This may be especially true in the groups that seek to reduce their contact with mainstream society. Defectors report that they sometimes delayed leaving for fear that their eighth-grade education and limited use of English would hinder them from making a living in the outside world. Finally, some wavering youth may simply remain Amish because of inertia. It is much easier to stay than to go through the inevitable changes and stresses required by leaving.

Despite concerns about the future of Amish society, many Amish adults discount the predictions that Amish youth and Amish life in the large settlements are drifting. Some cite signs of a conservative shift among the youth.

As evidence, they point to the growth of alternate adult-supervised singings in the large settlements as a healthy sign. An Amish grandfather who attended an Eagles singing in Lancaster County remarked, "I could hardly believe what I was seeing. The young folk came in, sat down, behaved, sang well all evening—it was amazing to know that this kind of singing was possible."

Growing numbers of young people are joining groups that require an alcohol- and drug-free environment for young people who are tired or disgusted with the party life and who are looking for "a more decent way." For example, in Lancaster County, the Hummingbirds and the Eagles, organized in the late 1990s, were two of the first supervised Lancaster County groups. By 2006 both groups had grown so fast that each had divided into five regional groups. Two additional supervised groups, the Parakeets and the Falcons, formed in the early part of the twenty-first century. Altogether, these alternative groups involved a thousand young people, more than 40 percent of the estimated youth in Lancaster County in 2006.

In other large settlements, the alternative groups are among the fastest growing. Observers maintain that in many communities, young people in general are drinking, smoking, and partying less than their parents did in the 1960s and 70s. Some adults report, "We had band hops and hoedowns way more often in our day than our own children have."

A minister's comment is typical: "I am thankful but sort of ashamed to say that my own children have been much easier for me to handle than I was for my parents." Also, a mother who was with the youth in the late 1970s believes that the kind of parties they had then may be over. "It's very rare to have one band hop a year now. Most of the youth just aren't into it anymore," she said.[14]

Finally, in some communities, parents indicate that the age of joining the church is again going down, a trend they interpret optimistically. However, some Amish still express concern about the integrity of the church. "I believe," said a mother, "we have become so tolerant of things that the *Youngie* can now join and still do what they want."

In most Amish communities, it is debatable whether times are better or worse today. Certainly many youth continue to stray for a time and "sow their wild oats" during their *Rumspringa*. Almost all Amish parents decry the worldly excesses of the youth. However, some adults still wonder if it is not a good idea for the *Youngie* to "go and get it out of their system."

In her extensive study of the early *Rumspringa* experience in a large settlement, Reiling concluded that their youth overwhelmingly believed that the adults of the community expected them to experiment with worldly behavior for a time in order that the weak and unworthy "be 'weeded out early lest they infect the rest of the group.' . . . For this selection process to be fully effective, the individual must have the opportunity to deny the profane by being exposed to temptation. This belief prevents Amish parents from acting against, and in many cases causes them to condone and even encourage, the more serious forms of deviance, such as the consumption of alcohol" (2002, 148).

Whether or not her conclusions are valid, it is true that for most plain youth their friends remain their primary reference group, whether wayward or obedient. Not only can one's peers pull him or her away, but they can also exert a potent influence on each other to become part of the fold. There is both danger and safety in numbers.

All who would become part of the Amish community, both obedient and rebellious, must choose to submit to the requirements of the *Ordnung*. Kraybill thinks that the very act of choosing whether to join or leave is the key to Amish viability and retention. He theorizes that such an act serves a strong sociological and psychological function by giving each youth a sense of having chosen his or her destiny. In whatever kind of community, perceived choice strengthens one's commitment and satisfaction. Kraybill believes that this freedom to choose is what helps bring the wayward youth back. Although they may taste and test the world, the majority return to become upstanding, responsible Amish members. In his judgment, the choice acts as the linchpin for increasing an individual's future adult loyalty.[15]

The Tug of the Family

Despite ongoing concerns and problems facing young people and parents, in most settlements their relationship appears strong, and the parent-teen stresses temporary and manageable. One reason may be that most Amish grow up in stable families. Couples commit to each other and to the well-being of their family members for life. Amish parents emphasize the importance of early "training" and the establishment of a strong parent-child attachment.[16] One cannot read the articles, letters, and editorials in the Amish periodicals without sensing the central position that family and parenting play. Parents want their children to learn obedience at home as a precursor for later obedience to the church and to God.

Some developmental psychologists might characterize Amish parents as coercive and oppressive. They would likely cite the Amish belief in corporal punishment for children, the parents' rigorous work demands, and perhaps most of all, their requirement of strict, unquestioning obedience. However, Amish parents believe that these expectations in themselves are not the problem; rather, it is these expectations in the absence of warmth and loving care that produce rebelliousness or emotional maladjustments. On the other hand, they also believe that warmth without boundaries too often produces questioning, dissatisfied youth who tend to abandon the Amish faith.

Outsiders likely underestimate the amount of love and security that most Amish children feel. A young man described as "independent-minded" explained, "Most of us really respect our parents and do not want to hurt them. That's one of the main reasons we stay Amish." Of course, parents are not the only ones who offer a sense of acceptance and belonging to the youth. When it becomes apparent in the community that one of their own is on a seriously wayward trajectory, many relatives, friends, and ministers exert their considerable influence on the errant individuals. Shachtman (2006) shows how the community can mobilize to bring the lost one back. Simply knowing that these pressures will be brought to bear may serve as a deterrent to some who consider leaving.

Ultimately, however, the extent to which parents succeed in establishing a bond and a secure attachment with their children is probably the critical factor in whether a child decides to leave or stay. Amish parents certainly believe that their influence is the key. It is this belief that makes parenting such a high-stakes endeavor and such a high priority in their lives. Meanwhile, they take seriously the scriptural admonition to "train up a child in the way he should go." They believe that this early training is crucial in that it occurs at the time when their children are open to receive the parents' instruction and example. With confidence, parents also take comfort in the promise attached to the early training admonition: "and when he is old, he will not depart from it" (Proverbs 22: 6).

Coming Home

The enduring power of those early teachings and experiences reveals itself in the way some wanderers, young and old, return. Pauline Stevick (2006) recounts the story of Andy, an Amish prodigal son who left home to live with English friends, returning months later, "filthy and penniless." Andy did not immediately repent or change his ways, but he eventually took instruction for baptism, sold his truck, and quit drinking. Today he is "with the church," and his parents confided that they would not be surprised if he becomes a minister. A man who grew up in Lancaster County rejected the Amish way in his youth and lived more than sixty years in the world. He would spend many winters in Pinecraft, Florida, and most people regarded him as an eccentric troublemaker. "Jakie was loud, obnoxious, and aggressive—not very loveable," said an Amish grandfather who knew him for years. "I always felt sad when people talked about him and treated him badly. But he needed to be loved, just as all the rest of us sinners."

When Jakie was eighty-six, he returned to Lancaster County and asked if he could be "taken back up" into the church. Not everyone was convinced that it was a good idea, but when he repented for his unfaithfulness, he was fully restored into the church. The following spring he took communion, died in less than a week, and was buried in the Amish cemetery. Everyone believed that even though he had lived a wayward and tragic life, God was merciful and the church could be no less.

Another example of mercy and forgiveness occurred about a year before Jakie's return in the way the Lancaster Amish community responded to the two young men arrested for trafficking in cocaine. Parents universally expressed sadness that such events had transpired among their youth. The fact that the offenders were not church members but "in the world" at the time of their arrest did little to diminish the pain. A minister who sought to distance the Amish community from the two offenders by pointing out that they were not really baptized Amish was roundly criticized for his statements.

Although everyone was relieved that the two were discovered and apprehended, the community grieved that their own offspring had become caught up in such illegal, destructive, and ungodly practices. Adults were shocked to learn that the culprits bought the cocaine from members of the Pagans motorcycle gang. They were even more dismayed to learn that these connections developed when the defendants hired some Pagans to work for them on their roofing crews. The Amish evidently began to do drugs with the Pagans, then bought drugs from them, and eventually sold drugs to their Amish peers.

When they were finally arrested, the defendants initially pleaded not guilty at the advice of their attorney. This strategy met with universal disapproval by the Amish community. Most Amish agreed: "If they're guilty, they should plead guilty, even if their lawyer says that this is not the best strategy." The Amish ideal has always been to tell the truth, confess one's wrong, and accept the consequences. Many Amish hoped that the court would make an example of these young men. "They should be found guilty and serve time in jail for what they did," some elders explained. "It will be a lesson to all of the *Youngie* who have been doing wrong," said a grandmother. Few, however, hoped for the forty-year maximum prison term.

More than three months after their arrest, the two defendants changed their plea to guilty of conspiracy to deliver cocaine. They had been charged with buying, using, and distributing cocaine with a street value of $100,000. The community regarded this shift as a hopeful sign for the *Youngie*: they had indeed done wrong, but they were willing to repent.

Actually, the offenders had been cooperating for months as informants for the FBI since the police discovered their dealings with the Pagans. After their arrest, the FBI required that as part of their community service they should speak at a series of meetings to inform and warn Amish and plain Mennonite youth and parents about the dangers of drug use. The eight public meetings reached several thousand individuals with testimonials from the two convicted youth and warnings from the FBI, Pennsylvania State Police, defense and prosecuting attorneys, and drug experts.

The meetings sometimes lasted four hours. Those in charge knew that if the press found out about them and wrote about it, many plain people would shy away from the events. Consequently, the organizers charged the parents and youth to keep news of what was happening totally confidential. At times they even asked all in attendance to look at the person on either side of them and immediately report the presence of anybody they did not know to those in charge. Everyone complied.

Consequently, the media never learned about the meetings until after they were completed. One Amishman said, "We feel this was inspired by a higher power, like it was just orchestrated by the good Lord. It seemed that as soon as one meeting was over, the leaders thought there should be more. It's ironic that a conservative group like ours needed help, but we needed help."[17] Skeptics, both within and outside the Amish community, expressed doubts about the two young men's motivation. "Sure they're willing to speak out about drugs now since it certainly won't hurt them when it comes time for sentencing."

On the day of sentencing at the U.S. Federal Court in Philadelphia, dozens of reporters and photographers from state and national news services thronged the courthouse, awaiting the outcome for these young men who had shamed their community, saddened their families, and grabbed unwanted national and international attention. But unlike many confessed felons, these two did not have to face the judge and their sentencing alone. As they waited inside the courthouse, more than a hundred solemn relatives, friends, and supporters strode somberly together with their errant sons' attorney to the judge's chamber. Their *Youngie* had done wrong—terribly wrong—and nobody knew this better than this group of supporters. But like the prodigal son, these two sons had also come to their senses and confessed their wrongdoing.

At their sentencing, each expressed his apologies to the community for what he had done: "When I was a teenager, I got into the wrong crowd," Abner Stoltzfus, of Ronks, said. "It was a miserable life I led. I didn't know it then, but I know it now. I apologize from the bottom of my heart to my family for the embarrassment and pain I've caused." Abner King Stoltzfus, pausing several times to collect himself, also expressed remorse. "We lived a terrible life for awhile," he said, stopping to wipe his eyes, as many others in the gallery did. "We want to make it better."[18]

Everyone agreed that after they had completed their obligations to the state, they were welcome to return and to be reconciled with their families and community. The community would be ready to receive their fallen ones—their precious fallen ones—back into the fold.[19] What was required of them to be fully "taken up" was the same as for other youth: a desire to be part of the church, repentance for their sins, instruction in the beliefs and practices of the church, baptism, church membership, and a willingness to submit to the church *Ordnung* for the rest of their lives.

Despite their past offenses, they could be accepted as full-fledged Amish. One became a member of the Old Order church and subsequently married an Amish girl in 2001. The other first joined the conservative Spring Garden Church, a church with Anabaptist roots, and later switched to a local charismatic Bible church.

Not all Amish are forgiving, nor do all stories end happily or redemptively. Sometimes parents harbor bitterness along with their sorrow and shame when their children leave the faith, and the breach is never restored. However, in many ways the Amish are realists when it comes to human shortcomings and sins. "We are human just like everybody else," they often say, "and we struggle with sin and must be forgiven." As collectivists, however, they may worry less about personal sins than about losing their communal soul, their core, their distinctives, and their identity. They believe, of course, that only God knows the future. All they know is that even if the way is perilous, they have been called to faithful obedience to God and to vigilance in their duties.

As the Swartzentruber bishop who as a teenager joined the U.S. Air Force explained, "I don't think that the Amish are the only ones who will get to heaven. But I do believe that if you have been born Amish, you should stay Amish and be a good Amish member." Thus parents, both Old Order and New Order, labor to impart their faith and lifestyle to their children and youth so that when they arrive at their time of decision, they will naturally choose the Amish way, just as their parents and ancestors have done for more than three hundred years. Parents believe that by remaining faithful, they can confidently entrust the future of their children and the future of their society to God. This was the hope that prompted the mother of that straying son to frequently set his place at the family table for four years while he was in the air force.

His homecoming and others like it serve as a reminder to Amish parents of God's loving faithfulness and helps provide them with a sense of comfort and purpose amid the inevitable uncertainties, disappointments, and vicissitudes of life. Stories like this also remind wayward youth, even Amish in the city, that they can return to the church and their families if they will repent, renounce their non-Amish ways and ideas, and commit themselves to the demands of the church and the faith.

Parents see themselves as co-laborers with God, both to shape the direction of the lives of their children and to cultivate and nurture their growth as the next generation of Amish adults. Although parents believe that God will surely help them, they also believe the adage that "God helps those who help themselves." Thus, as an Amish community and as individual couples, they diligently and intentionally work to construct for themselves and their children a social world that includes extended family, schooling, work, social events, courtship, and marriage. All of these provide gravitational forces that keep their youth in the Amish orbit and exert strong pressures to pull the wayward back from their *rumspringa* wanderings. This careful attention, along with high parental and community involvement with their sons and daughters, provides a strong Amish identity and helps explain the amazing retention, growth, and longevity of the Amish. They trust that as long as they maintain their vigilance, with God's help their future viability will continue through the generations to come.

German Word Usage

Use in Text	Form	English Translation
Ahroth	PG	Sunday morning ministers' council
Ausbund	SG	the principal Amish hymnal
Bann	SG	to excommunicate (v.); excommunication (n.)
Bouve	PG	young men
Deutsch	SG	German
Eck	PG	wedding corner
Eck balle	PG	cornerball game
Ecktender	PG	wedding corner helpers
Freindschaft	PG	extended family
Fressdisch	PG	midnight meal of wedding leftovers
Grumbierleit	PG	team in charge of preparing mashed potatoes at weddings
Hochmut	SG	pride
Hochzeit	SG	wedding
Kapp	PG	female's head covering

Note: PG, Pennsylvania German; SG, Standard German.

German Word Usage, *continued*

Use in Text	Form	English Translation
Liedersammlung	SG	the "thin" songbook
Loblied	SG	Praise Song, the second hymn sung in all Amish churches
Mosch	PG	cornerball playing field
Nacht Roch	PG	night dress
Newehocke	PG	wedding attendants
Newesitzer	PG	wedding attendants
onstlich	PG	in earnest
Ordnung	SG	church rules
Ring spiele	PG	traditional Amish dance
Roascht	PG	chicken and stuffing dish at weddings
Rumspringa	PG	running-around period for youth
Schnitz	PG	dried apples
Schul	PG	school
streng Meidung	PG	strict shunning
Sunndaagschul	PG	Sunday school
Uneheliche beischlof	PG	bed courtship
Unpartheyisches Gesang-Buch	SG	an important German songbook
Vorgeher	PG	ushers at a wedding
Vorsingers	PG	church song leaders
Youngie	PG	young people
Yung-g'heierditricks	PG	entertaining tricks and stunts
Zeugnis	SG	testimony

Note: PG, Pennsylvania German; SG, Standard German.

Notes

Preface

1. Luthy (1997) writes that the Japanese interest in the Amish was evident as early as 1972, when the *Japan Times*, a leading newspaper, provided major coverage of *Wisconsin v. Yoder*, the U.S. Supreme Court ruling that exempted Amish youth from attending high school.

2. Films such as *King Pin*, *For Richer or Poorer*, the Hallmark Hall of Fame presentation *Harvest of Fire*, the Cinemax documentary *Devil's Playground*, and even the MTV parody *Amish Paradise* revealed the media's interest in the Amish. David Weaver-Zercher (2001) has written an excellent and engaging study on the marketing of the Amish.

3. The five youths lived with six non-Amish young adults for several weeks in a house provided by UPN in Hollywood Hills. Several members of Congress, including Representative Joe Pitts, who represents portions of Lancaster and Chester counties in Pennsylvania, tried to block the show's release, claiming that it would ridicule the Amish. The UPN Web site www.upn.com featured several positive reviews of the series, along with biographies and video clips of each participant.

4. The media have also portrayed the Amish less favorably. ABC's *20/20* aired a segment, "The Secret of the Amish," that focused on alleged child abuse, incest, and a power-hungry bishop in an Ohio settlement. ABC ran the segment on 21 February 1997 and again on 25 July 1997. In October 1998, CBS's Bryant Gumbel featured an interview with two young men describing drug use

among Amish youth in their community. Late in 2004, ABC and NBC featured segments on the same night on sexual abuse in two conservative Amish families. Other negative depictions include those by Ottie Garrett (1998) and his Amish-reared wife, Ruth Garrett (2001, 2004). Lucy Walker's *Devil's Playground* (2002) portrays deviance among some Amish youth in northern Indiana, one of whom spent $100 per day on his methamphetamine addiction. Tom Shachtman (2006) based some of his book *Rumspringa* on transcripts of unused interviews and on follow-up interviews with several of the principals in *Devil's Playground*. Burkholder's (2006) description of growing up in Iowa portrays a dysfunctional family and community.

5. The division occurred in 1966 and eventually resulted in the formation of several small, more progressive groups. See one perspective of the division in *New Order Amish Directory* (1999, 127).

6. I was not alone in forecasting the demise of the Amish. Hostetler (1977, 353) reports that academics in the 1950s were predicting that the Amish would be assimilated into mainstream society "within a few decades."

7. A mother objected to my talking to her twenty-two-year-old son for this study, so I discontinued our conversations about youth activities and issues. I still remain friends with both of them. Also a great-grandfather wondered why I needed to write in such specific detail. We had a good-spirited conversation on the nature of cultural studies and research, and we also remain friends.

Chapter One. Amish Life

1. *Amish in the City* did not become the 2004 reality series hit that its producers might have wished for, although initially it did attract a flurry of media attention. UPN reported that it was its Wednesday night program most watched by young adult viewers in three years, with 5.4 million viewers its first night. It also attracted more viewers in its time slot than any of the three major networks that night.

2. All scripture in this book is quoted from the King James Version of the Bible, the preferred version of the Amish when they refer to an English translation.

3. Six months after the series was over, thousands who attended the Gordonville, Pennsylvania, fire department's annual fund-raising auction and "mud sale" saw four non-Amish teenage girls carrying a placard with a picture of Mose Gingerich that asked, "Have you seen this man?" As ardent fans, they

were evidently hoping to get information of his current whereabouts from one of the many Amish who were at the sale. On 14 August 2005, an article on theage.com.au Web site reported that Mose and his unbaptized 18-year-old brother had started a construction business in Missouri, but Mose had not returned to the Amish fold.

4. See P. Yoder (1993) for an excellent discussion of the Amish view of the state.

5. See Dyck (1993) for his treatment of the formative years of Anabaptism.

6. In a marked departure from their commitment to nonresistance, a group of zealots from Germany opted to establish an Anabaptist state by force. These radicals captured Munster in 1534 but were decisively defeated by a makeshift local army of Catholics and Reformed Protestants. This incident further incited resentment and hostility against the Anabaptists, who were already widely persecuted. See Nolt (2003, 15–18).

7. This tome, first published in 1660, is nearly 1,500 pages long and includes more than one hundred graphic illustrations of Anabaptist persecution and death (Braght 1998). A good introduction to the book is *Mirror of the Martyrs* by Oyer and Kreider (1990).

8. Some of this historical material appeared originally in R. Stevick (2001, 159–72). Clasen (1972) provides a detailed treatment of this turbulent period in Anabaptist history. The most comprehensive treatment of Amish history is Nolt's *History of the Amish* (2003).

9. The major biblical passages used to support this belief are 1 Corinthians 5:9–11; 2 Thessalonians 3:14; Titus 3:10–11; Romans 16:17.

10. Some Amish are not averse to voting in local issues that directly affect them, such as road or zoning decisions. In one area, according to a local resident, a number of them "voted against Clinton" in the 1996 presidential election. In the swing states of Ohio and Pennsylvania, Republicans actively sought the Amish vote in the 2004 presidential elections.

11. The Amish specifically refer to Matthew 5:33–48.

12. Ministers frequently quote 1 Corinthians 11:3, 1 Peter 3:1–6, and Titus 2:3–5 in support of male headship.

13. Baby girls are excluded from this requirement, and in some settlements, girls do not regularly wear coverings until they are about twelve or thirteen years old.

14. Perhaps for the historical reason of traveling long distances to church by horse and carriage, the Amish in North America have always held their worship

services every other week. The "off" Sunday is typically spent at home or visiting other churches, relatives, or friends.

15. "Dutch" is a corruption of the word *Deutsch,* the German word for German. Their spoken dialect should actually be called Pennsylvania German.

16. In reality, more than three affiliations exist because of ongoing internal divisions. For example, even though the Nebraska Amish look alike, they have subdivided into at least three distinct groups, each with its own *Ordnung.*

17. Another split occurred in Holmes County in 1986 that resulted in a group known as the *New* New Order Amish. They have many of the same values and tendencies of the original New Order group, including the propensity for many of their youth to defect to the Beachy Amish and conservative Mennonite churches. "It's not a large group because many of the youth have left," a New Order member observed.

18. The two largest settlements, Lancaster County, Pennsylvania, and Elkhart-Lagrange counties in Indiana, are much more homogeneous than the Holmes County, Ohio, settlement. One reason for the homogeneity in the Lancaster settlement is that all of the bishops meet together semi-annually to form policies and work out differences. This leads to more uniformity in Lancaster than in the other large settlements.

19. See Kraybill and Bowman (2001, 105); Kraybill (2001, 336); and Kraybill and Hostetter (2001, 177–208).

20. A highly regarded Lancaster County Amishman recognized as a community historian (personal conversation with the author, July 2000).

21. For example, in 1960, Lancaster estimates for total Amish population were 5,570; in 2000 they were 22,300. "Lancaster's settlement expanded from merely six church districts in 1878 to sixty-five by 1980. In the twenty-year period between 1980 and 2000, the number of districts more than doubled" (Kraybill 2001, 17, 335).

22. S. Stoltzfus (1994) describes how the area of one of the original church districts in Lancaster County was divided and subdivided over the years to accommodate a growing population. These divisions dramatically reduced the size of each district.

23. See the section on population and density in Hostetler (1993, 355–60).

24. Social psychologists call this phenomenon group polarization. It helps to explain why one's initial tendencies toward certain behaviors or beliefs intensify in the presence of like-minded peers. David G. Myers (2005, 303–11), one of

the early researchers in group polarization, has written an excellent summary of the theory and findings of this phenomenon.

25. Sociologist Ruth Benedict (1934) first discussed the continuous-discontinuous distinction. Also see Steinberg (2005, 113–18) for a helpful discussion of the topic.

Chapter Two. Socialization

1. For whatever reason, this lack of attention to adolescent religious experience also occurs in developmental textbooks on adolescence. Typically, authors devote fewer than five pages to this subject.

2. Some Amish believe that the ability of the young to understand German has actually increased since the rise of the Amish private school movement and subsequent instruction.

3. Although Sunday schools are usually associated with New Order Amish, a few Old Order churches in Indiana, Iowa, and elsewhere, have Sunday school in the summer.

4. Quoted in Bachman (1961, 143).

5. Occasionally Amish men and English outsiders teach in Amish schools, but the bulk of the teachers are single Amish women. Regardless of their background, teachers need to be sympathetic with Amish beliefs and practices.

6. In 1984 Pathway Publishers of Aylmer, Ontario, published an English translation of this book entitled *A Devoted Christian's Prayer Book*.

7. An Amish bishop estimated that fewer than 15 percent of Amish members have struggled with whether or not to remain Amish. However, a nearby married couple in their thirties estimated almost twice that many.

8. Both periodicals are produced by Pathway Publishers in Aylmer, Ontario. A few of the most conservative affiliations, such as the Swartzentruber Amish and the Lawrence County, Pennsylvania, group do not approve of these publications.

9. Most church districts offer membership instruction annually or bi-annually, following the spring communion. If a young person decides not to enroll in instruction, it could mean a delay of at least a year and possibly two, unless he or she receives permission to take instruction in a neighboring church district that is on a different yearly schedule. In some places, youth are permitted to miss the first two instruction sessions and still join their peers on the third.

10. Pathway Publishers produced an English translation of the *Dordrecht*

Confession of Faith. M. Miller (2000, 114–47) also has a parallel translation of the Articles.

11. The latter point was one of the divisive issues which caused Jakob Ammann to split from the main Mennonite body in 1693.

12. The exact wording may vary slightly among the affiliations, but the basic questions remain the same. *Handbuch fur Bischof* (1978, 26), *In Meiner Jugend* (2000, 190–191), and *Gemein Ordnungen von Lancaster Co., PA* (n.d.:6) demonstrate the variations. M. Miller (2000, 246–47) has an English translation of the vows used in Lancaster County, Pennsylvania.

13. *Handbuch fur Bischof* (1978) details ministerial procedures.

14. Lecture given at Elizabethtown College, May 1993.

15. Quoted in Bachman (1961, 144).

16. A number of anonymously written booklets identified as "An Amish Brotherhood Publication" can be found in certain bookstores and tourist venues in Holmes County, Ohio. For example, they have published *What Makes for a Strong Nation? A Sure Path for Mankind, What Shall I Wear?* and *Teaching Emphases That Hinder Discipleship.* A longer book, *The Truth in Word and Work,* explains some New Order beliefs and practices in more detail.

17. See Lapp's *Weavertown Church History* (2003) for details on the group's origins and distinctives.

18. R. Stevick (2001, 171). The Amish always emphasize the quiet witness of their deeds over theology or creeds.

19. Some New Order churches will switch to English if they have visitors who do not speak Pennsylvania German. Ministers in one New Order settlement with several converts preach all of their sermons in English, and at least two Old Order churches provide simultaneous translation in English for guests who do not understand the language.

20. An Old Order man related that when the young men returned late to the church service from an extended break, interrupting the sermon of a visiting minister, he stopped preaching and exclaimed, "You boys really get on my nerves coming in late like this." However, a public rebuke like this would be very rare from either Old or New Order ministers.

21. A number of Old Order churches also reject these practices.

22. One must use caution in extrapolating these findings to all New Order groups. Also, these questions may have been edited or screened by the elders before they were distributed.

23. The conservative Swartzentruber Amish also reported disruptions of

their singings by other Amish. Therefore, the harassment may have been indiscriminately targeted at any outside Amish youth rather than just at the "goodie-goodies."

24. *Family Life* (October 1968), in Igou (1999, 188).

25. *Family Life* (December 1974, 7).

26. Responding to this statement, one church member stated, "It makes me feel sad to hear comments like this, but it is true. Our ministers warn us all the time that this is not the true way to salvation, and deep in their hearts most Amish know this. We are told living the Amish lifestyle is very important, but without salvation it is nothing."

27. Even though New Order youth have fewer cars while at home, many of their parents concede that Old Order youth are likely to give up their cars, whereas New Order youth with cars are more likely to leave the Amish for a Mennonite group.

28. *New Order Amish Directory* (1999).

Chapter Three. Adolescence

1. James Marcia (1994, 153), the leading contemporary researcher in adolescent identity issues, defines identity as follows: "Identity refers to a coherent sense of one's meaning to oneself and to others within that social context. This sense of identity suggests an individual's continuity with the past, a personally meaningful present, and a direction for the future." Also Steinberg (2005, 264–65) has a succinct but helpful introduction to identity theory.

2. Developmental psychologists James Marcia (1980, 1994) and Erik Erikson (1968, 1980) describe this period of exploration as a moratorium, a by-product of a complex society that temporarily relaxes expectations for mature performance and behavior.

3. After reading this paragraph, a mother from a large settlement wrote, "For the most part yes, but 50 dresses for a teenage girl is frugal?" She reported that by the time they counted their outfits for Saturday night, Sunday church, and Sunday night, her daughters and their friends easily had that many dresses. Obviously those girls do worry about looking good and keeping up with the latest fashions. (Letter to the author, 10 August 2004.)

4. An exception to plain, utilitarian attire is that boys in the conservative horse-and-buggy groups in Lancaster County wear bow ties when they dress up.

5. An informal survey was done among Amish attending a county fair and discussed on an ABC special, *Happiness*, by John Stossel, aired 15 April 1996.

6. Upon reading this section, a convert to the Amish wrote, "I agree. The children are *so* loved and accepted."

7. Presentation at Young Center, Elizabethtown College (May 1991).

8. Platte et al. (2000) concluded from their research that "young Amish people do not show the body image problems characteristic of young persons in Western industrial society." The only documented case of anorexia occurred in a Swartzentruber Amish settlement in Tennessee, where five teenage girls exhibited anorexic behavior. Community members attributed the problem to parasites. Medical specialists at Vanderbilt diagnosed it as a form of mass hysteria (Cassady et al. 2006). The possibility of underreporting always exists, but this author has heard of fewer than ten cases of anorexia in his fifteen years of contact with the Amish. An article, "A Thin Shadow," in *Young Companion* (July 1999, 14–15) featured the first reference to the dangers of excessive concern about thinness. The first extensive treatment of eating disorders appeared in the "Problem Corner" section of the May 2006 issue of *Family Life*. The entire section (29–34) was devoted to anorexia and bulimia among Amish and Old Order Mennonite young women. Ten girls or women wrote in, all of whom had either personally experienced such a disorder or had a family member who did. The editor received more letters on the subject than he could print. Meanwhile, most Amish and outside observers believe that the plain people have proportionately fewer incidences of these disorders than do mainstream adolescents. An Amish writer speculated, "Girls in your society have to be more concerned about their appearance than our girls do. Your girls have to attract a boy from such a wide field. Our girls have a much smaller field to worry about and they can be pretty sure that somewhere in their group is a boy for them." In time, it should become apparent whether there is an increase in these disorders or simply a more open attitude to recognize this problem among the plain people.

9. In the faster gangs of the large settlements, on the other hand, it is likely that the young person's sense of well-being resembles that of the mainstream culture with its emphasis on consumerism, fashion, and pleasure. Their identity acquisition may be tied into the kind of autonomy and achievement issues that face youth in mainstream America.

10. See 1 Timothy 2:11–12; 1 Corinthians 14:34–35.

11. Moustaches are forbidden among all Amish men except in one or two

New Order settlements. Amish explain this prohibition as a reaction against the moustaches worn by their European military persecutors.

12. Kraybill found that 20 percent of Amish businesses are operated by women, but their ownership is traditionally gendered, e.g., women will not own construction businesses or welding shops. See Kraybill and Nolt (2004, 208–9).

13. When the Amish monthly, *The Diary*, prints its column requesting pen pals, the seekers are virtually all females.

14. Adults in a large settlement reported in 2006 that a few young men had their own small outbuildings behind their houses equipped with a TV, DVD player, and computer. Another observer reported spotting a small satellite dish attached to the corner of the barn. It was connected to a son's *rumspringa* TV.

15. An Amish father wrote, "This sets the pattern of a male being dominant because girls must get rides from boys to go to gangs and singings. Girls are dependent on the boys."

16. This parallels Batson and Ventis's (1982) findings, which indicate that in North America women typically outnumber men in religious expression and church attendance.

17. Despite their weekly waywardness, virtually all youth still wear traditional clothing for church. However, a Lancaster County Amishman claimed to have seen an Amish girl dressed in blue jeans at house church in Indiana.

18. If one's family also leaves, or if several families leave together because of a formal church division or split, the emotional consequences on individuals are likely less severe than if an individual leaves alone. Also, most Amish would agree that not joining the church and thereby avoiding shunning is less painful than joining the church and then leaving.

19. See McNamara (1997).

20. In October 1998, a significant exception to their silence occurred in an interview with two young men from Amish families shown on the CBS program *Public Eye* with Bryant Gumbel. Besides stating his belief that 10 to 15 percent of Amish youth in that settlement experimented with drugs, one of them demonstrated in precise detail how he smoked crack cocaine at an Amish party. Another notable exception occurred when several youth from northern Indiana cooperated with Lucy Walker, director of *Devil's Playground,* and allowed themselves to be interviewed and photographed extensively.

21. Even the young man who demonstrated how to smoke crack cocaine on CBS's *Public Eye* indicated that he planned eventually to "settle down" and join the church.

Chapter Four. Schooling

1. Johnson-Weiner (2006) has written the most comprehensive scholarly book on Amish education.

2. *Wired* magazine featured an article on the Amish and cell phones. See Rheingold (1999, 128–31, 160–63). Umble (1994, 1996) provides an excellent background regarding telephones and the Amish.

3. See Huntington (1994, 77–95), and Meyers (1993, 86–106).

4. See Nolt (2003, 306–7) for excerpts of the *Wisconsin v. Yoder* decision. Also see Kraybill and Bowman (2001, 114).

5. Kraybill (2003) extensively covers these conflicts, past and present in chapter 5.

6. An important update would be to compare the academic performance of Amish children in parochial schools with those who are still in public schools and also to compare Hostetler and Huntington's (1992) findings with current achievement scores.

7. Indiana's regulations state that "the teacher will have passed the eighth grade satisfactorily and will make a passing score on a General Education Development [GED] High School Equivalency Test or on a standardized 12th grade achievement test furnished, administered, and graded by the State Department of Public Instruction" (Articles of Agreement, 3). Although some teachers have obtained the GED, according to Johnson-Weiner (personal letter, 4 August 2005), nobody in Indiana knows of the regulation's being enforced. In some places, such as Pennsylvania, home school teachers must have either a high school diploma or GED. At least one New Order church permits their children to attend a local Christian high school if the student needs a diploma for nursing or teaching.

8. In a rare case, an Amish teacher from a plain group in the Big Valley of Pennsylvania reported that some of their teachers still resorted at times to Pennsylvania German for instruction. He recognized that if state education officials learned of this, those particular schools would face serious sanctions.

9. Personal letter (26 July 2004).

10. From Maryalice Yakutchik, *Amish Online,* Among the Amish, Day 5, on the Discovery Web site.

11. In her excellent book on Amish schooling, Johnson-Weiner (2006) reviews all of the important curricular materials used by various Amish groups in her chapter "Publishing and Old Order Education."

12. Occasionally girls as young as fifteen have taught school. Also an occasional teacher from a Mennonite or other Anabaptist group, or even an outsider sympathetic to Amish values, will be hired. These non-Amish teachers are sometimes criticized for "spending too much time on frills rather than the three R's" and on being too lax in disciplining the disobedient students. On the other hand, a convert to the Amish who taught in the Big Valley of Pennsylvania received criticism for pushing his students to learn too much.

13. In certain areas, teacher shortages have reputedly grown in recent years. "What can we expect," complained an Ohio father, "if we don't pay a decent wage to our teachers. Things will only get worse."

14. Personal letter (26 July 2004).

15. On this issue, see Meyers (1993, 92) and Nolt (2003, 276–78).

16. Librarians in Holmes County, Ohio, for example, indicate that Amish children and youth use their services and borrow books in disproportionately higher numbers than their other youthful patrons, although their choice of reading matter tends to be restricted to history, biographies, nature, farm, religious, and family themes.

17. Books can be ordered from Linda Byler, Buggy Lane Press, 11942 Weaver Rd., Orrstown, PA 17244.

18. New Order parents usually forbid their children from reading romance novels, westerns, or any novels portraying violence or fighting.

19. In Wojtasik's 1996 novel, *No Strange Fire,* a parent objected to the implied sexual behavior and use of the word "condom," a term that he thought most Amish readers would find offensive. Both an Old Order and a New Order reader who read a pre-publication copy of this chapter agreed that the word was objectionable, even in its present context.

20. *One Way Street* (E. Stoll 1972) and many other books published by Pathway typically do not list the author's name. This is a traditional practice to reduce the likelihood of pride or attention-seeking. A complete list of Pathway publications can be obtained at Pathway Bookstore, 2580 N-250W, LaGrange, IN 46761.

21. Several years ago a bishop from a tobacco-growing settlement required one of his ministers who served on Pathway's board to terminate his tenure.

22. Also see *Family Life* (Aug–Sept 1986): 8–10.

23. One youth discovered Thomas Paine and Herman Melville, and read all of Mark Twain's works.

24. Hostetler (1992). For decades, John A. Hostetler (1918–2001) was re-

garded as the foremost scholar on Amish life and culture. He wrote or coau-thored dozens of articles and several books on Amish culture for both profes-sional journals and popular magazines. His most noteworthy was *Amish Society*, published in four editions between 1963 and 1993. David Weaver-Zercher has analyzed Hostetler's place in Amish studies and also compiled some of Hostetler's most important contributions in *Writing the Amish* (2005).

25. To the dismay of state licensing boards, several Amish "dentists" and den-tal technicians even extract teeth or make dental plates for Old Order friends and acquaintances.

26. For an example of the kind of critical thinking and precise writing that some Amish attain, see a book review by Elmer Stoltzfus in *Pennsylvania Men-nonite Heritage* (April 1996): 19, 37. Also see Pauline Stevick's chapter, "An Amish Intellectual," in her book, *Beyond the Plain and Simple: A Patchwork of Amish Lives* (Kent, OH: Kent State University, 2006).

Chapter Five. Parenting

1. See P. Stevick (2006).

2. Kraybill (2001, 16; 333–34). Although these data are from Lancaster County, most Amish report retention rates that compare with or exceed these figures.

3. Exact numbers of deviants are difficult to obtain. Most estimates are based on observations of parents of teenagers. Some Amish adults in larger settle-ments estimate that as many as 50 percent of the youth over the age of sixteen have tried alcohol and that 25 percent use it weekly. In some of the Lancaster County youth groups, or gangs, all of the males and some of the females drink regularly. However, several groups, including two whose young men drive mo-torized vehicles, have virtually no drinking. Also drinking is very rare in most of the small settlements and in the New Order Amish affiliations.

4. All Amish adults and children know that they are to honor their parents and that children are to be obedient: "Children, obey your parents in the Lord for this is right. Honor thy father and mother" (Ephesians 6:1–2a). This verse quotes from the Fifth Commandment: "Honor thy father and thy mother that thy days may be long upon the land which the Lord thy God giveth thee" (Exo-dus 20:12).

5. A notable exception is that in Lancaster County, a non-Amishman de-scribed by the Amish as a "motivational expert" not only conducts Dale Car-negie-type seminars but also regularly conducts ten-week sessions on family

issues and dynamics. In the winter of 2003, one hundred plain people enrolled in his family seminar. Another exception occurred in 2005–6 when dozens of Amish paid $4,975 each to attend a 5-day "business/motivational workshop" conducted by an outsider. The bishops eventually agreed to forbid all attendance. *Lancaster New Era* (13 October 2005).

6. A conversation with an Amish woman related by Donald Kraybill to the author.

7. *Blackboard Bulletin* (April 1999, 5).

8. When asked about this relatively quiet period, a mother from a Lancaster County daughter settlement said, "It is generally true among our people, but it is not nearly so simple for those of us who are more liberal parents. We have more to deal with during those years. Our younger children want the same kind of independence that they see their older brothers and sisters experiencing."

9. *Young Companion* (January 1991, 10).

10. *Family Life* (January 1975, 8).

11. According to Reiling (2002, 151), "The Amish believe that listing the names of those who defect will function to limit defection."

12. A minister who moved to another settlement asked that he not be placed in the lot for bishop there because his children were "out in the world." His request was honored.

13. *Young Companion* (January 1979, 16–17).

14. *Die Botschaft* (2 December 1987:5).

15. *The Budget* (11 August 1960).

16. (Lancaster) *Intelligencer Journal* (30 November 1984, 9).

17. Nanette Varian's article, "Escaping Amish Repression: One Woman's Story," appeared in *Glamour* (August 1999, 114–20) and chronicled an Amish couple's worst fear when their daughter left their Iowa community to marry a divorced English man. The daughter, Ruth Irene Garret, has since written her own books, *Crossing Over* (2001) and *Born Amish* (2004) with Deborah Morse-Kahn.

18. Speaking of an "English" young man who was seeking to join the Amish, a mother asked rhetorically, "Would you want him marrying your daughter?"

19. Exact figures are unavailable, but reputedly in one western Old Order settlement virtually all of the young men in CPS left the Amish.

20. One former Old Order man recounted how his volunteer work project among Native Americans put him in contact with more progressive Anabaptist youth who influenced his eventual defection to the Mennonites. Ironically, his

Amish home church district had supported his voluntary service involvement that resulted in his leaving. The problem of defection became so worrisome that it led to the formation of the National Steering Committee in the 1960s. Committee members tried to work out alternatives to urban assignments in hospitals.

21. Parents and ministers would have been upset to know that according to the rental clerk, the most popular rentals in the local convenience store were *Strip Tease* for Amish males and *That Thing You Do* for Amish females.

22. Letter to the author (5 March 2001).

23. *Family Life* (February 1986, 12).

24. *Blackboard Bulletin* (April 1999, 5).

25. For an excellent discussion of the concerns that many Amish have with the decreased percentage of children growing up on farms, see Kraybill and Nolt (2003).

26. "Singing and Hymns," *Young Companion* (March 1990, 9).

27. *Die Botschaft* (3 June 1987, 10). Although this statement was made before the advent of supervised groups, it still applies to many youth who are not in those groups or who live in other settlements.

28. *Lancaster New Era* (8 November 1984, 6).

29. *Elkhart* (Indiana) *Truth* (8 September 1973).

30. *The Budget* (1 April 1909).

31. See Associated Press article in the Lubbock *Avalanche Journal* entitled "Amish teen drinking, vandalism worries parents" (12 June 1999). Thirty years earlier, the *Des Moines Register* reported a similar incident from the same community (27 September 1968) when nine youth were picked up for overturning a wagon and an elevator, breaking windows, decapitating chickens, and dumping sand and gravel into machinery.

32. *The Budget* (29 September 1949).

33. *Die Botschaft* (5 December 1984).

34. One reason such situations are rare is that Amish youth have traditionally been more likely to leave home than to act out. For example, young men might join the armed forces or go west to work on a ranch.

35. *Family Life* (April 1999).

36. An Amish minister claims that a realtor who worked with the Parke County settlement refused to bring certain interested families to check out the community "because he knew they didn't fit in."

37. Being small and isolated is no guarantee to concerned parents that life

will be like it is in Parke County, Indiana. On the other side of the state, another small daughter settlement has the reputation of resembling Lancaster County more than it does Parke County. The youth dress less conservatively, spend more time with each other, and reputedly violate more community standards. One observer wondered if this settlement began in an attempt to have more relaxed standards. For whatever reasons, these two daughter settlements in the same state provide a contrast in youth standards.

Chapter Six. Teen Culture

1. This poem written by nine-year-old Esther Zook was one of two poems about work on the cover of *The Diary* in March 1998.

2. For a description of this relief effort, see Unruh (1952, 227–29), and for a fascinating first-hand account, see Newswanger (1996, 110–13).

3. Of course, long hours of work in the heat or cold can become tiresome. An Amish writer from Iowa reminisced about the drudgery of endless hours of picking beans and cucumbers in "Pity Party in the Pickle Patch," *Plain Interests* (April 2004, 1).

4. Unpublished letter from 2 April 1978 on file in Heritage Historical Library, Aylmer, Ontario.

5. *Die Botschaft* (23 July 1997, 45).

6. Kissinger (1983, 87–93) devotes an entire chapter to tobacco cultivation and culture.

7. Traditionally, Amish youth have turned over the bulk of their earnings to their parents, who either used some or all of it for family expenses or kept it on behalf of their children until they "came of age" at twenty-one. Many families in large settlements have dropped this practice.

8. The word *frolic* comes from the German word *fröhlich*, which means "joyous." See Hostetler (1993, 243).

9. Shachtman (2006, 196–205) summarizes the struggle between the Amish and OSHA, especially around the turn of this century.

10. To a lesser degree, organized sports are an integral part of the youth culture in other large settlements. A scribe from Mt. Hope, Ohio, wrote in *The Budget* that the Holmes County Merchant volleyball team, composed of Amish players, won the state finals and went on to Kansas, where they placed second in the national finals (29 July 1992).

11. *Young Companion* (June 1993, 7–8).

12. *Young Companion* (May-June 1990, 20).

13. The "Can You Help Me" column in one issue of *Young Companion* was devoted to the question of playing ball on Sunday. Predictably, every letter printed stated that Sunday should be kept holy and reserved for worship and visiting (May-June 1990, 20–21).

14. By 2006, a number of baptized adults, including parents, had returned to the ballparks to see the *Youngie* play.

15. *Family Life* (March 1982, 9–12).

16. Outsiders can watch cornerball at the volunteer fire company auctions and sales held in Lancaster County in late winter and early spring. Sometimes called "mud sales" by outsiders, they attract thousands of buyers and spectators, who inadvertently turn the frozen ground into a quagmire.

17. Cornerball was also popular among many German-speaking rural Pennsylvanians from the Lutheran, Reformed, and United Church of Christ traditions. Kline (1990) has written an informal history of the game.

18. Some young men have apparently solved this problem by moving to Rexford, Montana, an Amish settlement two miles from the Canadian border. "We get quite a few unattached boys who are here primarily for the hunting," said a longtime resident.

19. Lancaster County has only a handful of serious birders. When an Amishman from Ohio was asked about this dearth, he allowed that "the Lancaster Amish are too busy working to pay off their big farm mortgages." Some Lancaster residents agreed.

20. Apparently, birding and hunting are both regarded as male activities, since females are rarely involved in either.

21. Shortly after the in-line skating craze hit mainstream culture in 1990, rollerblades entered some of the large communities. Major news organizations featured photos of smiling Amish youth skating along rural roads. By the turn of the century, not only the youth but many adults were lacing up to go to work or to sales, or simply for fun. For his revision of *The Riddle of Amish Culture* (2001), Kraybill chose two young women from Lancaster County on rollerblades for his cover photo. In that settlement, rollerblades are permitted, even though bicycles are forbidden.

22. See "Amish Going Modern, Sort of, About Skating" in the *New York Times* (11 August 1996, 20).

23. Amish skaters were featured on http://inlineskating.about.com/library/bl-Amish-photos.htm.

24. When the *Lancaster Intelligencer Journal* (16 December 2003) reported that five members of the Blazers hockey team were killed when their Jeep Grand Cherokee collided with a snow plow after competing in a local hockey league, many readers learned for the first time of Amish youth involvement in organized ice hockey in Lancaster County, Pennsylvania.

25. All Old Order affiliations prohibit flying except for health or family emergencies. Three single Old Order members were temporarily excommunicated for flying to Central America on a Mennonite-sponsored work project. Many New Order groups, however, permit members to fly.

26. In most Amish communities, some local people, often Mennonites or retirees, supplement their income by "hauling" Amish to nearby and distant destinations when horse and carriage transportation is inconvenient or impossible. Of course, in settlements where youth have their own cars or pickups, hiring a "taxi" is unnecessary for them. See Butterfield (1997).

27. Despite looking thoroughly English, most of the breakfast crowd, both diners and waitresses, in the family-style seating room of Troyer's Dutch Heritage Restaurant (formerly *Der Dutchman*) in Pinecraft grew up plain and can still converse in Pennsylvania Dutch.

28. *Boston Globe* (22 March 1999) and *Philadelphia Inquirer* (15 February 1999).

29. *Elkhart* (Indiana) *Truth* (22 September 1973). Writers and headline editors, unaware of the distinction between the Sunday night singing and Saturday night parties, have sometimes confused the two in their reporting. A headline proclaimed, "Amish 'Sing' Busted—Two Arrested." The article then described a Saturday night party instead of a Sunday singing. The same mistake had been made six years earlier, when a reporter confused a Saturday night party with a Sunday night singing (*Elkhart Truth*, 18 July 1967). Anyone observing a band hop or party would recognize that they are in a different category from a singing.

30. Personal letter (24 September 1999).

Chapter Seven. Singings

1. Personal conversation (18 June 2004).

2. In some parts of Indiana, this Sunday evening event is called a "crowd," and according to one informant, "Not much singing takes place. It's mostly a bunch of socializing and carrying on."

3. In some new settlements made up mostly of young families, adults may

get together at times to sing in the evenings, but children rarely attend youth singings until they turn sixteen. In some cases, singings have been held sporadically or suspended because of rowdiness when parents have refused to host the youth at their homes. Both of these situations are fairly rare; however, in one large settlement, regular singings were suspended for several years because of excessive drinking and rowdiness.

4. In the 1990s a gang for the older unmarried Amish formed, and they called themselves the Chess Nuts since many of them liked to play chess. By the turn of the century, the gang had dissolved, since "most of our gang had gotten married," a bachelor reported. However, they were soon replaced by the Drifters, a new gang of twenty- or thirty-somethings who boasted a membership of nearly 80. A bachelor from another state who attended a singing reported, "They started right on time and had a very good singing."

5. The underlying message may be that it would be disrespectful of parents and other adults to be overly excited about going with the young folk.

6. This practice varies among communities, depending on tradition and income. Sometimes boys will receive their carriages in their early teens if the family needs extra transportation for church or visiting. In some communities or families, sons must obtain their own carriages.

7. In 2001, a young man in Ohio sported a kind of sunroof in his carriage.

8. *Lancaster Sunday News* (27 October 2002).

9. See Scott (1981) for a comprehensive treatment of carriage styles in a variety of Amish settlements.

10. An older couple recalled that several singings were held "on the lawn under the trees" in Lancaster County in the 1950s, but their son responded, "If we would hold ours outside these days, people would freak out. It would be the joke of the year!"

11. In a few settlements, usually in the Midwest, boys and girls alternate along the benches.

12. *Die Botschaft* (30 June 1993, 8).

13. Some of the songs have a decidedly nonpacifist bent: "The Battle of New Orleans," "Hello, Viet Nam," "I Died for the Red, White, and Blue," "Geisha Girl," "Rolling in My Sweet Baby's Arms," "Pistol Packing Mama," and "Camptown Races," to name a few (see Schwartz and Schwartz 1980). Other than the oldest songs with no copyright restrictions, virtually all of the lyrics have been pirated.

14. Many New Order and some of the more progressive Old Order Amish

permit part singing in the youth gatherings. In fact, some Lancaster County gang members attend weekly music classes, where they learn to sing harmony from old-fashioned shaped-note songbooks. Amish adults with a love of music teach these classes.

15. A minister who knew about this song was apparently more concerned about the rhythm than about the references to the radio or rock and roll in the lyrics: "This music is just not Christian. Listen to it. It has a rock and roll beat!" he asserted. Lyrics used with permission of Mrs. Wayne Raney.

16. "Bluebird on Your Window Sill," written by Canadian Elizabeth Clarke in 1948, was the first Canadian song to sell one million copies. It was popularized in the United States by Bing Crosby, Doris Day, and Tex Williams, among others, and obviously caught the attention of many Amish youth (*Canadian Encyclopedia*, 2000, Historica Foundation of Canada).

17. This distinct singing quality may have originated from the nasal singing style common in colonial America and mocked by the British. More likely, it stems from the popularity of country and western music among Amish youth, who listen to country music on the radio, cassettes, and CDs.

18. Perhaps the compilers assume that because no music notes are included, they need not obtain permission to reprint the words.

19. When asked about the quality of the translations, one informant admitted that occasionally translators "had to sneak in some Pennsylvania Dutch to make things come out right."

20. Unpublished letter in Heritage Historical Library, Aylmer, Ontario.

21. *Die Botschaft* (24 January 1989).

22. *Die Botschaft* (19 August 1987, 14).

23. Young people from Somerset County, Pennsylvania, who attended a youth-only singing at one of the plainest groups in the state reported with obvious surprise that the boys actually smoked during the singing and that even some of the girls smoked and used chewing tobacco.

24. The conservative settlements are often repositories of games popular in the eighteenth and nineteenth centuries.

25. In one large settlement, local law enforcement officials sent school busses to the site to transport the revelers to town for booking.

26. Despite reports of heavy drinking over the years among a significant number of Amish youth, most Amish believe that, with some exceptions, there are relatively few Amish adult alcoholics. One bishop offered an explanation: "In mainstream society, young people often drink as self-medication to

get away from their troubles. Most of our youth who drink do it for fun with their peers instead of trying to escape from bad situations. When they decide to settle down and join the church, most of them have little trouble in giving up their drinking." Nevertheless, 50 youth in the fourth-largest settlement in northern Ohio were required by law enforcement officials to receive counseling at Turning Point, an alcohol prevention program. See www.enquirer.com/editions/2000/05/21/loc_ohios_amish_seek.html.

27. "Hard to Forget," *Family Life* (July 1969, 24–25).

28. *Gemeinde Brief* (5 March 1986), a local Indiana publication.

29. *Lancaster New Era* (23 May 1981). With characteristic humility, an Amish parent wrote back, thanking the writer for his or her concern, promising to do his best to "plant many seeds of love, joy, peace, and respect" in his children, and with the Lord's help do something to alleviate the problems the writer pointed out. The Amishman's entire letter, from which this excerpt came, filled nearly eighteen column inches.

Chapter Eight. *Rumspringa*

1. *Hollywood Outsider*, www.hollywoodoutsider.com.

2. *Calgary Film Festival Guide*, www.sharbean.ca.

3. In parts of Indiana, according to Langin (1994), youth join groups similar to the Lancaster County gangs but do not use the same terminology.

4. *Die Botschaft* (22 December 1993, 36).

5. Today some of these peace-loving parents might wonder about what attitudes and behaviors are reflected in more recent gang names such as Cruisers, Crystals, Diamonds, Drifters, Rangers, Rockies, and Sawed-off Shotguns, a split from the Shotguns, one of the longest-standing gangs in Lancaster County.

6. Gideon L. Fisher in *The Diary* (August 1982), describing the beginning of his *Rumspringa* in 1929.

7. The late Abner Beiler, a Lancaster County historian, remembered the Happy Harrys as being the first youth group. He also recalled, "I was in the Chow-chows. It was called that because we had a real mixture of youth." (*Chow-chow* is the name of a pickled mixed vegetable dish served as an accompaniment to a meal.) Conversation with the author (July 2000).

8. Since the drug arrests in 1998, this gang has dissolved.

9. Many Amish elders say that car ownership or the boys' haircuts are the best indicators of the "decency" of a gang and its members.

10. Some of the counties adjacent to Lancaster have developed their own similar gang structure. For example, nearby Perry County had three gangs in 2001 but only one three years later. At the same time, the Amish in the ridge-and-valley counties of central Pennsylvania had four gangs, the Mountaineers, Chipmunks, Rangers, and Meadowlarks, that the nearly four hundred youth chose from. Most of the youth from Sugar Valley, Nitanny Valley, Penn's Valley, Brush Valley, Buffalo Valley, White Deer, and Nippenose belonged to one of these groups, although a few youth traveled to Lancaster on weekends to participate in a gang.

11. Out-of-county teens can also belong to conservative gangs.

12. On Memorial Day weekend in 1999, five Amish youth from both western Pennsylvania and Lancaster County traveling from the Sunday night singing in Lancaster were killed, along with their driver, in a pre-dawn crash. See *Lancaster Intelligencer Journal* (4 June 1999).

13. Similar age groupings or cohort groups occur in most settlements, but without the "buddy bunch" designation.

14. In developmental psychology terms, the Amish gang is equivalent to the adolescent "crowd" in public schools, a loose aggregation of peers who share common interests and find their identity and status through membership in this group. In contrast, the Amish buddy bunch is similar to what the developmentalists call the adolescent "clique," a smaller group of friends that provides intimacy and socialization needs. See Steinberg (2005, 175–91).

15. In Arthur, Illinois, a teenager explained that their buddy bunch equivalent usually takes the name of the first—and therefore the oldest—member who turns sixteen. "I belong to the Katie group," she explained.

16. Three college students visiting an Orioles group singing thought that all the girls from a particular buddy group could actually be identified through their distinctive perfume. When asked about it, an Amish mother laughed and said that each girl likely tried on their hostess's perfume before coming down to the singing.

17. In light of these kinds of experiences, advisors of one of the supervised gangs in Lancaster County have abolished the practice of having sidekicks in an effort to avoid cliques.

18. Young people in a few smaller settlements also spend part of Saturday and all of Sunday with their peers.

19. For this reason, some parents refuse to go away overnight during a weekend. "Of course our children say that the group came to our place without an

invitation, but either way, it's a mess," reported a father. One couple revealed that the only time they left the farm over a weekend was when their children were out of town.

20. Crowding can cause its own problems. In 1977 a Lancaster County newspaper ran a Monday story with the headline, "Seven Amish injured when barn collapses." So many young people had crowded into the barn where the Sunday night party and dance were being held that the main floor collapsed. No fatalities were reported, but one girl sustained serious back injuries (*Lancaster New Era*, 10 October 1977).

21. The description of this hop held in the summer of 1996 was provided by a college student and friend of the author. The student had grown up plain and had attended school with the Amish boy who accompanied him.

22. Virtually no females cut their hair short, and in most places, relatively few who live at home appear anywhere in jeans or shorts. However, some girls from Amish families in northern Indiana reportedly wear jeans or shorts in public.

23. A Beachy Amish historian reports that as an Old Order youth in the 1950s, he knew of two rival gangs in Ohio that would occasionally fight each other at a singing. A man from another large settlement who later left the Amish reported that when he was a teenager in the early 1960s, at 90 percent of those hoedowns there was always a "big brawl" between one or two of the guys. See McNamara (1997, 214).

24. When the same observer, his girlfriend, and another couple decided to crash the barn party two weeks later, they reported a very different reception. By the time they arrived, he discovered that his Amish friend who had invited him before had been drinking heavily and was in no state to host them. Almost immediately the two girls became the object of unwanted attention from several of the boys who were drinking. "We quickly decided that this was not the place for us to be, especially for the girls, so we left as fast as we could." He did not believe that they were in physical danger, but he feared that the girls would be harassed by inappropriate behavior and comments. It was the last barn party he attended. Other uninvited outsiders have reported being threatened or even ejected when they tried to crash one of these events. (This information comes from a conversation between the author and a man who is now a Mennonite minister.)

25. Unpublished letter on file in Heritage Historical Library, Aylmer, Ontario.

Chapter Nine. Courtship

1. James Hurd (1997), who has done extensive research among the Nebraska Amish in Pennsylvania, points out the difficulties that young people in some of the small splinter groups have in finding a spouse from such a limited pool of eligible mates.

2. Research studies by Miller et al. (1986), Thornton (1990), Dorius et al. (1993), and Small and Luster (1994) all show a significant positive correlation between early dating and early sexual intercourse.

3. Functionally, this may result from a developmental difference between males and females.

4. The father added, "A boy gets a desk during his running-around years. He has things just like the girl that his mother made, just not as much."

5. Although the social setting is nonthreatening, the physical setting of walking along a dark road at night is a different matter. A group of horse-and-buggy Mennonites playing walk-a-mile after a singing were struck by a car in rural Franklin County, Pennsylvania, and five youth were injured.

6. Occasionally boys have been so humiliated when they were "told off" (refused) that they quit attending the singings.

7. Related in Goldstein (1997, 140–41).

8. Ibid., 141.

9. *Family Life* (February 2000, 28), printed in Special Section: Journey to Freedom.

10. A deacon reported that a church member had found condoms while cleaning up after a youth activity

11. Technically, the "wedding season" runs up to spring communion, but first marriages rarely occur after Christmas. Couples in their thirties or older marrying for the first time may choose a wedding date after the traditional October to December season.

12. In the same settlement, married couples will occasionally confess in a members' meeting that their courtship was "impure" and ask to be placed in the ban. They are not asked to specifically describe their wrong behavior. After being excommunicated for six weeks, they are again accepted into full membership. Some members report as many as 20 percent of their married couples in their district have made such confessions.

13. Donald Kraybill relates that when he traveled to Switzerland in 1993, an

older man recalled participating in bundling as a youth in a rural part of southern Switzerland. Letter to the author (30 May 2003).

14. See the chapter "Bed Courtship" in Folsom (1994, 117–18). Folsom reports that among the Nebraska Amish, the pink patches in the normally subdued quilts come from remnants of the night dresses or *Nacht Roch*.

15. See Gingerich (1939, 244).

16. See Yoder (1998, 7, 61–62).

17. Several Old Order Amish who knew Levi Miller criticized him for betraying family secrets. Some bookstore managers in Holmes County, Ohio, claim that this is the primary reason that they do not stock or sell the book.

18. His observation illustrates that an action viewed from two different cultures or sub-cultures may mean one thing to the person in the culture and something quite different to the person outside the culture.

19. A father from a large settlement that once condoned bundling wrote the following: "[The boy] held his girl on his lap on a rocking chair or the girl laid on the couch and the boy laid on top of her. This latter practice was *very* awkward because the couple could feel each other's body parts through their clothing. Couples in the 1960s hated this and realized it was not a Christian way to court." Letter to the author from Amish father (Spring 2001).

20. Letter to the author (6 November 2002).

21. Letter to the author (11 April 1998).

22. Older informants in the largest settlements say that bundling was widespread at least through the first half of the twentieth-century.

23. Folsom (1994, 121) writes that a minister who spoke out against bed courtship fifty years ago was silenced by his bishop for five years.

24. *Ein Risz in der Mauer: Treatise on Courtship* (n.d., 30, 34).

25. Editors and writers in *Family Life* and *Young Companion* wrote against bed courtship almost from the magazines' inception. In October 1971, *Die Schaedliche Uebung* (The Shameful Practice) strongly criticized bundling. The editor used Martin Luther's Bible German and wrote in the Fraktur script, a practice sometimes used when the author or editorial staff judged the content to be too private or too provocative for outsiders or children to read.

26. *Young Companion* (1999).

27. Conversation with the author (July 1998).

28. Besides prohibiting early dating, the Amish prohibition of listening to popular music may also relate to sexual activity. Martino et al. (2006) report a positive correlation between hours spent listening to popular music and sex-

ual activity and especially between listening to degrading sexual lyrics such as found in rap music.

Chapter Ten. Weddings

1. Stephen Scott (1988), an Old Order River Brethren writer, provides the most comprehensive description of wedding customs in Lancaster County, Pennsylvania, and elsewhere. He notes correctly that practices vary considerably among communities after the wedding. Many of the customs described in his book, as well as some in this one, reflect traditional practices in Lancaster County, Pennsylvania.

2. Because the Amish rarely write for outsiders about their weddings, English guests who attend often assume that what they observe in a particular community is true for all Amish. Also, because the guests do not understand either High German ("church German") or Pennsylvania German, they often miss the meanings or nuances of the ceremony and some of the subsequent activities.

3. Since the wedding season in Lancaster County traditionally consists of no more than eight Tuesdays and eight Thursdays on which to be married, courting youth face the formidable task of finding a day that "suits" their families and friends. An unprecedented change occurred in June 2005, when the Lancaster County community learned that the daughter of a prominent bishop would be married in a June wedding. Except for weddings involving pregnancies or widow-widower weddings, this was likely the first "traditional" wedding to be held outside the "sacred" fall wedding season. Some undoubtedly hoped that this would be the beginning of a more flexible, less-stressful wedding season option.

4. A bishop commented that proposing when the strawberries are in flower is not mandatory. "Although this timing may be traditional, there is constant variation," he explained.

5. Deacons in a horse-and-buggy Amish settlement in Ontario reportedly read the wedding announcement or banns during three successive services before the couple may marry.

6. In other affiliations, such as some New Order groups in Ohio, the young man simply receives verbal approval from the bishop and reports this to his future bride's home bishop. In parts of Central Pennsylvania, the *Zeugnis* is mailed to the bishop of the bride.

7. A young Amish man reported that his community learned that before one

of his peer's wedding, the young man had sexual relations with an English girl. As a result, the ministers decided that the couple could not have the traditional attendants during the church service and ceremony but would be permitted to have them for the rest of the day's and evening's activities.

8. According to Scott (1988, 9–10), the father may stipulate the age of those who are invited, depending on how much room the family has for guests. If the house or premises are small and the family has many relatives and friends, they may limit invitations to guests who are eighteen and older instead of offering the more typical invitation for sixteen- and seventeen-year-olds.

9. In Kalona, Iowa, not only does the bride-to-be attend, but her future in-laws and family will also come to her district to hear the announcement.

10. One young man claimed that many youth are relieved when they are not invited, since there are so many weddings and date conflicts in the short Lancaster County wedding season. A grandfather commented that guests are attentive for the first and last weddings of the season but suffer from "wedding shock" for most of the rest.

11. See "A Wedding and a Wedding Tale" in P. Stevick (2006).

12. In St. Mary's County, Maryland, the parents of the large wedding described above invited one hundred relatives and friends to help. This description appeared in an earlier version of www.amish-heartland.com and was contributed by George and Marty Kreps and used by permission of Amish-heartland.

13. With the decrease in farming and the increase in businesses among many Amish, more families are opting to buy cases of chicken and celery from commercial sources.

14. Printed invitations are common in some of the other large settlements. "In Lancaster County," a mother reported, "invitations are discouraged. Some do send them about a month before. A verbal invitation is encouraged. With the rubber stamp craze, some make pretty (home-made) invitations with them. Only the 'fastest' people use engraved invitations, a very small percentage." One bride-to-be reportedly sent out a "pretty fancy card" that included a photo of the couple. The bishop required her to ask each person who received the photo to destroy it. See *Lancaster Sunday News* (17 November 2003) or www.lancasteronline.com/articles/4441.

15. Donnermeyer, Kreps, and Kreps (1999, 153–55) reported that many Amish in their tri-county area of Ohio scheduled their weddings based on the availability of the wagons. One reason this service may not occur in Lancaster County is that the wedding season is generally compressed into six weeks, requiring an

inordinate number of vehicles to meet the intense demand. A Lancaster County father explained that some Amish individuals provide "wedding chests" with dishes and silverware to rent, but the owners charge "a meager fee."

16. Donnermeyer, Kreps, and Kreps (1999) describe this service in Holmes County, Ohio.

17. The day after the wedding, the entire addition is dismantled, and many of the materials may go to a relative or friend whose daughter is getting married in the next few days or weeks. Occasionally, the addition will be incorporated permanently into the house or the shop. See *Lancaster Sunday News* (17 November 2003).

18. In Lancaster County, at least one bottled gas company has a thriving business of transporting and hooking up gas stoves at the wedding sites. Families may rent as many as ten propane stoves for the occasion, depending on the size of the wedding. The Renno and Byler Amish in Big Valley hire a vehicle to bring in as many as a dozen kerosene-burning stoves to their sites.

19. A couple who has been part of the *Grumbierleit*, or potato crew, described the difficulty of cooking potatoes for 400 or 500 people: "It's hard to make mashed potatoes for hundreds of people. It's not something you can practice. One time we underestimated how many to do, but fortunately the wedding was at a farm with a bulk food store, and we got powdered potatoes and added them with cream cheese and butter to try and make them taste right." The husband explained that mashing such a huge quantity is physically demanding and that somebody came up with the idea of breaking down the potatoes with beaters attached to the Makita battery-operated power drills used by carpenters. "Women in the local church district with nothing else to do help to peel and slice the potatoes for cooking," they reported.

20. More recently, one or more young married men oversee the hostlers to avoid some of the past problems of these young teenagers "getting involved in pranks or other mischief."

21. In most places, the couple chooses unmarried siblings who are close to their own age as their *Newesitzer* (side-sitters) or witnesses, the most honored participants in the day's events. If the bride or groom have no available siblings, they will choose cousins or nieces or nephews. However, in parts of Lancaster County many couples choose their friends rather than relatives. Tradition dictates that none of the attendants are to be dating each other.

22. A minister's wife reported that a woman who was married in 2006 was "disciplined by the church"—that is, she had to make a public confession at the

close of a Sunday service because she wore a green wedding dress instead of the traditional blue or purple. The minister's wife said, "The color is not actually written into the *Ordnung*, but everyone knows what is expected."

23. In some youth gangs and some settlements, young men begin wearing the broader brimmed hat as soon as they join the church.

24. Pauline Stevick (2006) captures this self-effacing attitude from her observations of three Old Order Amish weddings, two in Pennsylvania and one in Ohio.

25. When the couple initially seeks the church's approval for their marriage, both are approached by their respective deacons and asked if they were free of fornication. A deacon explained, "At this point, nobody admits to an improper courtship. If they would confess to having done wrong, they would have to postpone their wedding, be excommunicated and placed in the ban for six weeks. Some couples or individuals have voluntarily confessed to an impure courtship and remove themselves from 'full fellowship' for six weeks during the summer." Likewise, some couples may confess to an improper courtship sometime after they are married. Generally these confessions are not detailed.

26. Letter to the author (8 August 2002).

27. A middle-aged couple from one of the most conservative settlements reported that when they were married, their ministers routinely instructed couples that when they had children they were "not to tell their boys" about menstruation. They did not know the reason for such admonitions.

28. Tobit, chapter 8. A father wrote that all ministers urge the couple to follow Tobias and Sara's example of abstaining from sexual relations immediately. A great-grandmother from Ohio stated, "Starting your life together with prayer and fasting is a good way to begin." However, a newly ordained minister expressed surprise that some of the bishops no longer admonished the new bride and groom to observe the three-night fast. "I think very few follow it," said a bishop. When an elderly father was asked how faithful he thought newlyweds were in abstaining, he answered, "Who knows? Nobody is there to check on them." With regard to the admonishment to abstain, another father replied, "If I was a betting man, I'd bet a million to one that it don't happen."

29. In a settlement in southern Indiana, the deacon is charged to counsel the couple when they seek the church's approval to marry.

30. Although this description shows the order of the Lancaster wedding service, weddings in the other affiliations are similar, with a few exceptions, such as selection of hymns and standing/sitting protocol. Mary M. Miller (2000,

243–88) provides a thorough description of the scriptures, hymns, and prayers used in most weddings.

31. In some settlements, if the bride's father is a bishop, he may preach the main sermon and perform the wedding rites.

32. A New Order couple reported that in their affiliation they do not even use the Tobit narration or blessing because "Tobit is Apocryphal and has strange passages we shy away from." Similarly, an Old Order minister reports, "This practice is being dropped by the New Order groups and slowly seems to be losing out in the more progressive (Old Order) areas" (letter to the author, 8 August 2002). A couple who was married in Daviess County, Indiana, reported that the book of Tobias was not used in any weddings performed in the early 1940s.

33. Because of the length of the service and the language barrier, non-Amish guests are usually invited to arrive a little before 11:00 a.m., in time for receiving the vows.

34. In some places, this question takes place earlier in the service.

35. I am indebted to Stephen Scott of the Young Center at Elizabethtown College, Pennsylvania, and to a Swartzentruber Amish bishop for their help in translating the wedding vows. Also see Hostetler (1993, 192–200) for a description of a wedding in central Pennsylvania.

36. Translations from *Die Ernsthafte Christenpflicht* are from M. Miller (2000).

37. A man who was married in the 1940s recalls that in his settlement "the ceremony was to take place before 12:00 noon because if the hand on the clock was going up, it was thought that the marriage would be strong." Upon hearing this, someone wondered aloud if the functional purpose of this belief was to keep the preachers from preaching on into the afternoon.

38. Hostetler (1993, 198). In a wedding he attended in the Big Valley, Hostetler noted that the bride and groom were served baked oysters and ice cream. Actually, oysters were a traditional treat at many weddings in the past. However, an Amish father from that area reports that "oysters were usually served for the evening meal, but lately that has changed perhaps due to the cost of good oysters! Now it's usually meat loaf, ham, or some other specialty. The bride's parents choose what to serve the guests."

39. In Lancaster County, immediate family members, relatives, and close friends sit at the "second table." Everyone else is served in the "final sitting."

40. See Lasansky (1990) for a history of the dowry among the Pennsylvania German groups.

41. Letter to the author (26 September 2002).

42. See Scott (1988, 24–25) for other Lancaster County evening meal customs.

43. See the Kreps's Web site: www.amish-heartland.com/newdisc_toc.htm.

44. Until the early 1990s, the boy had to ask the girl if he could "take her to the table in the evening." With the possibility of being rejected, this created its own stress for him.

45. In the past, according to Hostetler (1993, 198), reluctant sixteen-year-olds were caught by older siblings or friends and forcibly thrust together to enter with their assigned partners.

46. See the Kreps's Web site: www.amish-heartland.com/newdisc_toc.htm.

47. The change from cigars to beef sticks began in the mid-1980s, probably as a nod to health concerns or propriety. Nobody knows for sure why beef sticks became the replacement. "It gives them something to nibble on instead of smoking," an Amishman conjectured. Couples may order several cases from which to distribute to well-wishers before they leave the wedding.

48. See the Kreps's Web site: www.amish-heartland.com/newdisc_toc.htm.

49. In Lancaster County, the bride's family traditionally has a table set up with leftovers for anybody who still wants to eat in the evening or before going home. It is called the *Fressdisch, fresse* being the Pennsylvania German verb used to describe the ways animals eat and gorge themselves. At Swartzentruber weddings, unmarried youth pair up and eat leftovers at midnight.

50. *Lancaster Intelligencer Journal* (15 October 1985, 36).

51. *Die Botschaft* (12 December and 19 December 1990).

52. *Die Botschaft* (1 November 1986, 23).

53. Letter to the author (8 August 2002).

54. The word *Infair* or *Infare* originated as a Middle English word that has virtually disappeared from modern parlance except among the Amish. *Infair* originally meant "a feast and reception for a newly married couple usually at the home of the groom's family a day or two after the wedding," from *Webster's Third New International Dictionary* (1986).

Chapter Eleven. The Future

1. A young father thought that young couples in their twenties or thirties were more vulnerable to leaving for liberal or progressive churches because, when they joined the Amish as teenagers, most had not really thought through or understood their decision.

2. Kraybill quoted in *Lancaster New Era* (13 July 1998).

3. Greska et al. (2002) point out that the Lancaster study is more than twenty-five years old.

4. See Igou (1999, 113–38) for concerns that many Amish have about father-absence because of working away.

5. Deborah J. Johnson has assembled a comprehensive listing of studies on the impact of fathers in "Father Presence Matters: A Review of the Literature" for The National Center on Fathers and Families (NCOFF). See www.ncoff.gse .upenn.edu/litrev/fpmir.htm.

6. Most Amish would consider the loss of Pennsylvania German as a prerequisite for membership to be a major loss for Amish identity. Acquiring skill in old German and Pennsylvania German has been one of the chief barriers to assimilating outsiders into the Amish.

7. Since these are correlational data, it is difficult to determine whether the proximity of the town influences youthful attitudes and behaviors, or whether being part of a family that chooses to live near town may be the critical ingredient. Perhaps marginalized Amish prefer to live near town; perhaps proximity to town life allows worldly influences to penetrate the family.

8. In defense of their group, one New Order spokesman said that his group's attrition rate is inflated because they are the last step out for some Old Order members who planned to leave the Amish without being shunned. See Kraybill (1994a).

9. Iannaccone (1994) provides a comprehensive discussion as to why conservative sects have a stronger holding power. He also cites clear examples of groups on both ends of the strictness-lenience spectrum.

10. Each community periodically prints a directory listing information on each Amish family unit. The number of single women listed is higher than single men in almost all settlements.

11. Batson and Ventis (1982, 36) write, "There is considerable evidence that women are more likely to be interested and involved in religion than men."

12. The occasional exposé on Amish sexual abuse featured on national network news programs may lead to exaggerated estimates of the frequency of this problem. Nobody really knows whether incest or other sexual deviancies are higher among the Amish than among the non-Amish.

13. Quoted in Reiling (2002, 156). One cannot generalize from one person's experience because individuals vary as to how salient or significant a particular belief is for them. Many Amish youth who deviate from adult norms apparently feel much less guilt and fear during their *Rumspringa*.

14. Others believe that more strict law enforcement may be the key to the diminished number of band hops and alcohol use.

15. Kraybill (2001, 186–87) argues that even though this act of joining appears to be freely taken, it is somewhat constrained, since everything in the community has funneled youth into making this decision to join. Shachtman (2006) believes that freedom to explore during the *Rumspringa* is the key to high Amish retention success.

16. An extended series, "Leading the Lambs," in *Family Life* featured letters from parents on child-rearing. The two themes of discipline and the development of warm, loving attachments were equally emphasized. This series started in 1998 and appeared regularly until early 2000.

17. *Lancaster Intelligencer Journal* (1 July 1999).

18. Ibid.

19. The defense attorney was impressed with the participation and cooperation of the Amish leaders and parents with the legal and judicial systems. He described this case as the "the zenith of his legal career"(ibid.).

Selected References

This listing of references includes all major sources cited in the notes as well as selected works related to Amish youth. Most bibliographic information for archival sources such as pamphlets, newsletters, newspaper articles, and articles from Amish periodicals, as well as radio or television segments and information from electronic databases, appears in the notes.

Ausbund, Das ist: Etliche schone Christliche Lieder. 1997. Lancaster, PA: Lancaster Press. First edition in 1564.

Bachman, Calvin George. [1941] 1961. *The Old Order Amish of Lancaster County.* Pennsylvania German Society, vol. 60.

Batson, C. Daniel, and W. Larry Ventis. 1982. *The Religious Experience: A Social-Psychological Perspective.* New York: Oxford University Press.

Baumrind, Diana. 1971. "Authoritative vs. Authoritarian Parental Control." *Adolescence* 3:255–72.

———. 1978. "Parental Disciplinary Patterns and Social Competence in Children." *Youth and Society* 9:239–76.

Beechy, William, and Malinda Beechy. n.d. Comp. *Experiences of CO's in CPS Camps, in I-W Service in Hospitals, and During World War I.* LaGrange, Ind.: authors.

Benedict, Ruth. 1934. *Patterns of Culture.* Boston: Houghton Mifflin.

Blackboard Bulletin. 1957–. Aylmer, Ont.: Pathway Publishers. Published monthly for Old Order teachers.

Botschaft, Die. 1975–. Lancaster, PA: Brookshire Publications and Printing. The masthead describes its mission as "a weekly newspaper serving Old Order Amish Communities everywhere."

Braght, Thieleman J. van, comp. [Dordrecht, 1660] 1998. *The Bloody Theater; or Martyrs Mirror of the Defenseless Christians*. Trans. Joseph F. Sohm. Scottdale, PA: Herald Press.

Budget, The. 1890–. Sugarcreek, OH: Sugarcreek Budget Publishers. A weekly newspaper serving Amish and Mennonite communities.

Burkholder, Chris. 2005. *Amish Confidential*. Argyle, IA: Argyle Publishing.

Butterfield, Jim. 1997. *Driving the Amish*. Scottdale, PA: Herald Press.

Cassady, Joslyn D., David L Kirshke, Timothy F. Jones, Allen S. Craig, Ovidio B. Bermudez, and William Schaffner. 2006. "Case Series: Outbreak of Conversion Disorder Among Amish Adolescent Girls." *Journal of American Academy of Child and Adolescent Psychiatry* 44(3):291–97.

Clasen, Claus-Peter. 1972. *Anabaptism. A Social History, 1525–1618: Switzerland, Austria, Moravia, South and Central Germany*. Ithaca, NY: Cornell University Press.

Cooksey, E. C., and J. F. Donnermeyer. 2004. "Go Forth and Multiply: Changes in the Timing of Marriage and Childbearing Among Young Amish Women." Paper presented at the annual meeting of the Population Association of America, Boston, April.

Devil's Playground. 2002. Directed by Lucy Walker. Wellspring Media Inc. Videocassette.

Devoted Christian's Prayer Book, A. 1984. Aylmer, Ont.: Pathway Publications. An English translation of *Die Ernsthafte Christenpflicht*.

Diary, The. 1969–. Gordonville, PA: Pequea Publishers. A monthly periodical devoted to Amish history and genealogy.

Directory. 2005. *Amish of Holmes County and Vicinity*. Sugarcreek, OH: Carlisle Press.

Donnermeyer, Joseph F., and Elizabeth C. Cooksey. 2004. "The Demographic Foundations of Amish Society." Paper presented at the annual meeting of the Rural Sociological Society, August. www.ruralsociology.org/annualmeeting/2004/Donnermeyer,Cooksey.pdf. Accessed 9 August 2006.

Donnermeyer, Joseph F., George M. Kreps, and Marty W. Kreps. 1999. *Lessons for Living*. Sugarcreek, OH: Carlisle Press.

Dorius, Guy L., Tim B. Heaton, and Patrick Steffen. 1993. "Adolescent Life

Events and their Association with the Onset of Sexual Intercourse." *Youth and Society* 25(1):3–23.

Dyck, Cornelius J. 1993. *An Introduction to Mennonite History*, 3rd ed. Scottdale, PA: Herald Press.

Ein Risz in der Mauer: Treatise on Courtship. n.d. Sugarcreek, OH: Schlabach Printers.

Ericksen, J. A., E. P. Ericksen, and J. A. Hostetler. 1980. "The Cultivation of the Soil as a Moral Directive: Population Growth, Family Ties, and the Maintenance of Community among the Old Order Amish." *Rural Sociology* 45:49–68.

Erikson, Erik Homburger. 1968. *Identity, Youth, and Crisis.* New York: Norton.

———. 1980. *Identity and the Life Cycle.* New York: Norton.

Family Life. 1968–. Aylmer, Ont.: Pathway Publishers. A monthly Amish periodical.

Folsom, Jan. 1994. *The Amish: Images of a Tradition.* Harrisburg, PA: Stackpole Books.

Friedrich, Lora, and Joseph F. Donnermeyer. 2003. "To Be or Not To Be: An Analysis of the Baptism Decisions of Young Amish Men and Women." Paper presented at the Ritual in Anabaptist Communities Conference, Hillsdale College, Hillsdale, Michigan, June.

Garrett, Ottie A. 1998. Comp. *True Stories of the X-Amish.* Horse Cave, KY: Neu Leben Inc.

Garrett, Ruth Irene. 2001. *Crossing Over: One Woman's Exodus from Amish Life.* Allen, TX: Thomas More.

Garrett, Ruth Irene, and Deborah Morse-Kahn. 2004. *Born Amish.* Paducah, KY: Turner Publishing Company.

Gehman, Richard. 1965. "Amish Folk." *National Geographic* 128(2):227–53.

Gemein Ordnungen von Lancaster Co., PA (Church ordinances of Lancaster County, PA). n.d. Trans. Noah G. Good.

Gingerich, Melvin. 1939. *The Mennonites in Iowa.* Iowa City: State Historical Society of Iowa.

Goldstein, Michael A. 1997. "Party On, Amos." *Philadelphia Magazine* 40 (August): 137–44.

Greska, Lawrence P., and Jill E. Korbin. 2002. "Key Decisions in the Lives of Old Order Amish: Joining the Church and Migrating to Another Settlement." *Mennonite Quarterly Review* 76 (October): 373–98.

Handbuch für Bischof (Handbook for bishops). [1935] 1978. Trans. Noah G. Good. Gordonville, PA: Gordonville Print Shop.

Harter, Susan. 1999. *The Construction of the Self: A Developmental Perspective.* New York: Guilford.

Horst, Irvin B. 1988. Ed. and trans. *Mennonite Confession of Faith* (Dordrecht). Lancaster, PA: Lancaster Mennonite Historical Society.

Hostetler, John A. 1977. "Old Order Amish Survival." *Mennonite Quarterly Review* 51 (October): 352–61.

———. 1992. "An Amish Beginning." *American Scholar* 61:552–62.

———. 1993. *Amish Society,* 4th ed. Baltimore: Johns Hopkins University Press.

Hostetler, John A., and Gertrude Enders Huntington. 1992. *Amish Children: Education in the Family, School, and Community,* rev. ed. Fort Worth, TX: Harcourt Brace Jovanovich.

Huntington, Gertrude Enders. 1994. "Persistence and Change in Amish Education." In *The Amish Struggle with Modernity,* ed. Donald B. Kraybill and Marc A. Olshan. Hanover, NH: University Press of New England.

Hurd, James P. 1997. "Marriage Practices Among the 'Nebraska' Amish of Mifflin County, Pennsylvania." *Pennsylvania Mennonite Heritage* 20(2):20–24.

Iannaccone, L. R. 1994. "Why Strict Churches Are Strong." *American Journal of Sociology* 99:1180–1211.

Igou, Brad. 1999. Comp. *The Amish in Their Own Words.* Scottdale, PA: Herald Press.

In Meiner Jugend: A Devotional Reader in German and English. 2000. Aylmer, Ont.: Pathway Publishers.

Intelligencer Journal. 1794–. Lancaster, PA: Lancaster Newspapers.

Johnson-Weiner, Karen M. 2006. *Train Up a Child.* Johns Hopkins University Press.

Keim, Albert N. 2003. "Military Service and Conscription," in *The Amish and the State,* 2nd ed., ed. Donald B. Kraybill. Baltimore: Johns Hopkins University Press.

Kissinger, Warren S. 1983. *The Buggies Still Run.* Elgin, IL: Brethren Press.

Kline, Edward A., and Monroe Beachy. 1998. "History and Dynamics of the New Order Amish of Holmes County, Ohio." *Old Order Notes* 18 (Fall–Winter): 7–19.

Kline, John B. 1990. Ed. *Rural Recreation: The Traditional Adult Game of Cornerball Plus Country Schools and Their Recess Games.* Denver, PA: Hill Barn.

Kraybill, Donald B. 1994a. "Plotting Social Change Across Four Affiliations." In

The Amish Struggle with Modernity, ed. Donald B. Kraybill and Mark A. Olshan. Hanover, NH: University Press of New England.

———. 1994b. "The Amish Encounter with Modernity." In *The Amish Struggle with Modernity,* ed. Donald B. Kraybill and Mark A. Olshan. Hanover, NH: University Press of New England.

———. 1994c. "War against Progress: Coping with Social Change." In *The Amish Struggle with Modernity,* ed. Donald B. Kraybill and Mark A. Olshan. Hanover: Hanover University Press of New England.

———. 2001. *The Riddle of Amish Culture,* rev. ed. Baltimore: Johns Hopkins University Press.

———. 2003. *The Amish and the State,* rev. ed. Baltimore: Johns Hopkins University Press.

Kraybill, Donald B., and Carl Deportes Bowman. 2001. *On the Backroad to Heaven: Old Order Hutterites, Mennonites, Amish, and Brethren.* Baltimore: Johns Hopkins University Press.

Kraybill, Donald B., and C. Nelson Hostetter. 2001. *Anabaptist World USA.* Scottdale, PA: Herald Press.

Kraybill, Donald B., and Steven M. Nolt. 2004. *Amish Enterprise: From Plows to Profits,* rev. ed. Baltimore: Johns Hopkins University Press.

Kraybill, Donald B., and Mark A. Olshan, eds. 1994. *The Amish Struggle with Modernity.* Hanover, NH: University Press of New England.

Lancaster New Era. 1877–. Lancaster, PA: Lancaster Newspapers.

Lancaster Sunday News. 1923–. Lancaster, PA: Lancaster Newspapers.

Langin, Bernd G. 1994. *Plain and Amish: An Alternative to Modern Pessimism.* Scottdale, PA: Herald Press.

Lapp, Aaron, Jr. 2003. *Weavertown Church History.* Sugarcreek, OH: Carlisle Printing.

Lasansky, Jeannette. 1990. *A Good Start: The Aussteier or Dowry.* Lewisburg, PA: Oral Tradition Project of the Union County Historical Society.

Luthy, David. 1986. *The Amish in America: Settlements That Failed, 1840–1960.* Aylmer, Ont.: Pathway Publishers.

———. 1997. "Japanese Interest in the Amish." *Family Life* 30 (December): 21–24.

———. 2003. "Amish Settlements across America: 2003." *Family Life* 36 (October): 17–23.

Marcia, James C. 1980. "Identity in Adolescence." In *Handbook of Adolescent Psychology,* ed. Joseph Adelson. New York: Wiley.

———. 1994. "The Empirical Study of Ego Identity." In *Identity and Development: An Interdisciplinary Approach,* ed. H. A. Bosma et al. Thousand Oaks, CA: Sage.

Martino, Steven C., Rebecca L. Collins, Marc N. Elliott, Amy Strachman, David E. Kanouse, and Sandra H. Berry. 2006. "Exposure to Degrading versus Nondegrading Music Lyrics and Sexual Behavior among Youth." *Pediatrics* 118 (August): 430–41.

McNamara, Timothy. 1997. *Uses of Popular Music by Old Order Amish Youth in Lancaster County, Pennsylvania.* Dissertation Abstracts International. 58:03A.

Meyers, Thomas J. 1993. "Education and Schooling." In *The Amish and the State,* ed. Donald B. Kraybill. Baltimore: Johns Hopkins University Press.

———. 1994. "The Old Order Amish: To Remain in the Faith or to Leave?" *Mennonite Quarterly Review* 68 (July): 378–95.

Meyers, Thomas J., and Steven M. Nolt. 2005. *An Amish Patchwork: Indiana's Old Orders in a Modern World.* Bloomington: Indiana University Press.

Miller, Brent C., J. Kelly McCoy, and Terrance D. Olson. 1986. "Dating Age and Stage as Correlates of Adolescent Sexual Attitudes and Behavior." *Journal of Adolescent Research* 3:361–71.

Miller, Levi. 1989. *Ben's Wayne.* Intercourse, PA: Good Books.

Miller, Mary M. 2000. *Our Heritage, Hope, and Faith.* Sugarcreek, OH: Carlisle Printing.

Myers, David G. 2005. *Social Psychology.* 8th ed. New York: McGraw-Hill.

Mystery of Happiness: Who Has It, How to Get It. 1994. Directed by John Stossel. ABC News. Videocassette.

New Order Amish Directory. 1999. Millersburg, OH: Abana Books.

Newswanger, Xtian. 1996. *Amishland.* Intercourse, PA: Gordonville Print Shop.

Nolt, Steven M. 2003. *A History of the Amish,* rev. ed. Intercourse, PA: Good Books.

Oyer, John S., and Robert S. Kreider. 1990. *Mirror of the Martyrs.* Intercourse, PA: Good Books.

Plain Interests. 2001–. Millersburg, PA. A monthly periodical dedicated to interests of plain readers.

Platte, Petra, Joan F. Zelten, and Albert J. Stunkard. 1998. "Body Image in the Old Order Amish: A People Separate from 'the World.'" *International Journal of Eating Disorders* 28 (December): 408–14.

Reiling, Denise M. 2002. "The 'Simmie' Side of Life: Old Order Amish Youth's

Affective Response to Culturally Prescribed Deviance." *Youth and Society* 34 (December): 146–71.

Remnick, David. 1998. "Bad Seeds." *New Yorker*, 20 July, 28–33.

Renno, John R. 1993. *Growing Up Amish*. Petersburg, OH: Pilgrim Brethren Press.

Rheingold, Howard. 1999. "Look Who's Talking." *Wired* 7(1):128–31, 161–63.

Rice, Charles S., and Rollin C. Steinmetz. 1956. *The Amish Year*. New Brunswick, NJ: Rutgers University Press.

Schwartz, Christian, and Elizabeth N. Schwartz. 1980. *Schwartzs' Song-Book*. Gordonville, PA: Gordonville Print Shop.

Scott, Stephen E. 1981. *Plain Buggies: Amish, Mennonite, and Brethren Horse-drawn Transportation*. Intercourse, PA: Good Books.

———. 1988. *The Amish Wedding and Other Special Occasions of the Old Order Communities*. Intercourse, PA: Good Books.

Shachtman, Tom. 2006. *Rumspringa*. New York: North Point Press.

Small, S., and T. Luster. 1994. "Adolescent Sexual Activity: An Ecological, Risk-Factor Approach." *Journal of Marriage and the Family* 56:181–92.

Standards of the Old Order Amish and Old Order Mennonite Parochial and Vocational Schools of Pennsylvania. 1981. Gordonville, PA: Gordonville Print Shop.

Steinberg, Laurence. 1990. "Autonomy, Conflict, and Harmony in the Family Relationship." In *At the Threshold: The Developing Adolescent*, ed. S. Feldman and G. Elliot. Cambridge, MA: Harvard University Press.

———. 2001. "We Know Some Things: Adolescent-Parent Relationships in Retrospect and Prospect." *Journal of Research on Adolescence* 11:1–19.

———. 2005. *Adolescence*. 7th ed. Boston: McGraw-Hill.

Stevick, Pauline. 2006. *Beyond the Plain and Simple: A Patchwork of Amish Lives*. Kent, OH: Kent State University Press.

Stevick, Richard. 2001. "The Amish: Case Study of a Religious Community." In *Contemporary Spiritualities: Social and Religious Contexts*, ed. Clive Erricker and Jane Erricker. London: Continuum.

Stoll, Elmo. 1972. *One Way Street*. Aylmer, Ont.: Pathway Publishers.

———. 1982. "Why I See Danger in Games and Sports." *Family Life* (March): 9–11.

Stoll, Joseph. 1966. "The Police Came." *Blackboard Bulletin* (September): 27–29.

Stoltzfus, Louise. 1998. *Traces of Wisdom: Amish Women and the Pursuit of Life's Simple Pleasures*. New York: Hyperion.

Stoltzfus, Samuel S. 1994. "Our Changing Church District." *Pennsylvania Folklife* (Spring): 124–31.

Tomlin, Jimmy. 2003. "Be not Conformed . . ." *Our State* 71(4):152–56.

Thornton, Arland. 1990. "The Courtship Process and Adolescent Sexuality." *Journal of Family Issues* 3 (April): 239–73.

Triandis, Harry C. 1990. "Theoretical Concepts that are Applicable to the Analysis of Ethnocentrism." In *Applied Cross-cultural Psychology*, ed. R. W. Brislin. Newbury Park, CA: Sage.

———. 1995. *Individualism and Collectivism*. Boulder, CO: Westview Press.

Troyer, David A. 1920. *Hinterlassene Schriften*. Comp. and trans. by Paton Yoder in *The Writings of David A. Troyer*. Aylmer, Ont.: Pathway Publishers, 1998.

Umble, Diane Zimmerman. 1994a. "Amish on the Line: Telephone Debates." In *The Amish Struggle with Modernity*, ed. Donald B Kraybill and Mark A. Olshan. Hanover, NH: University Press of New England.

———. 1994b. *Holding the Line: The Telephone in Old Order Mennonite and Amish Life*. Baltimore: Johns Hopkins University Press.

Unruh, John D. 1952. *In the Name of Christ: A History of the Mennonite Central Committee and Its Services, 1920–1951*. Scottdale, PA: Herald Press.

Weaver-Zercher, David. 2001. *The Amish in the American Imagination*. Baltimore: Johns Hopkins University Press.

———. 2005. *Writing the Amish: The Words of John A. Hostetler*. University Park, PA: Pennsylvania State University Press.

Wittmer, Joe. 1973. "Amish Homogeneity of Parental Behavior Characteristics." *Human Relations* 26(2):143–54.

Wojtasik, Ted. 1996. *No Strange Fire*. Scottdale, PA: Herald Press.

Yoder, Joseph Warren. [1940] 1995. *Rosanna of the Amish*. Scottdale, PA: Herald Press.

Yoder, Paton. 2003. "The Amish View of the State." In *The Amish and the State*, rev. ed., ed. Donald B. Kraybill. Baltimore: Johns Hopkins University Press.

Index